america

at twelve miles an hour

a view from the edge of the road | phil shrout

To Merj
Without whom this book would have been much shorter.

PROLOGUE

Seventy miles into the long, hot, windblown day, a sign finally announced our arrival at the outskirts of Rawlins, Wyoming, the evening's destination. The day had been the most difficult of the trip, and two fifty-something cross-country bicyclists were "gassed." The mountain passes of Colorado and the searing heat and headwinds of the Kansas plains still awaited us. After that, the rolling hills of Missouri, a state often referred to as Misery by fellow cyclists, would follow. Then the Appalachians.

After thirty-one days and 1,560 miles, and with 2,300 yet to ride, questions originating in our tired bodies made their way to our equally exhausted minds. Had this forty-year dream been a mistake? Were we going to be able to make it the rest of the way? Was it time to get on a bus and head home? There were fourteen hours until tomorrow's ride would begin. We had fourteen hours to decide.

It's sometimes surprising the things a middle age baby boomer remembers from his youth. Those things seen or experienced that somehow left an impression and reappeared as the years passed, much like a hungry mosquito leaving an itch that had to be scratched.

My itch started at the age of ten or eleven while growing up in rural northeastern Ohio in the late 1950's. Like many of the other boys in my hometown, I was a member of the local Boy Scout troop. One summer an article appeared in the monthly scouting magazine, *Boys Life*; it chronicled a bicycle trip by an older scout who had cycled across the entire United States. I recall reading the article, and feeling that such an undertaking was just about the limit of human capability. A summer's worth of riding around the neighborhood on my old Sears Roebuck J.C. Higgins three speed was but a few miles of a cross country journey. I wondered how anyone could accomplish such a seemingly impossible feat. Although not knowing it at the time, the mosquito had done his deed. An itch had started.

Years passed with the usual experiences of life. School, marriage, career, and children all became part of a happy and rewarding passage from youth to middle age. The typical busy lifestyle of a family going about daily activities pushed the idea of a cross-country bicycle trip to a place to the side. The itch never really disappeared, but scratching it was something that would have to wait.

Not long after celebrating my fiftieth birthday, there came a point in time when thoughts of the long held dream began to occasionally make their way into my consciousness. Maybe it was the watershed event of turning fifty years old that had prompted a feeling that it was time to accomplish long held aspirations. Maybe it was the feeling that good health could change at any time and make the goal an elusive one. Maybe it was the practical realization that our children had completed college, and my career was at a point where a reduced workload could allow time to make the trip. Whatever the reason, it was time to begin serious consideration of the venture.

Merj, my wife of thirty plus years, had been somewhat aware of my cycling objective and the time had arrived to discuss preliminary planning with her. I had always assumed the trip would be a solo undertaking, but as we talked about very preliminary plans, Merj, surprisingly said she wanted to be part of the experience. As a retired teacher, she also had the time, and having her with me would be a welcome addition. We decided it was a good temporary cure for the empty-nest syndrome that we were both experiencing.

Previously we had completed weeklong bicycle tours together in Yellowstone, Alaska, and France, and had enjoyed the experiences. The trips were organized by bicycle tour companies that moved our gear from hotel to hotel. All we had to worry about was the cycling. This trip would be different. We would carry all of the gear on the bikes and manage our own planning, maintenance, and repairs.

Merj's only requests were that she be given an option of

other short term non-cycling transportation should fatigue or injury limit her ability to ride, and that we spend each night at a hotel or motel. Even though I had a personal drive bordering on obsession to ride every inch of the way, neither of her requests presented a problem for me. Three days of constant rain and mud during bivouac at Fort Knox, Kentucky in the early seventies, and a similar family outing some years later, had already permanently soured me on camping. Staying in motels would get no objection from me.

We began planning for the trip by becoming members of a national organization, Adventure Cycling, and purchased their excellent cross-country route maps. We dutifully gathered and cataloged information about lodging and points of interest from each of the eleven states that would be part of the trip. State tourism departments were researched on the Internet and calls were placed to real live humans to learn about each state's "must sees."

As an engineer by education and training, there was an unfortunate need to compulsively plan the details of the trip. Before long, the painstaking research resulted in a thick loose-leaf notebook containing day-by-day summaries of distances, riding conditions, rest stops, food, and lodging. To continue the effort to create the perfectly choreographed bicycle experience, the information was reduced and bound into a lightweight document that could be easily carried on a bike.

Early on it became obvious that our bicycles needed to be upgraded. Our current bikes, although only about ten years old, would not be up to the task of crossing the country, so we decided to buy two identical Cannondale T2000, twenty-seven speed, touring bicycles. Since they were identical, one could be used as an example of what a properly equipped bike should look like in case there were problems with the other one. My engineer friends called it "redundancy." Merj referred to it in less flattering terms, but accepted the marginally rational reasoning in the interest of sustaining team morale. In reality, a primary reason for buying the

Cannondales was that their bright yellow color would be clearly visible to passing motorists; plus they really looked pretty good fully loaded with all our gear.

We decided it was important to agree on a philosophy for the trip. What exactly was to be achieved as a result of spending a summer on a bicycle seat? Other than the obvious physical effects of three months on the narrow seat, we came to the conclusion that the trip had to be about much more than just the cycling. The bikes were a means to traverse the country at a pace that would allow an opportunity to experience the scenery, and especially the people, in a way most travelers never could. Taking time to enjoy the country and talk to locals and fellow travelers along the way became our primary objectives. Although heartily endorsing the agreed upon approach, it ran contrary to my normal "getting from Point A to Point B as quickly as possible" way of thinking. I decided to put a small reminder in the form of a note on the front pack of my bike that simply stated two words: SLOW and STOP.

Having maintained a good fitness level over the years through a regular running program, there was a confidence bordering on arrogance that the physical challenges of the trip were within my capabilities. Merj, though, was more than a little concerned, and in turn, that caused more than a little concern on my part. Merj's fitness level would play a big part in our enjoyment of the trip, so training became a priority.

Since the bikes had been purchased while on an extended winter stay on Hilton Head Island, South Carolina, the training began there. Hilton Head is one of a number of barrier islands lying along the Atlantic coast, and although there are numerous bike paths throughout the island, trying to find conditions similar to those we would find crossing the country was a real challenge. The highest naturally occurring point on the island is only about thirty feet above sea level; some 11,000 feet lower than we would encounter in the Rocky Mountains. Not to be deterred, we found a high level arched bridge and did countless laps up and down the bridge. Not only did the bridge laps lead to strange looks from the toll collectors at one end, but they also gave us an unwarranted confidence as to our hill climbing ability.

When we returned to Ohio in early spring, we found more challenging riding conditions, but along with the training-hills, came less cooperative weather. After about five hundred miles on the bikes, it was decided the trip itself would provide our training. We naively believed that the coastal hills would afford enough training to effortlessly tackle the inland mountains of Oregon and beyond. I was banking on the miles of running to carry me through, but Merj was still apprehensive. A lessening of her fears came from an unexpected source.

Merj's parents had been talking for some time about an extended driving trip through the western United States. A suggestion was made to combine our two trips, which would allow them to support us through a portion of the ride. Their presence would make available an opportunity to lighten the load on the bikes and have supplies such as food and drinks brought out during the day's ride. They could also transport Merj if the need arose and help by arranging lodging in the town that would be the evening's destination. After a short discussion, it was agreed that Merj's folks would meet us near Boise, Idaho, and offer support for about four weeks. Merj's optimism took a quantum leap, and a quantum leap in her optimism directly translated to a similar rise in that of the other half of the cycling twosome.

As the June departure to our Oregon starting point approached, many friends became inquisitive about details of the trip. The two most frequently asked questions were about the anticipated discomfort after many hours on a bicycle seat, and the survivability of a long marriage. The bicycle seat was far and away the biggest concern. The standard answer lay with a book on bicycle touring that we had purchased; we never read the book, but instead, placed it on its edge and sat on it for extended periods of time. It was the quickest way to prepare for the seat.

As word spread about the trip, it became obvious there could be no backing out. Too many people knew about our plans. That fact became crystal clear when friends decided to give us a bon voyage cocktail party at a local hotel. It was a fun filled evening of sharing our anticipated adventure with friends and family. The words of encouragement were greatly appreciated. On the way home in the car, a quick look at Merj showed that we shared the same thought: there was *absolutely* no way to get out of this now.

The remaining two weeks before our departure were filled with final preparations. Early on, there had been much discussion about ways to record experiences and keep in touch with family and friends back home. Since this trip was likely a once-in-a-life-time event, recording details that could be easily recalled later was a priority.

It was decided to use a couple of methods. Each of us would carry a small tape recorder on our bikes that would allow a chance to record events and first hand impressions as they occurred. A friend volunteered to transcribe the tapes as they were mailed back during the progress of the trip. Since each of us would separately record our observations, there would be two unique viewpoints of the same situations. It was sort of a *Men Are From Mars, Women Are From Venus* approach. Past experience showed it was quite possible that anyone reading both sets of transcripts would not believe that we had been on the same trip. The second method of record keeping would be an old-fashioned, hand-written, daily diary.

Keeping in touch with the folks back home was another important consideration. Having a daughter with a degree in computer information science made the problem comparatively easy to solve. She would create a web site that would give a daily update and would also provide a means for anyone to e-mail questions, concerns or encouragement. To update the site and receive the e-mails, we planned to carry a small pocket sized computer with an attachable fold out keyboard. Whenever access to the

Internet was available, we would send updates to our daughter who would then update the site. After way too much deliberation, we decided on the web address: www.usabiketrip.com. Twenty-first century technology had invaded our quaint tour of rural America.

The fact that most of the cycling would be through sparsely populated portions of the country was not lost on a number of friends. We were most often asked how we intended to protect ourselves in the event of an unwanted incursion by a two-legged or four-legged adversary. Admittedly, the problem had not been given much thought. Many had suggested carrying a firearm, but we weren't comfortable with the idea.

It was with a certain relief that a local police chief told us carrying a firearm would be impossible due to the many state lines that we would cross. He suggested pepper spray, so two canisters of pepper spray were soon purchased from a local outdoor recreation store. Just for good measure, and not to forget potential four-legged adversaries, we also bought two canisters of dog repellent spray from a bike shop. It was a little disconcerting when the pepper spray salesperson included instructions to spray downwind so as to not spray the stuff on ourselves. Now, apparently, it would be necessary to add a weathervane to an already lengthening list of items to be packed.

When it came to packing, there was cause for concern. The feminine member of our team had earned a well-deserved reputation over the years for packing solutions to every trip eventuality. Past overnight automobile trips that had included three or more full sized suitcases gave sufficient reason for trepidation about the packing for this trip. Since weight was a concern, packing would have to be as economical as possible. On one of the earlier week-long bicycle tours, a guide had talked about a trip across the Australian Outback. She was so concerned about weight, that she drilled holes in the handles of her toothbrush to make it lighter. We didn't intend to be quite that economical.

We expected wide variations in weather, so the choices of what to include and what to leave behind were not easy. To lighten the load, we planned to send the cool weather gear home after leaving the Rockies. To begin the process, all the gear, clothing, and various bicycle packs were laid out on the bedroom floor. It was an impressive collection of every conceivable thing two people would need to survive a summer on the road. Toiletries, cameras, underwear, tools, gloves, shoes, rain gear, sunscreen, power bars, and clothing for all seasons covered the floor. Somehow, through judicious negotiation, there was eventual agreement as to what should go and what should stay. In the back of our minds though, just like the overnight trips of the past, we both knew there was probably far more than we would need.

About a week before leaving for Oregon, the bikes and gear were taken to a local shipper who disassembled the bikes, mounted them on pegboards, and boxed them for the trip across the country. While impatiently waiting to leave, we tracked the progress of the bikes and a summer's worth of gear toward Oregon. In a few days verification was received that they had safely arrived at our bed and breakfast in Astoria. The equipment was now on the West Coast. It was time for us to get this show on the road. The itch was about to be scratched.

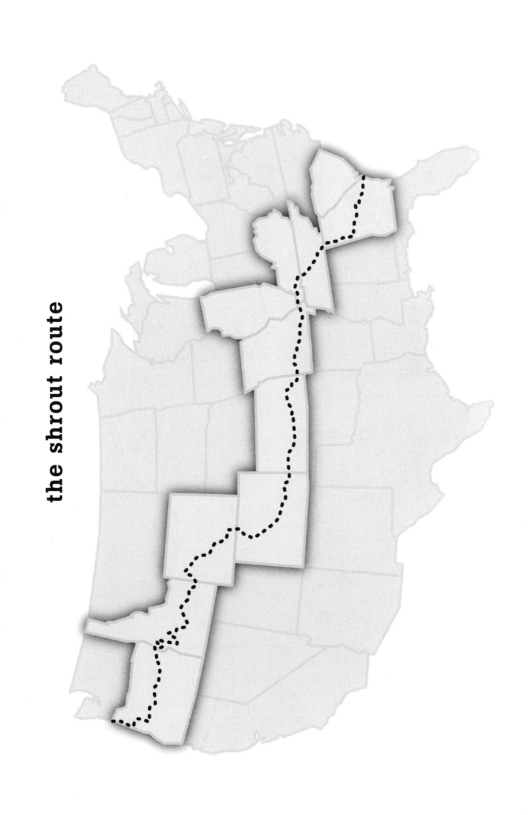

the shrout route

oregon

"You gotta do what you gotta do"

NO TURNING BACK NOW

To the young Coast Guardsman who shared the well-worn interior of an airport shuttle, we looked like any other middle age married couple heading out on an early summer vacation. Unknown to him, or our talkative driver behind the wheel, an anxiety was taking up residence inside our finely tuned, albeit somewhat weathered, bodies.

There are those that say worry takes many equally valid forms. Such was the case as we neared our destination in Astoria, Oregon. While I fretted about the upcoming hills and weather, Merj worried whether she had left the iron on back home. After assuring her that the same fear had proven unfounded a hundred or so times in the past, a legitimate concern took its place. Maybe our finely tuned bodies weren't as tuned as we thought. Maybe the padding in the cycling shorts wasn't thick enough to deal with the "agony of the bicycle seat." Maybe we weren't ready for this.

As the battered shuttle van rolled closer to the night's lodging with a loud cacophony of rattles and squeaks and a cloud of blue exhaust smoke, one thing became perfectly clear: No matter what fears occupied our increasingly apprehensive minds, there was no turning back now.

WHEN YOU'RE WRONG, ADMIT IT; WHEN YOU'RE RIGHT, KEEP YOUR MOUTH SHUT

The picturesque town of Astoria, Oregon traces its roots back to the early 1800's and fur trader John Jacob Astor and explorers Lewis and Clark. Astoria's location near the juncture of the Columbia River and the Pacific Ocean contributed to its growth as a thriving seaport. As the town grew, it developed a reputation in the mid 1800's of being second only to San Francisco in sin and moral decadence. Strict enforcement of new regulations controlling unruly behavior successfully changed Astoria's image. As the years passed, the town became home to a great many Scandinavians. The Finns, Swedes, Norwegians, and Danes became an integral part of Astoria's growth and prosperity.

Today, Astoria, a community of about 10,000 inhabitants, has become a preferred vacation spot for many in the Northwest. Astoria has also served as the backdrop for movies such as *Goonies*, *Kindergarten Cop*, *Teenage Mutant Ninja Turtles 3*, and *Free Willy*. The town's prominent feature is the Astoria Column, a 125-foot structure that sits atop Coxcomb Hill and represents a history of the Northwest through scenes on its exterior.

Over the previous few months, we had formed images of what to expect in this small coastal Oregon town. On the ride into Astoria in the cramped back seat of the airport shuttle van, our first sights were of logs piled like toothpicks awaiting shipment to mills and the wide expanse of the Columbia River.

Victorian homes nestled on the sides of steep hills looked down on the town's business district, and sea lions barked loudly a short distance off the river's edge. As we imagined it would, Astoria had all the look and feel of a coastal Pacific Northwest town. More importantly, it was the point of departure for a long anticipated adventure.

A bed and breakfast appropriately named the Astoria Inn provided lodging for our first night in Oregon. Our welcome by Mickey, the owner and hostess, left little doubt that the evening's stay would be a comfortable one. Her warm greeting, an affectionate bulldog named Blossom, and a pet raccoon inhabiting the back yard all contributed to the relaxed feeling she had created at the Astoria Inn. Blossom's deeply wrinkled face made our multiple "laugh lines" look youthful by comparison.

I couldn't wait to begin readying the bikes for the start of the trip the following day. The bikes had arrived in wooden crates that were neatly stored in Mickey's garage, but unfortunately had been disassembled beyond our expectations. Reassembling them would take more than the tools we had brought from home. Mickey, recognizing my well practiced look of despair, disappeared only to return quickly with an assortment of tools.

After some gnashing of teeth, breaking of skin, and unorthodox utterances of the English language, the bikes were finally assembled. Even though no unassembled parts remained on the garage floor, the two keenly observant females looking over my shoulder clearly questioned my assembly skills. To afford some reasonable assurance that the bikes were properly assembled, I confidently suggested a trial ride around the block. The chosen route, although a short one, included a hill of sufficient grade to give Merj some difficulty. The combination of the hill, and slipping of the gears on her bike, resulted in an unmistakable look of frustration and worry on her face.

Doubts about Merj's ability to handle the rigors of the trip manifested themselves during the short trial ride. My own concern for her ability to enjoy the three months to come, always in the back of my mind, had inched closer to the front. My "body language" evidently showed the building tension and worry. Such an obvious display of emotion only added to Merj's frustrations. For a brief period, the worry expressed by friends back home about the effect of constant companionship on a long term marriage reared its ugly head. The fact that a cycling "misunderstanding" had arisen, and we hadn't even started the trip yet, was further cause for concern. Merj made a not so subtle suggestion that we visit a local bike shop to have the assembly of the bikes checked by an expert. Quick acceptance of her request was deemed a judicious course of action.

Contemplation of the unknown and a long travel day had made us hungry. For dinner Mickey suggested a restaurant overlooking the Columbia River and tossed us a set of keys. "Take my car, it's in the garage," she insisted. Her trust of two people she had just met was a bit of a surprise. Watching my bicycle assembly skills earlier in the afternoon had probably raised Mickey's comfort level. She probably figured that anyone that inept wouldn't make it very far in a stolen car.

The drive was a short one to a restaurant that offered a relaxing view of the late day sun over the still waters of the bay. The restaurant ambiance gave us an opportunity to assess our status, and share feelings on the evening before launching our journey. The test ride had caused some angst, but the effects of the dinner and the setting sun had helped quell the worries for the time being.

As we headed for the restaurant exit, Angela, the youthful hostess, slipped us a piece of paper with her name and address. "Please send me a post card from your trip," she whispered. Her nearly inaudible request made it seem that she was somehow self-conscious living a travel adventure through someone else's eyes. It didn't matter; her request would happily be fulfilled.

A very eventful day ended with deep slumber induced by the background serenade of barking sea lions in the Columbia River.

In what seemed like minutes, dawn arrived and day one of the trip began with a sky of rolling clouds, a sprinkle of rain, and an unease in the pits of two stomachs. We pushed the bikes up a short grassy hill to get a picture in front of the Astoria Inn; it became clear, fully loaded, they were cumbersome and heavy. Regardless, it was time to head downtown to the bike shop to have yesterday's handiwork validated by an expert.

The kindly older bike shop owner took a personal interest in our plight and adjusted the bikes himself. "These bikes are really in pretty good shape," he said, "I only needed to adjust the gears." A quick glance at Merj showed her justifiable pride in the skill and mechanical aptitude of her talented husband. It also showed a sense of relief that it really was the gears, and not her cycling ability which had caused her difficulties the evening before.

FINALLY, we were ready to get the show on the road. The odometers were set to zero and the watches were synchronized. It was 10:14 am. Like a well-coached team with an unbeatable game plan, two fifty something "athletes" charged onto the field.

A NEEDLE IN A HAYSTACK

The morning passed easily as we cycled out of Astoria and along the Pacific coast to the small town of Cannon Beach. Experiences that would soon become common were sources of questions while the first day's ride continued up and down the coastal hills. Was the morning's headwind a bad one or no big deal? Was that last hill a challenge or nothing compared to what lay ahead? How was Merj doing? Was it safe to ask? Since this was the first day, there was no basis of comparison. The wondering continued through the rest of the morning.

In Cannon Beach, Betsy, a friendly waitress at a seafood lunch stop, patiently answered questions about alternate routes to the evening's destination of Manzanita. It was already evident that waitresses would be great sources of information. Getting the information, however, required that I ignore Merj's frequent and sometimes vigorous kicks under the table. It was still early in the trip, but her "reminders" were already becoming an obstacle to my naturally inquisitive nature.

Pre-trip research had shown that a cross-country cycling trip properly began with a ceremonial dipping of the rear wheel in the ocean of departure. The ritual would be repeated at the conclusion of the journey by dipping the front wheel in the ocean of destination. Both events were to be treated as near religious experiences. As we cycled out of Cannon Beach along the hilly coastline, we began a search for the ideal spot. It had to be the perfect setting, one which would always remain in our memory as the place where a significant event in our lives began. With the help of a local resident, we found a location south of Cannon Beach matching the required description. It was a wide sandy beach that fronted large stone monoliths lying just off the shore.

The monoliths, large basaltic rock outcroppings rising from the ocean floor, were formed from prehistoric volcanic eruptions. Unbeknown to us, we had decided to dip our wheels into the Pacific Ocean in front of an especially prominent monolith called Haystack Rock. Haystack Rock rises 235 feet above sea level and gets its name from its shape. The rock and the water surrounding it are the home for a variety of birds and aquatic life. Protection of Haystack and the nearby water is taken seriously; there is a substantial fine for climbing on it. Fortunately there was no fine for taking pictures and a young couple walking the beach graciously took ours in front of the rock. The journey was officially underway.

As we pushed the bikes through the sand back to the hard surface road, we drew the attention of three Oregonian couples. The encounter was friendly, but unremarkable, except that it provided a bit of useful information. Like most Midwesterners, we had been referring to the state as Ore-e-gone. "You guys are saying it all wrong," we were informed by one of the natives. "You gotta call it Ore-gun."

The local pronunciation triggered conversation as we remounted the bikes and continued south along the coast. If the folks in the Northwest wanted it pronounced that way, why wasn't the state name spelled Oregun? And if the Oregon spelling was to reflect native pronunciation, what about neighboring Worshington, or how about Minnesooota, or Takesus, or Nawth Carolina, or New Yawk, or Illinoy? Even our native Ohio, when not confused with Iowa, was many times referred to as Ohia. As the cycling continued, we agreed that the classic case had to be Arkansaw. If that was the way residents pronounced their state name, should Kansans refer to their state as Kansaw?

The first day on the road came to a successful completion in the small coastal town of Manzanita. The day's ride had included some wind, some hills, and some traffic. We had survived it, but we both knew that many more challenges lay ahead. As we turned out the light in a forgettable hotel, there was also pleasant anticipation of many more adventures to come.

Day 1 - 46 Miles Down, 3741 To Go

DID YOU BREAK WIND?

Shortly after leaving Manzanita early the next morning, the rainy reputation of the Northwest was reinforced as the skies opened. The rain bounced off our helmets and useless sunglasses and we dreaded the expected discomfort of wet, cold cycling. It was only our second day on the road and we worried: Was the rain an omen of things yet to come? Who knew, and besides, there were only so many things that could be accommodated in a pair of minds already cluttered with information and worries.

Duly prepared for any meteorological event, we quickly donned our rain gear, and just to be safe, headed for the protection of a covered porch on a real estate office. Fortunately the office had not yet opened. The sight of two wet cyclists imitating escapees from an aquarium display would likely have caused a prospective homeowner to come back another day. Before long the rain ended, and the paranoid fear of bad omens lessened.

The morning ride through the cheese-producing town of Tillamook and along the edge of Tillamook Bay provided a scenic contrast. The mountains in the distance nicely framed the nearby bay and flat road along the water's edge. A brisk wind whipped up the water's surface creating the melodic sounds of waves hitting the rocky shore, but the wind ceased to be our friend as we rounded the bay and turned directly into it. Our plan to have Merj ride in front to set a comfortable pace required a different approach when riding into the head wind. As I took over the lead, Merj remarked, "This is one time I don't mind if you break wind." She had obviously chosen the lesser of two evils.

Tillamook Bay is a popular destination for Northwestern sportsmen as evidenced by the number of fishermen casting lines from shore. While stopped for a break in the middle of one such group, we had the opportunity to chat with a grandfather fishing with his daughter and grandson. The elderly man's enjoyment went beyond the mere act of catching fish. It was an opportunity to pass skills down two generations, and to spend unfettered time with his family. A bucket of rainbow trout offered proof of his teaching ability. His grandson, probably four or five years old, happily posed for a picture while holding one of the day's catch. As the grandfather shared stories of local lore, our conversation turned to what lie ahead. He grinned and pointed down the road. "You've got a tough hill right around that bend," he told us. Not knowing whether one man's mountain was another man's molehill, we bid the old gentleman goodbye and headed for the ominous bend.

We always welcomed descriptions of what lay ahead of us from locals, but realized their warnings needed to be taken with a grain of salt. In the case of the hill around the bend, however, the elderly fisherman was pretty much on target; it was a good one. The first real challenge was dealt with by my dogged determination to ride every inch, and a rational, calm, approach by Merj to walk the portions of the hill that were especially steep.

Ultimately, both methods proved successful, and our reward for the climb was a panoramic view of the ocean from a high coastal bluff. There had been a bit of a self congratulatory feeling while I patiently waited for Merj at various stages of the climb. The calmness and patience were good signs. They foretold an attitude that would be important in the days to come. Maybe the SLOW and STOP reminders on the front pack were a good idea after all.

A cabin facing the Pacific Ocean in Netarts, a tiny coastal town, was the evening's lodging. The last remnants of the orange sun over the ocean provided the setting for a relaxed assessment of the first two days on the bicycles. Merj reported significant soreness in her legs, and we both experienced a little more difficulty in sitting comfortably than a short forty-eight hours earlier. Maybe the shorts did need a little more padding, but we agreed things would probably be better in the morning.

Day 2 - 86 Miles Down, 3701 To Go

HANG TEN, DUDE

The road out of Netarts followed the shoreline of Netarts Bay and was rightfully designated as a scenic Oregon highway. A sea lion raised its head above the early morning, misty, water surface and followed our progress just a few yards away. It seemed that he (or she) wondered why two humans on strange looking machines had

entered its domain. The riding was free and easy, and the morning cool and pleasant. Despite some aches and stiffness, optimism
became the emotion of the moment.

Before beginning the trip, the idea of using individual tape
recorders to record our progress was heralded as a stroke of
genius. In practice, however, a problem arose that proved difficult
to overcome. As it turned out, Merj had a previously undiagnosed
case of lalophobia, a fear of speaking; at least when it came to the
recorder. Even after considerable coaxing, she was unmoved. For
Merj, the daily written diary would have to suffice. That said,
Merj did memorialize her experiences by recording an occasional
quote of the day into the tape recorder; succinct descriptions, such
as "This wind sucks!" and, "I'm walking," accurately summed up
her attitude part way up a coastal hill. What early quotes lacked in
length, they made up for in short and snappy descriptiveness.
More gems were certain to follow.

The road turned away from the bay and headed into a lush
forest. The abundant rainfall of the Oregon coast had nourished
a thick green growth of plantlife that included varieties of fir,
spruce, hemlock, and ferns. Slivers of sunlight passed through the
canopy formed by the branches overhead. A long climb through
the forest past Cape Lookout State Park was again rewarded by
another panoramic view over the Pacific. We were reminded of
the oft-quoted phrase, "The spectacular viewed on a daily basis
becomes the ordinary." So far that hadn't happened.

Another reward for the long climbs was a near effortless ride
down the other side. Such was the case cycling down from Cape
Lookout State Park. A few miles down from the top, however, the
lush green surroundings were abruptly interrupted. The forest
was replaced by a wide expanse of sand dunes known as Sand
Lake, and the quiet was replaced by the drone of dune buggies. As
we stood looking at acres and acres of dunes we wondered, how
had a desert come about in the middle of a coastal forest? The
uniqueness of Sand Lake, especially its stark contrast to the

scenery of the earlier part of the day, was fascinating. With considerable reluctance, we decided to move on toward a planned lunch destination of Pacific City. In addition to SLOW and STOP, maybe a third note on the front pack should have read, DON'T WORRY ABOUT PLANNED LUNCH STOPS.

The road from Sand Lake to Pacific City flattened out and was filled with pickup trucks towing dune buggies of all sizes and designs. The ride passed large dairy farms that announced their presence from some distance away by the distinctive odor of grazing dairy cattle. The sights and smells resembled the Ohio countryside we knew well.

As we entered Pacific City, the ocean again made an appearance. Surfers rode the white crested waves a short distance off shore. The beach setting left a comfortable feeling in a babyboomer whose youth had been filled with the harmony of the Beach Boys. So, after the last oyster at the Pelican Pub had met its match, I made a beeline to the sandy beach nearby.

Before long, a group of five young surfers found themselves the focus of an eager surfer wannabe with a camera and recorder. The boys had customized a '58 GMC pickup and made it into a surf wagon that looked like it had jumped right off a Beach Boy album cover. The young men realized that the guy befriending them was obviously stuck in some king of sixties time warp and wasn't likely to go away anytime soon. "If you want a picture, go right ahead mister," one of them offered. The offer was quickly accepted.

Day 3 - 117 Miles Down, 3670 To Go

WE'RE NOT ALONE OUT HERE

The night in Neskowin was the last on the Oregon coast; it was time to turn inland. The early morning ride out of town was generally typical of the coastal region as it passed through canopied forests and up and down terrain. The idyllic surroundings soon ended as traffic picked up and speeding logging trucks became a worry.

Fortunately attitudes improved early in the afternoon when three other cross-country cyclists, a husband, wife, and brother, joined us at a rest stop. Although it was still early in the trip, the chat along the side of the highway afforded a chance to share experiences and concerns about what might await down the road. There was a certain comfort found in the similarity of our observations. We took pictures, exchanged addresses, and bid each other good-bye for the day. We expected to see each other again.

The last few miles into the evening's destination of Monmouth, Oregon were along a flat, smooth bike path bordering the Willamette River. The Willamette River Valley lies east of the coastal range and is a prominent feature in western Oregon. The valley stretches along the 230 mile length of the river and is home to two-thirds of the state's population. Acres of grapes showed evidence of the fertile soils of the valley floor. The wineries that sprung up over the years have made the Willamette Valley a favorite destination for vacationers. A stop at a winery on this warm early summer day was a topic of serious contemplation, but the evening's destination of Monmouth and a warm shower beckoned.

Day 4 - 176 Miles Down, 3611 To Go

JUST CALL ME PHILBERT

The Willamette River provided a wide, flat valley conducive to easy cycling. The pleasant, but warm, ride south from Monmouth took us past large farms toward the City of Corvallis. Fields of rye, strawberries, and nursery stock covered the valley floor. We considered a dash into one of the strawberry fields for a quick treat, but discarded it as a bad idea.

Corvallis, a town of about 45,000 people, was the largest city of the trip so far and the home of Oregon State University. Since we had broken the pocket PC two days earlier, we needed the well-equipped public library to supply Internet access to check e-mails and send updates home. A replacement PC would wait in Idaho, but Idaho was five hundred miles away. It was again necessary to remind ourselves to stay flexible.

While cycling out of Corvallis, we set our sites on the small town of Harrisburg as a good stopping place for a late lunch. Harrisburg was typical of the one-stoplight towns in rural Oregon, and a small restaurant with a few outside dining tables became our choice for a break. Soon after ordering, we struck up a light-hearted conversation with a couple of older diners; Don, whose real name was Laverne, and his buddy Al. "If you call me Laverne, you better be careful!" Don advised.

Don had ridden into town on his motorcycle and parked it just off the sidewalk. He wore a black tee shirt proudly displaying the classic Harley Davidson logo. He had a collection of twenty motorcycles, and professed love for the freedom the bikes offered. Don, a cross-country, tractor-trailer driver in his earlier years, shared many stories of the open road. "Why would anyone want to travel on two wheels without an engine?" he asked. It was a good question for which Merj's aching legs had no good answer. He asked our names, and prompted by mine, said, "We got a bunch of filbert trees just outside of town." We laughed and told him that good friends back home often jokingly referred to me as Philbert.

Al, the more reserved of the two, was duly proud of a couple of '53 Chevys he had restored. The ensuing discussion of the merits of the small block Chevy V8 would have gone on for the better part of the afternoon if not for Merj's increasingly noticeable yawns, and the number of miles yet to cover to reach the evening destination of Coburg. As we left the company of two newfound friends and prepared to leave town, Don jumped on his motorcycle and roared out ahead of us. Less than a mile out of Harrisburg a large grove of filbert trees appeared on the right side of the road. Such trees are not common in the Midwest and normally their identification would have remained a mystery. We knew they were filberts because Don was waiting by the grove to identify them for us. Don and Al had made it difficult to leave the friendly confines of Harrisburg, Oregon.

The evening in Coburg was interrupted by a cab ride into nearby Eugene. Eugene, located near the juncture of the Willamette and McKenzie Rivers, is home to 140,000 residents and is the second largest city in Oregon. It's also home to the University of Oregon. Since Eugene was the last city of any significant size for a while, we took time to enjoy shopping and a relaxing supper, and to deal with a problem that had developed with the female half of our team.

Merj's condition after four days on the road had caused some concern. Recurring pain in her legs had not responded to medication and the day's ride had been less than enjoyable for her. She expressed worry about the upcoming Cascade Mountains and a fear that her condition might get in the way of my enjoyment of a long held dream. Merj's worry about my enjoyment was an example of the type of thinking that would insure a successful completion of the trip and preservation of a long marriage.

Eugene's size offered alternative travel options that would soon be unavailable in the upcoming small towns, so a decision was needed quickly. The disappointment in having to consider another travelling option was evident as Merj weighed the possibilities. She fretted that we should have trained harder before we began the trip, and agonized over her plight to such a degree that tears replaced her normally happy demeanor. She would say later that no decision during any part of the remainder of the trip caused such agony as this one. No amount of consoling and encouragement from me would matter. Only Merj knew how she felt. Only she could make the decision.

After much discussion and more internal debate on Merj's part, we rented a vehicle in Eugene and bought a bike rack at a local Target store. Over the next ten days or so, Merj planned to provide support. With strategic placement of the vehicle, she would also continue to accompany me on her bike for significant portions of the remaining ride across Oregon, including some pretty good climbs. I admired Merj's ability to objectively examine her state of affairs and make a difficult choice. I wondered if under similar circumstances I could have made the same decision.

Day 5 - 234 Miles Down, 3553 To Go

"THE GUY THAT USED TO BRING IT MUST HAVE DIED OR SOMETHING."

The route east out of Coburg followed the McKenzie River through more lush forests. The lack of traffic and the sounds of the babbling water as it rushed over the nearby streambed made for a pleasant ride. The rapid flow of river water in the opposite direction gave further verification that the road was rising quickly. There are images and feelings one anticipates when considering a bicycling journey. The peaceful ride along the McKenzie River satisfied many of them.

The river's flow made available a ready source of energy for generating electricity as evidenced by the appearance of hydro power stations. We weren't sure what the structures were at first, but a restroom stop at a feed store gave us an opportunity to ask the lady behind the counter to verify our assumption. The affable woman explained the importance of the hydro stations, and gave detailed directions to the restroom in the back corner of the store. After weaving through a narrow maze framed by stacked bags of feed and fertilizer, we finally discovered the bathroom. Dropping breadcrumbs along the route to find the way back was a passing thought. The cramped cubicle barely allowed the door to close; it was a classic "one holer." Privacy wasn't a real concern, though, because Lewis and Clark couldn't have found this particular restroom. Although still early in the trip, restrooms and roadside respites had already become an unanticipated adventure.

A short time later we stopped at a small general store to chat with the owner about the road ahead. The store was similar to those that we had seen throughout rural Oregon. It sold a little bit of everything, and it wasn't unusual to find the owner behind the counter. Back home a daily dose of *USA TODAY* had become addictive. The news and sports coverage was great, but the daily challenge came from the crossword puzzle. Although it was difficult to find the newspaper in the small towns, it was always worth asking for it.

When we asked this general store owner for a copy of *USA TODAY*, we were not surprised to find none were available. "It used to come, but just quit a year or two ago," he told us. "The guy that used to bring it died or something." *USA TODAY* was not an important item in the daily routine of rural Oregonians. When we did come across a copy, we expected it to be more appropriately titled, *USA YESTERDAY*. The news of the day and the crossword would have to wait, and that was okay.

FINN ROCK

Merj was born in Finland and came to the United States with her family at the age of six. Immigrating at such an early age allowed her to learn English with no hint of a Finnish accent, so most people never knew of her Scandinavian heritage. She and her family became US citizens many years ago, but they still spoke Finnish within the family. Like many proud immigrants, they also retained a number of the customs and foods from their native land. So when we arrived at Finn Rock, a very large chunk of geology located just off the side of the road, it was of particular interest to us.

Did this thing really have a connection to Finland? Finding answers to perplexing questions was usually not difficult. Such was the case with Finn Rock. Just beyond the rock was a restaurant in the later stages of a major remodeling. We soon struck up a conversation with Jordan and Al, two young carpenters working inside the restaurant. Both of them had lived their entire lives in the area and enjoyed taking a break and sharing what they knew of the history of Finn Rock.

According to the two young men, a large group of Finns came to the area in the early nineteen hundreds to work for a Finnish landowner who intended to harvest trees from his land on the opposite side of the McKenzie River. The Finnish loggers set up camp and worked along the banks of the river. The landowner decided the large rock should be a lasting monument to the Finnish enclave and pronounced it Finn Rock.

A second version had the name of the rock originating with Old Pete Finn. Old Pete supposedly moved the rock from the center of the road, where it blocked passage, to the side. He purportedly accomplished the feat by wrapping ropes around the rock and pulling it with a team of oxen. Legend has it, the grooves circling the base of the rock are evidence of his accomplishment. Jordan and Al were pretty sure the Finnish monument version was the correct one. It was plausible enough to be accepted by Merj, and that was good enough for me.

A RIVER RUNS THROUGH IT

The afternoon ride was a hot one and the day warmed considerably. Heat had been expected, but not in the Pacific Northwest. Was this another troublesome bad omen? Whatever, the warm pavement continued to steadily pass under the spinning bicycle wheels toward McKenzie Bridge.

The evening's destination, the Log Cabin Inn in McKenzie

Bridge, was a welcome end to the day's ride. The Log Cabin Inn, a rustic lodge situated on the banks of the McKenzie River, was reconstructed after a fire in 1907, and has remained essentially unchanged since. The inn was a budget-busting extravagance; a departure from the norm - although it was already becoming evident that any semblance of a budget was quickly disappearing. Departure from the norm was becoming the norm.

After checking in, I headed down to a pair of dusty horseshoe pits behind the lodge. Those who have never been initiated into the world of horseshoe pitching cannot fully understand the simple pleasure derived from throwing an oversized two and a half-pound horseshoe forty feet toward a metal post. Growing up, it was not unusual for my dad and me to spend part of a warm summer evening pitching horseshoes behind the back yard tool shed. Many nights the metallic clanging of the shoes attracted a neighbor or two, and a mini round-robin tournament ensued.

Some years later it was discovered that the joy of horseshoe pitching had apparently spread throughout the civilized world. During a visit to Finland, Merj's Finnish cousin, having heard of my enjoyment of the game, made a thoughtful attempt to accommodate his American visitors by pounding two stakes into the ground and rounding up four horseshoes. Unfortunately the horseshoes were real shoes used to shoe real horses. Their smaller size made it necessary to take into account the effects of a brisk wind off the Baltic Sea on the light horseshoes as they flew toward their targets. Needless to say, ringers were a rare occurrence. Regardless, his desire to please was met with great appreciation. The horseshoe pits behind the lodge were a magnet pulling a middle age Ohioan back to his youth. Fortunately the art of horseshoe pitching is much like riding a bike; once you learned how to do it, you never forgot. An occasional ringer was still possible in the billowing dust of the lodge's horseshoe pits.

Dinner was a pleasant experience as we chatted with Chuck and Carolly, newfound friends from Hawaii. Carolly was an

accomplished author who had published books recounting the
lives of prominent historical figures. She talked in great detail
about a book she was currently writing, and held our rapt attention as she discussed the main character and the writing experience. Carolly encouraged us to record details of the trip and write
about them later.

At first I greeted her suggestion with an, "Awe shucks,
you're kidding me," response. But, after listening to her enthusiasm about the writing process and her encouragement to follow a similar path, I had a strong desire to get started as soon as
we returned to the lodge. Although not evident at the time,
another mosquito had landed. Another itch had to be scratched.
Life was going to get busy; maybe it was time to buy some mosquito repellent.

Our discussion was interesting enough to draw the attention
of an older nearby couple. The husband was a retired shoe salesman from Cleveland. "I sold over a million work shoes in my
career," he was quick to inform. There was a hesitancy to ask
whether he meant a million pair, hence two million shoes, or one
million individual shoes consisting of say five hundred left shoes.
It was always interesting to learn how various professions meas-
ured success.

River, our friendly, early-twenties waiter, brought dessert and
the check. Earlier in the trip we were served by a waitress named
Wind. She shared an interesting story of how she got her name,
so River's name couldn't go without questioning. We needed to
know why young people in Oregon were so "natural." Would Sky
be waiting at tomorrow's supper? "My mother grew up in the
60's," River informed us with a, "you know what I mean" look.

We too were products of the 60's and would have liked to pursue the story, but remembering bits and pieces of the 60's ourselves, we decided it might be a story he didn't want to tell.

River told us that he and his buddy, another waiter at the
lodge, represented one seventh of the local high school's recent

graduating class. This personable young man was planning on attending college soon. It was comforting to know that his college application could honestly represent that he was in the top fifteen of his high school class.

Day 6 - 292 Miles Down, 3495 To Go

SOONER OR LATER IT HAD TO HAPPEN

We left McKenzie Bridge before dawn with anticipation of a climb over the Cascade Mountains at McKenzie Pass; the first identified mountain pass of the trip. There had been a few climbs during the first six days that had provided a reasonable challenge, but none of them had names. This one did and we expected a test of our cycling stamina; both physical and mental.

As we approached the turnoff to McKenzie Pass, a large sign told travelers that the road was closed. A longer, but more grad-ual, detour over Santiam Pass was the alternate route. The long climb to Santiam was along a well-paved road through lush growths of pine. Typically, the road rose for a mile or two and then dropped for a shorter distance, only to repeat again. To most normal people, the periodic downgrades were a welcome respite. In our case, knowing the climb eventually ended on Santiam Pass at an elevation of 4,817 feet, we regarded the drops with a certain amount of loathing. They represented a loss of elevation that we'd already paid for.

Regardless, the ascent to Santiam Pass began as an enjoyable event. That changed when Merj, distracted by a cascading water-fall spilling over the face of sheer rock near the road, rode off the pavement onto the soft shoulder. The sandy surface stopped her bike in its tracks and tossed her onto the pavement. The resulting spill caused a hard landing on a bare knee, and an ugly, large knot.

Fortunately, after cleaning and bandaging the wound, Merj announced, "I'm ready to go."

We accepted the fact that minor accidents were probably inevitable. Based on past experience, we expected them to occur at dead stops when we couldn't get a foot out of a shoe clip. Merj's fall was of that nature. The only good news for her was that the first spill was over. Anticipation of my eventual accident loomed large.

The pine growth quickly gave way to acres of gray and black lava rock. Millions of years prior to our visit, volcanic eruptions had covered the landscape with molten lava that had eventually solidified. The lava fields along both sides of the highway stood in stark contrast to the lush green growth of the earlier part of the morning.

As we pedaled past the lava fields, the road became steeper and significant headwinds made the remaining climb to Santiam Pass a challenge. At the top we experienced a feeling of accomplishment that would be repeated over and over at mountain passes yet to come. It hadn't been a cakewalk, but the first identified challenge had been conquered; and the confidence that came with success in the face of challenges, was growing. The rest of the day's ride into Sisters was generally downhill and greatly appreciated after the morning's climb and wind.

HIGH JUMPING LLAMAS

Sisters, Oregon derives its name from three prominent volcanic peaks rising southwest of the city, collectively known as the Three Sisters. During the town's infancy the logging and lumber industry supplied work for early settlers. As time passed, livestock and farming became the staples of the local economy. Sisters survived two serious fires in the 1920's and is now part of the fastest growing area of Oregon. High technology, light manufacturing, and the wide-open spaces of central Oregon have attracted an influx of new residents, mostly from California. Today, this small town is home to about 950 residents.

As we checked into our lodging for the evening, other contributors to the local economy munched their evening meal in a field next to the hotel. The herd of diners consisted of a dozen or so strange looking critters that resembled a cross between a long-haired pony and a small giraffe. Having frequented zoos over the years, we recognized the animals as llamas.

Llamas are native to South America, and at the time of the Incas, there were about 23 million in existence. The Incas used them primarily for food, clothing, fiber, and transporting cargo. Today, there are about 3.5 million llamas in South America with the largest population outside South America being the 100,000 or so in the United States. Sisters is home to the largest llama farm in the country.

Llamas now serve a number of purposes in addition to the hauling and fiber producing roles of their ancestors. The Incas would be surprised to see modern day llamas participating in a show circuit or a llama-jumping contest. In fact, documentation from the 1993 Virginia State Fair shows that the greatest height cleared by a llama from a dead start is fifty-two inches. It was more than a little disturbing to discover that such a strange looking four legged animal with a name that begins with two l's could easily out jump the male component of our cross country duo.

Llamas, though, serve more practical uses, and that is what makes them commercially viable. Llamas have an instinctive nature that allows them to be effective guard animals. Western ranchers covet them as protectors of their livestock herds from predators such as coyotes. The llama's agile step allows them to tread lightly, and as a result, a few have been trained as golf caddies. The lack of sarcastic comments after a bad shot would be a much appreciated benefit of a good llama caddie.

Downtown Sisters is a reconstruction of an 1880's western town that begs for a walk along Main Street. Having little will power to resist, we headed downtown. The shops along Main

Street were like a light attracting a moth. In Sisters, the moth took the human form of Merj. "I'm in hog heaven!" she happily exclaimed. I had no idea she had such descriptions in her considerable vocabulary.

The late afternoon excursion had hardly begun when a voice from a passing car yelled our names. Realizing that there are a fair number of Phils inhabiting this planet, I wasn't sure that we were the objects of attention. But, hearing Merj's name raised our interest. The number of Merjs in Sisters, or west of the Mississippi for that matter, was a very small number; most likely just one. After six days on those damnable bicycle seats, there were still enough faculties remaining to realize that someone was trying to get our attention. It turns out, Chuck and Carolly, friends from the previous evening, had followed us in their car from McKenzie Bridge. An invitation to join them for sundaes in a nearby ice cream shop was accepted in a millisecond.

Sisters' two main annual events are an outdoor quilting show in July and a rodeo that had been held the weekend before we arrived. Both events draw substantial crowds to the small town. A friendly waitress at Bronco Billy's, the choice for supper, described the recently completed rodeo as, "A collection of flannel." She was a lifetime resident, and bemoaned the fact that a number of retail businesses opened along the nicely restored main street and failed within a year or two. The tourists that are such a large part of the new local economy frequent Sisters almost exclusively during the summer months. As a result many of the new entrepreneurs failed to sustain sufficient income during the remainder of the year to stay in business. After lingering over a tall mug of Harry Weinhard's Premium Root Beer, and soaking up the Old West atmosphere of Bronco Billy's, reality slowly returned. It was time for a trip to the local laundromat; a smell resembling that of a goat farm had become attached to our clothing. The laundromat was a welcomed cure for such fly attracting aromas.

Day 7 - 346 Miles Down, 3441 To Go

PHILIPPE

Leaving Sisters, a dramatic difference in terrain and scenery became quickly evident. The location of Sisters on the eastern side of the Cascade Mountains puts it between the lush pine forests to the west and the high desert to the east. The Cascade Mountain Range plays a major role in the weather patterns of Oregon as it provides a barrier between the generally moderate Pacific and more severe continental air masses. West of the Cascades a mild, moist climate is prevalent, while the high desert east of the mountains experiences very hot summers and cold winters with much less rainfall.

The ride out of Sisters took us through the spotty vegetation of the brown and tan high desert. A morning stop in the good-sized town of Redmond was a welcome opportunity for snacks and a short break. The day would get complicated, though, as we didn't discover a wrong turn out of Redmond for ten or twelve miles; sooner or later it had to happen. Not inclined to retrace the incorrect route on the bikes, we decided to flag down a pickup truck to catch a ride back to Redmond.

Normally we would have been reluctant to hitchhike, but a more comfortable, trusting feeling had developed as we became familiar with the people of central Oregon. The worries that would have been present at home, while not totally absent, were reduced. And, finding someone with a pickup truck was not a problem; pickups had shared the road surface with us during most of the morning.

Not surprisingly, within a few minutes a well used GMC pickup pulled along side. After my explanation of the navigational error in Redmond, the fellow inside the truck told me to load up for the ride back. The assortment of chain saws in the truck bed produced flashbacks to a particular horror film. My concern disappeared when the truck driver, a Swiss immigrant by the name of Philippe, mentioned that he owned a log home construction company. Now, the chainsaws made sense.

Philippe preferred to be called Phil, a particularly good name choice by most anyone's measure. He was probably in his late thirties, and had immigrated to this country thirteen years earlier. As we chatted on the ride back to Redmond, pleasant traces of Phil's native language punctuated his speech. He was particularly proud of the quality of his work and of the fact that his homes were built from scratch. Merj's Scandinavian heritage was, as to be expected, a topic of interest to this fellow European. A very pleasant individual, Phil talked about his young family and a successful battle with cancer two years earlier. His knowledge of the twists and turns in the road was evident as it seemed the old GMC was on two wheels for much of the ride back to Redmond.

When we finally arrived back on track, he refused any compensation and was prepared to help in any other way that may have been needed. The folks in central Oregon seemed accommodating by nature, but it was hard to imagine anyone more accommodating than Phil. He was an unassuming, hard-working person who deserved to have success come his way. I would have enjoyed spending the afternoon listening to Phil's melodic accent, but he had work to do, and I had miles yet to ride on this increasingly warm afternoon.

The ride from Redmond to Prineville was generally flat through low brown tinted hills and sagebrush. The warm temperature was apparent, but the very low humidity made it deceiving. The often stifling summer heat and humidity of northeastern Ohio had always warned that we were losing important fluids through heavy perspiration. Perspiration in the high desert was almost nonexistent even with the amount of cycling we were doing. We had to remember to drink from our frame mounted water bottles on a regular basis. Dehydration was a potential problem that had to be avoided.

Prineville represented the completion of our first week on the road and an opportunity to reflect. We had covered four hundred miles, and although it seemed to be a significant accomplishment, it represented only one-tenth of the expected total. For every revolution of the bicycle wheels that had already happened, nine more would be needed. More importantly, the energy expended for every pedal stroke to date would be called upon nine more times before the Atlantic Ocean came into view.

The physical aspects of the trip were obvious causes for reflection, but the mental and psychological effects of contemplating the remaining nine tenths of the journey could not be overlooked. We had been warned by experienced cyclists of the increasing difficulty of getting up early day after day with the anticipation of another day on the bicycle seat. So far that hadn't been a problem, but then again, only a tenth of the ride was behind us.

And what about the possibility of problems with two and four legged adversaries? In the more heavily traveled portions of western Oregon, such worries had not even entered our minds. In the sparse, wide-open stretches of highway in central Oregon, however, even with the apparent very accommodating nature of the local residents, the possibility of trouble was a little more of a concern.

Fortunately, the final assessment of a week on the road was one of accomplishment and the fulfillment of a small part of a summer's journey. We had legitimate worries of what lay ahead, but most of them were things that we could not control. The realization led to a newly developed philosophy that it was okay to be properly concerned, but not to a point of irrationality. The really good news was that after a week of constant companionship, our marriage was holding up quite well.

Day 8 - 404 Miles Down, 3383 To Go

A REAL BUCKAROO

The ride out of Prineville was flat and comfortably cool. A fifteen mile climb to Ochoko Pass began about a dozen miles into the morning. The rise to the pass was generally gradual as the road led through green forests bristling with wildlife that included deer and a variety of bird species. An especially annoying small black bird, plainly upset by the disruption caused by passing cyclists, insisted on taking out its frustrations by dive bombing the source of the problem. The birds nested in the roadway ditches and chose the technique to protect their nest. With helmets for protection, feeling claws on the top of our heads was not a real worry. Although the noise and proximity of the winged pests were a mild annoyance, they were preferable to a single minded Doberman Pincer in hot pursuit.

As I stopped to take photos part way up the long climb, a young cyclist pulling a small trailer and riding a bike fully loaded with gear passed. A short distance away he pulled over to rest and record the event with his camera at the top of Ochoco Pass. I joined him, and easy conversation followed as we compared our experiences so far. I soon learned that this single thirty-two-year-old Californian was named Andy, and that he was on his way to visit his parents in Iowa. A past member of the Peace Corps and a current member of the Army National Guard, he had just come off active duty.

We compared our Santiam Pass experiences of a few days ago. "That was a real struggle," Andy said as he slowly shook his head, "I really considered quitting right there and going home." It was comforting to find that a young man had also found the wind and climb a challenge. Andy was obviously fit, and even more significantly, he could have easily been our son.

Down the other side from Ochoko Pass, the green of the

morning turned into more of the high desert feel of the previous day. As the road flattened, the cool of Ochoko Pass was replaced by blasts of heat; a precursor of the hot afternoon that would soon follow. The ride into the night's destination of Mitchell was a hot, tiring experience.

Surprisingly, Mitchell, a small high-desert town of about 150 people, included a "business loop" off the main highway that was home to a collection of stores, a café, and a gas station. There was a real feeling of the Old West as we rode into town. We decided on a late lunch at the Little Pine Café and were greeted unenthusiastically by a gray-bearded man behind the cash register whom we dubbed "Captain Ahab." After consuming a hearty collection of western cuisine, we headed to our shelter for the evening, The Skyhook Motel. Little did we know that our opinion of the people of Mitchell, Oregon would soon change dramatically.

To engineers, a skyhook is a device that is used to support a structure when no man made alternative is available. It is a fictional last resort. The Skyhook Motel was indeed the only option for lodging in Mitchell, but favorable first impressions left us feeling that it was not a last resort. The Skyhook was located high above downtown and afforded a panoramic view of the whole community. A panoramic view of Mitchell, however, was not to be confused with the view from atop the Empire State Building over Manhattan. Denny and Becky, a husband and wife team, owned the motel, and as we checked in, they invited us to join them and their family for a barbecue dinner. We agreed, but only if we could supply the hamburger buns and beverages. The beverage of choice was Coors Light.

A trip back downtown included a stop at The Wheeler Trading Company for picnic supplies. The Wheeler Trading Company was a general/hardware/feed store that served most of the needs of the citizens of Mitchell. The kind, elderly, lady behind the counter was quick to inform us that her store didn't sell beer; it would have to be purchased across the street. After paying for hamburger buns and soft drinks, we engaged her in a discussion of the recent history of Mitchell. "The school only has about seventy students through the twelfth grade, and it's in trouble," she sadly informed us. "One of the teachers will be retiring soon and we'll be down to just four teachers."

While chatting with the storeowner, a second woman, the head of the visitor's bureau, joined us. Since we were curious about the occupations of the folks living in the small, western towns we passed through, we asked about the people of Mitchell. "Most of them work for the State or County Road Departments," the lady from the visitor's bureau told us. "The loss of the logging industry and closing of lumber mills has had a devastating effect on the local economy." Unfortunately, Mitchell's best days appeared behind it. Being the head of the Mitchell Visitor's Bureau had to be a tough job.

Across the street, through the sliding glass front door and around the random piles of various goods, we discovered a treasure trove of Coors Light in the back of Schnee's Grocery. We guessed that the gruff, disheveled, old man behind the counter was related to our lunchtime friend, Captain Ahab. The shopping trip completed, it was time to head back to the Skyhook.

We spent the rest of the afternoon in the shade of a large tree, partaking in some of our purchased beverages, and enjoying the good company of Denny and many of his family members. They had gathered at the motel for a mini-family reunion. Merj and I felt a little uncomfortable intruding in the family affair, but Denny and the others made it clear that we were more than welcome. In fact, our continued attendance had become mandatory.

Denny cooked chicken, pork shishkabobs, and hamburgers on the grill while we all chatted about the bike trip and what lie down the road out of Mitchell. Becky added potato salad, chips, carrots, and brownies and we had the trappings of an All-American cook out. Denny's daughter and son-in-law had brought their four-and-a-half month old daughter who, being the first grandchild, was clearly the apple of grandma's eye. The envious look in Merj's eyes showed her desire for the same grandmotherly opportunity.

The warm late afternoon slid into evening as we joined the family on the porch for more beverages and good conversation. Denny, the acknowledged and respected patriarch of the family, regaled the group with stories of life in the high desert. "I'm 58 years old and I moved here from Portland to get away from the city," he proclaimed. He popped open another Coors, hand rolled a cigarette (something I hadn't seen since watching my dad do it when I was six), propped his boots up on a chair, and commenced to describe his philosophies of life. We placed the recorder on the table in front of Denny and asked him to share those philosophies with the world. Unlike Merj, between the Coors and the good company of his family, Denny didn't suffer from lalophobia. He was more than ready to talk, and the assembled group was more than ready to listen.

When he wasn't doing odds and ends around the motel, Denny worked as a hand on a local ranch. He spent a big part of many days on a horse checking the outlying areas of the ranch. His life was centered on his family, and he accepted things and people for what they were. "You gotta leave things better than you found 'em," he told us while explaining part of his philosophy of life. Denny leaned back, took a drag on his hand rolled cigarette, and proudly proclaimed himself a buckaroo. We couldn't let him stop without finding out what made a buckaroo. After all, wasn't a buckaroo the same as a cowboy?

Denny didn't disappoint. In his no nonsense fashion that we had already come to expect, he explained, "A buckaroo is a guy who's gotta do what he's gotta do." Little did we know that Denny's concise definition would provide words of encouragement to us when facing the challenges that lay ahead.

Spending time with Denny and his family in Mitchell caused us to reflect about the people we had encountered since leaving the Pacific coast. The folks of the West were a truly different breed when compared to the Midwestern types that we had become accustomed to growing up. Many of the Westerners were there because of the wide-open spaces and a desire to live a life that "leaves things better than you found 'em." There was an independence, and a take-life-as-it-comes point of view that was remarkable. Each encounter reinforced the unique lifestyle and hard working characteristics of those who had decided to inhabit the vast reaches of the West.

The ride into Mitchell also showcased the differences in land-scape and topography from our customary environment. The stark-ness of the countryside and the red hills of central Oregon stood in sharp contrast to the hardwood forests and gentle rolling terrain of northern Ohio. Here, the stark landscape had a beauty all its own.

In Mitchell, as we turned in for the evening, we shared a common thought. The different but impressive countryside and the likeable independent people made it feel as though we had somehow left the United States; at least the U. S. that we knew. On the surface, it seemed that the English language was the only thing that we shared with the folks of the West. We were discov-ering the types of people and having the sort of experiences that we had hoped for when we left Astoria. While nodding off, we both agreed that it had been quite a day.

Day 9 - 449 Miles Down, 3338 To Go

FOR GOODNESS SAKE JOHN, PUT SOME CLOTHES ON

The ride out of Mitchell began with a tough, six-mile, six percent climb to Keyes Pass. The ascent was made a little easier by letting our thoughts wander back to the prior evening at the Skyhook Motel. It was a comfortable feeling as the morning began to warm.

The long climbs were a particular challenge for Merj, so we developed a technique that usually worked well. Merj began the climb ahead of me and stopped to rest when she felt the need. I rode past her and stopped and waited about the same distance up the hill. Merj then rode up to me and rested again. The whole procedure was repeated over and over until reaching the top. This approach allowed her to have twice the number of rests, and made our slow moving bikes a little less of a traffic hazard. We called the technique "leapfrogging." The procedure worked exceptionally well on the six-mile climb out of Mitchell.

The ride down from Keyes Pass began with a twenty-mile downgrade through the high desert toward the John Day Fossil Beds. Portions of the lightly traveled, twisting road passed through spectacular canyons with sheer walls rising from the road's edge. There was a real feeling of being alone, and a nagging concern that, if something happened, it would be a while before anyone else knew about it. Images of skeletons picked clean by high desert varmints made their way into our subconscious minds.

An occasional ranch interrupted the mostly uninhabited landscape. Barbwire fences bordered the ranches, and occasional rock filled bins served as fence posts. The unusual structures seemed to be prevalent at bends or where the fences crossed streams. My engineering logic told me that, much like guy wires on power poles, the boxes of rocks probably anchored points of high stress on the fence line. Since we were never able to discover their purpose, Merj had no choice but to accept my well thought out theory.

The road flattened and the John Day Fossil Beds National Monument soon appeared. This unusual national park encompasses 14,000 acres and is visited by 100,000 people a year. The animal and plant fossils found in the park have been exposed by the erosion of volcanic rock over millions of years. The fossil beds provide a record of forty million years of North American plant and animal life. To protect the fossils, the State of Oregon began purchasing the fossil beds in the 1930's for use as a state park.

Congress authorized the creation of the John Day Fossil Beds National Monument in 1974.

It was Father's Day and we decided to stop for brunch in Dayville at the appropriately named Dayville Café. The small restaurant was filled with celebrating families. It didn't take long to notice that some of the patrons sported boots outfitted with spurs. In a classic Midwestern naïveté, we asked the young lady behind the counter whether the spurs were functional or whether they were just used for western style adornment. "Those guys are working cowboys; they could care less about how they look," we were informed with an attitude that said, "take that you bicycling city slickers!" Thank goodness we hadn't asked one of the spur-wearing diners. We decided that a follow up question as to whether they may be buckaroos was probably inappropriate.

The ride to John Day was flat over generally barren terrain. An occasional ranch broke up the unremarkable scenery of the high desert. The day was turning out like most had been since crossing the Cascades, a comfortable morning followed quickly by a very warm late morning and afternoon. As we rode into John Day, a local bank sign showed a temperature of 90 degrees. A McDonald's restaurant on the western outskirts of the city supplied a welcomed respite. It had been a while since the golden arches had been part of the landscape.

The stop in the air-conditioned restaurant provided a refreshing break, but when I bit into my chicken sandwich it developed an unexpected crunch. As I wondered if the just swallowed bite contained ground up bones, or broken glass, or the cook's wedding ring, the source became obvious when I ran my tongue over the sharp edge of a molar. The back half of a dental crown had broken off leaving a noticeably jagged surface. A quick assessment showed no pain, and, other than a minor objection from my tongue, no need for immediate action. It was a problem that would have to be dealt with later.

Having passed through Dayville, the John Day Fossil Beds and with John Day the evening's destination, we wondered about this John Day fellow. We soon discovered that everything John Day was technically named after the John Day River, and not the man. That begged a second question. Who was the river named after?

With a little help from the National Park Service, we learned that John Day was a native Virginian who joined an expedition to form a fur trading post at the mouth of the Columbia River at what is now Astoria. Though the expedition party became widely separated, Day and one other member were eventually able to reach the mouth of the Mah-hah River on the Columbia. There, they were attacked by a band of Indians who, legend has it, took all of their possessions including their clothes. The duo was rescued and arrived in Astoria in 1812. As the years passed, travelers on the river would point to the mouth of the Mah-hah and recall John Day's experience. By the 1850's the river was officially renamed the John Day River.

In reality, John Day probably never came within 100 miles of any town or fossil bed named after him. The story was interesting, but we wondered how a guy who had been rescued naked at the mouth of a river could be memorialized forever by having the river named after him. It was too bad some of the escapades of my own youth hadn't received such similar notoriety. On the down side, we guessed the word spread quickly down river and the gang waiting in Astoria had a lot of fun with old John when he finally arrived.

Day 10 - 526 Miles Down, 3261 To Go

A RAAM IS MORE THAN A BARNYARD ANIMAL OR A DODGE TRUCK

An increasingly painful left hip had made for a restless night's sleep. Walking with a slight but painful limp was becoming the norm. With three climbs ahead on the day's ride, I worried that the hip could put a serious dent in our progress. I decided to take a quick test ride around the motel parking lot and was encouraged; the hip felt better on the bike than it did off it. Another encouraging sign was the much-diminished pain in Merj's legs. Her "leap frogged" participation in most of the climbs during the last week had significantly strengthened them.

The morning was still cool when we stopped at a scenic pull off about halfway up the climb to Dixie Pass, the first and longest of the day's climbs. An oversized Conestoga wagon that begged to be photographed marked the viewpoint. The high elevation of the rest area allowed a panoramic view of the surrounding mountains and an aerial view of an impressive valley below.

As we took pictures of each other on the Conestoga wagon, three fellows piled out of a van parked in the small adjacent parking lot and walked toward us. The van had attracted our attention when we rolled in because it carried bicycles on the roof and was marked by a sign designating it as a support vehicle. It looked like the trio had the right idea of how to do bicycle touring. When they got close, one of them asked us, "Are you guys part of RAAM?" Not knowing what a RAAM was, we told them we didn't think so, but who knows, maybe we were. "What is a RAAM?" I asked. What we learned was humbling, and made our little cross-country trip seem like a ride to a buddy's house on the old J. C. Higgins.

RAAM stood for Race Across America. The basic concept of RAAM is for a group of cyclists to mount their bikes on one coast and see who can be the first to the other coast. We remembered watching a television broadcast of this event a few years ago, and while admiring their fitness and mental endurance, we thought they were a bit crazy. It was now clear that, although many had placed us in the crazy category as well, we weren't part of RAAM.

This year's Race Across America began in Portland, Oregon and was to end at Pensacola, Florida slightly less than three thousand miles later. The racers were divided into a number of classifications such as solo riders, teams, age groupings, etc. The most highly acclaimed participant, however, was the solo rider who completed the trip first. The route would take cyclists through nine states and include 100,000 total feet of climbing. The winner would cross the country in a little more than nine days and average over thirteen miles per hour from start to finish. Because they would be on the bikes for most of 24 hours each day, a support vehicle and support staff was a necessity. The support group supplied the riders with food and drink, mechanical assistance, sleeping arrangements, clothing, speed and timing information, and motivation.

The friendly guys in the van were the support team for a 53-year-old entrant who happened to be the brother of one of them. Two friends, a doctor, and an electrical engineer, made up the rest of the crew. My first thought was that this guy is 53 and he's doing this thing? At 54 years old, I couldn't help but look at our trip as something relatively insignificant. I consoled myself by thinking that the one year between 53 and 54 must be a significant one, and that I probably could have done RAAM last year. The RAAM crew was very supportive of our significantly smaller effort, and they offered encouragement and nutrition bars as we snapped pictures of them in front of the Conestoga wagon. Our casual discussion abruptly came to an end when they spotted their rider coming up the hill a half-mile away. They quickly jumped into the van and repositioned it at the side of the road prepared to help their brother and friend in any way required.

I watched the rider pass before remounting the bike and heading out. I was surprised to find that gaining on him was not a real problem. Who cared if he may have been on his bike for most of the night and day; or that he had to pace himself to cover 300 miles a day. I was right there gaining on a RAAM cyclist! Approaching from the back, I noticed he wore headphones and that high decibel rock music was the entertainment of choice. I debated for a half-mile or so as to whether I should pass him. The question brought back my mild annoyance with perky runners who were part of a 10k race and found enjoyment in passing us crazies who had chosen to participate in the marathon.

At best, in this situation I represented one of those perky 10k runners. By the same token, I really admired what he was doing and wanted to tell him so. Merj, being the more rational of the two of us, had decided some time back that she would not take part in such tomfoolery. Whether it was a testosterone rush, the need to acknowledge his feat or a combination of both, I joined him for just long enough to give a heartfelt thumbs up and receive a smiling nod in return. I pedaled on to the top of Dixie Pass with a certain sense of false accomplishment. Soon the support crew joined me and offered more encouragement and nutrition bars. These guys were truly remarkable.

TAKE TWO ASPIRIN AND CALL ME IN THE MORNING

Reaching Dixie Pass, at an elevation of 5,277 feet, was another cause for photos and mild celebration. We were tempted to climb onto something three feet in height and lay claim to being a mile high. The pass was covered in pines and the air was cool enough to require donning cold weather gear for the ride down. A group of friendly touring motor cyclists had also stopped at the pass and we all traded exaggerated tales of the road. Although there was a certain two-wheel comradery with motor cyclists, we always felt a little inferior. As they roared off on their hogs, we dutifully followed on our piglets.

The day's roller coaster ride continued as the road fell from Dixie Pass only to rise five or six miles again to Tipton Pass. The process was repeated again and we eventually reached the final high point of the day, Sumpter Pass. By now I had developed an attitude of, "Once you've seen one, you've seen them all." The ride down from the pass toward Baker City was interrupted by a stop in the small town of Sumpter for lunch.

Sumpter is a very nicely restored tourist friendly community that was established in the 1860's by farmers who named the town after South Carolina's Fort Sumter. The fact that the town is spelled with a "*p*" was the result of a request by the U.S. Post Office to avoid confusion with another Oregon town. The early settlers were soon overrun by gold seeking prospectors, and the town peaked with a population of about 3,000 in the late 1800's. Today Sumpter is a community of about 175. A restored narrow gage railroad, The Sumpter Valley Railroad, transports visitors around the area.

The waitress at the Scoop and Steamer Restaurant, our choice for lunch, was an affable young lady who happened to be the restaurant owner's daughter. She and the rest of her family had pitched in to help while her mother recuperated from a leg broken in three places. When she discovered our northeastern Ohio origins, she informed all within earshot that Terrell Brandon, a former member of the Cleveland Cavaliers, was a good friend. As the discussion continued, the names of other professional athletes sprinkled her conversation. Each successive name heightened the curiosity of a sore-hipped male diner. Merj, sensing that I was about to explode with a series of rapid fire questions, began the customary under-the-table ankle kicking. Ignoring the growing pain in my lower extremities and the possibility of admonishment once outside the restaurant, I asked, "How in the world do you know all these people?"

We soon discovered that our name dropping waitress had a Master's Degree in sports therapy. She had worked with a number of pro-athletes over the years by helping them rehabilitate sports injuries. This revelation caused a thought to cross my furtive mind. I wasn't exactly a professional athlete, but maybe she had an idea on how to deal with the toothache in my hip. Although the left hip was not particularly troublesome on the bike, walking into the restaurant and sitting at the table caused a constant pain that made it difficult to get comfortable.

After patiently listening to my somber and maybe slightly embellished litany of symptoms, she confidently stated, "You've got bursitis and it's caused by repetitive motion." The diagnosis certainly sounded plausible. "Take two Aleve in the morning and two at night for a week, followed by one each morning and evening for another week," she added with equal confidence. "Unless you follow my instructions religiously, it's a waste of time to even start."

Her precise instructions gave the feeling that a snap to attention and a brisk salute were in order. Regardless, her confidence in the recommended cure and the pain in my hip made me decide to give it a try. If this worked, it would amount to the cheapest medical advice either of us had received in the past thirty years. After a generous tip, we headed out the door and on to Baker City.

The road to Baker City was comfortably downhill and it was easy to get into an easy cycling rhythm. Powder Creek paralleled the roadway for much of the ride and provided a pleasant burbling sound as the water passed over occasional rapids. Smaller versions of the previous day's canyons rose alongside the road. The ride into Baker City was unimpressive; junkyards seemed to be the business of choice in the outlying sections of town. The downtown area, however, was a pleasant surprise as it had the comfortable feeling of a nicely preserved small American community.

Baker City was granted its charter in 1870 and was once considered a social gathering point for travelers on the Oregon Trail and miners working the nearby gold mines. The early hard drinking, fun loving locals made Baker City a classic Wild West town. Today's population of 9,100 belies the fact that it was once Oregon's largest city.

As we checked into the hotel, an obliging lady behind the desk offered the name of a local dentist and suggested a Mexican restaurant for dinner. The restaurant was an obvious favorite with locals as the parking lot was filled to capacity. While being escorted to our table by a young waitress named Conchita, we discovered that she was the daughter of the owner. She quickly took our order and began running from table to table taking and filling other patron's meal requests. Soon the food suggested by Conchita arrived, and between her breathless sprints, we began a conversation with our delightful and efficient waitress.

Conchita, we learned, was thirty-years-old and had been in the United States for seventeen years; the last ten in Baker City. Her melodic voice had strong hints of her native Mexico. We tried to assure her that the self-consciousness that she felt about her accent was unwarranted. As the evening wore on and the number of patrons in the restaurant dwindled, Conchita was able to slow her frenetic pace and spend more time chatting. We laughed, as she talked about her life in a free-spirited, upbeat, almost childlike fashion. She mused about the plusses and minuses of working in her father's business, her early years in Mexico and life in Baker City, all the time with a bright smile on her face and a sparkle in her eyes. If hard work and positive outlook were the keys to success, Conchita was another of the people we had met that deserved success in life. The list was getting longer.

Day 11 - 595 Miles Down, 3192 To Go

WILL I NEED NOVOCAINE?

We had been looking forward to a rest day in Baker City since crossing Santiam Pass. The day began by waking up well after the usual 5:00 AM. It took a while to realize that on this day, we would not be facing the usual confrontation with the bicycle seats. When reality sunk in, a smile crossed both our faces.

My first productive endeavor of the day was a call to Dr.

Whitnah; the dentist who had been recommended the previous evening. An impassioned plea resulted in a 1:00 appointment. My early arrival at the dentist's office provided the unexpected pleasure of chatting with Betty, the very amiable lady behind the front desk.

Betty had moved to Oregon from southern California, and now lived with her husband on a ranch in Richland, a small town that would be part of the next day's ride. She was an admitted horse lover, who owned about sixty-five, and bred another ten or fifteen each year. Since I was in the presence of a real horse expert, I felt an urgent need to resurrect the spur question from a few days ago. Since Merj was no where in sight and her usual admonitions would not be forthcoming, I boldly asked Betty about the real motives of spur wearing Oregonians. "The spurs are used to nudge the animal along, but most people these days wear 'em for show," she patiently explained. Ah-ha, just as I thought! The trip to the dentist was already paying dividends.

Betty was curious about our trip and told me about her avid bicyclist ex-husband. I wondered if the bicycle obsession had contributed to their divorce, and my thoughts drifted back to the marital concerns expressed by our friends back home. Just to be safe, I briefly considered picking up some flowers for Merj on the way back to the hotel. One could never be too careful. Betty asked for the web site address and said that she and her ex-husband would enjoy following the progress of the trip. I was relieved to hear that they had obviously maintained a friendly relationship. Maybe his cycling hadn't been the problem after all. Maybe the flowers could wait.

Before long Betty escorted her jagged tooth patient back to a waiting dentist chair and a waiting dentist. Dr. Whitnah was a pleasant, professional looking individual, probably in his later 50's, who exhibited the easy going outlook on life that had become the norm in Oregon. "Patching the crown is an iffy proposition, but let's give it a try," he cautiously declared. After ten minutes or so of methodical dental diligence, he confidently stated, "This might be more successful than I first thought."

After the procedure, I sat in a comfortably reclined dental chair and we chatted about the trip. "You've got some pretty good hills coming up," he offered. In the interest of maintaining team morale, I made a mental note to avoid sharing this newfound information with Merj. After a sincere wish of good luck from Betty, I was out the door and back to the realities of laundry and taking care of that aching hip.

Day 12 - 595 Miles Down, 3192 To Go

LOOK OUT FOR THAT FRISBEE

The ride out of Baker City was a bit of a worrisome experience. A very brisk wind had kicked up and it blew directly from the side. Experienced cyclists had told us that crosswinds were more of a problem than headwinds. At the time we thought "Yeah, sure," but today's winds validated their warning. The wind gusts were so ferocious at times that staying on the bike required an awkward, severe lean to the side. Had the wind momentarily ceased, a knee onto the pavement would have been our certain fate.

About five wind-buffeted miles out of Baker City, we came upon the Oregon Trail Interpretive Center. The Interpretive Center is a 500 acre site with a museum housed in a modern look-ing structure located a short distance off the road. The museum displayed artifacts, exhibits, and dioramas that recreated the expe-riences of travelers on the Oregon Trail. Near the museum, a roadside plaque showed the place where the trail crossed the highway. Unbelievably, the wagon tracks of the westward bound settlers were still visible in the hard packed soil.

The Oregon Trail dates to 1843 when a thousand settlers formed a wagon train and traveled across the country to live in what are now the Pacific Coast and western Rocky Mountain States. At the time, there were few other travel options as the trail offered the only feasible way to get through the mountains. The westward trek on the Oregon Trail was a two thousand mile trip where one in ten died along the way. Many walked the entire distance barefoot. The greatest problems faced by the early settlers were not attacks by Indians, but disease, poor sanitation, and accidental gunshot wounds. The funerals of the many cholera victims were conducted quickly as delays could have endangered the whole party by the onset of winter.

The history of the Oregon Trail is filled with tales that are tragic and humorous. The travelers were much like those of today in that they over packed before heading west. As a result, the landscape along the trail was often littered with discarded furniture, stoves, and even food. Rumor had it that officer's quarters at forts along the route were remarkably well furnished.

It was also well documented that buffalo chips, dried buffalo dung, were prevalent throughout the plains. The dung's practical use was that it made good campfire fuel. Its recreational use, however, was providing a diversion for young pioneers who used them as early day Frisbees. The look on nineteenth century Labrador Retrievers as they jumped into the air to fetch a Frisbee, and instead sank their teeth into a dried cow pie had to be quite entertaining. Through 1869, when the Oregon Trail was pretty much replaced by the Transcontinental Railroad, over a half million people had traveled it in search of gold in California or the fertile farm land of the Willamette Valley. Our cross-country trip, again, seemed insignificant by comparison.

HOLE IN THE WALL

Today was the last full day in Oregon, and excitement started to build as the first state line crossing quickly approached. The scenery during the morning's ride was both stark and beautiful. To the southwest, the rolling landscape was covered by low sagebrush; views to the northeast were much the same as in the foreground, with snow capped mountains providing a pleasant distant diversion. The winds stopped as quickly as they had started, and the morning ride turned refreshingly cool through gently rolling topography under a cloudless, crystal blue sky. Reaching the top of an occasional knoll provided opportunities for panoramic views of the surrounding countryside. A minimal amount of traffic added to a very pleasant morning ride through the eastern Oregon high plains.

The sagebrush soon gave way to working ranches with herds of horses and cattle. A large ranch house situated on the top of a hill looked down on acres of grazing livestock and a newborn foal on wobbly legs at its mother's side. Irrigated fields and an occasional clump of trees was the typical scenery as the road headed toward Idaho. Remembering a popular television show, it felt as though real life had been pulled out of a scene from *Bonanza*.

The same Powder Creek that had provided company west of Baker City again gave noisy companionship as the road passed through small canyons. The glistening sun off the water's surface and the sonorous sounds of birds chirping in the background made for a delightful morning's ride. Thankfully, the birds bore no resemblance to their dive bombing counterparts from a few days ago.

After a short climb we came upon a large sign that described a recent event called the Hole-in-the-Wall Landslide. In 1984 a landslide covering the original roadway isolated hundreds of local residents and blocked the Powder Creek creating a half-mile long reservoir. The original road and reservoir could be seen when looking down into the valley below at a lake that seemed very much out of place in the middle of the surrounding terrain. Continuing to read the sign, I learned that the landslide had moved 10,000 cubic yards of rock and soil and was still moving about a half inch per day. It would continue to move until the year 2014.

Once again I had an obsessive need to know how someone had determined that this particular landslide would reach its demise in the year 2014. I quickly calculated that, at a half inch per day, the landslide would move about sixty yards between now and then. As I looked around for an obstacle sixty yards away that could stop this thing, none was visible. I left Hole-in-the-Wall Landslide with two thoughts: somebody smarter that me must know what they're talking about, and why in the world should I be concerned about the final resting place of a landslide in the wide open spaces of eastern Oregon? Apparently, time on the bicycle seat had given me way too much time to contemplate such things.

In Richland, while stopped at the Cappuccino Corral and Eatery for a rest and a Coke, an unsolicited comment from a local warned that a good-sized hill waited a few miles out of town. Since we were in no particular hurry to take it on, we slowly sipped our drinks and watched a young mother play with her two cowboy hat adorned ranchers in training.

The hill, another seven percenter, started soon enough, and we again incorporated the leapfrog technique to reach the top. Before leaving home, a group of friends had given us a hand held global positioning system. The GPS came in handy on the grades, as I would regularly give Merj status reports by reading off an elevation during a long climb. Since the route maps usually showed the elevation at the top, the GPS allowed both of us to gauge how much more climbing would be required to reach the summit.

There was always the temptation to add a few feet to the GPS readings to keep Merj's spirits up. Because of a character flaw, temptation often prevailed, and my reported elevations in the middle part of a climb were usually "elevationally enhanced." It was a delicate juggling of conscience and a desire to maintain team morale.

Reaching the top of the latest summit was a rewarding accomplishment. Merj's strength and confidence continued to grow with each mountain pass. We hadn't completely discarded worries about the physical and psychological challenges presented by the upcoming mountains, but they had diminished in magnitude; and reduced anxieties allowed for more enjoyment.

From the summit, the panoramic view to the east was filled with rugged snow capped mountains: Idaho was going to be beautiful and challenging. A large, yellow, Paul Bunyon sized ruler rose vertically a short distance off the road. The painted one-foot increments topped out at ten feet. Like the rock filled fence baskets, we never found the purpose of the over-sized ruler, but guessed that it was used to measure snow depth. If that were true, the winters at the top of the hill were truly something to write home about.

"YOU'LL JUST BE FOLLOWIN' RIVER GRADE."

The evening's stopping point was in Halfway, another typical rural Oregon town. An old timer resting with his cane on a park bench shared two versions of the origin of the town's name. Apparently during the boom times of the 1800's there were two villages, Pinetown and Cornucopia, that were located at either end of the Pine Valley. Because of the wide separation between the two towns, it was determined that a post office was needed between them. Application was made to put a new town at the mid-point and name it Midway. Since there was already a Midway, Oregon, the name was changed to Halfway. Ironically one of the original towns is now under water and the other no longer exists. The second version was based on the location of Halfway on the forty-fifth parallel, halfway between the equator and the North Pole. Either story sounded believable, and the old man certainly enjoyed telling us about them.

It's a good thing neither of us was in a hurry, because the old man's stories didn't stop there. We soon learned that the good people of Halfway had, in the year 2000, renamed their city Half.com. The story seemed more than a little bazaar, so further questioning was in order. Piecing together the stories of town folk and archived articles in *Time Magazine* and *The New York Times*, it appears that a visitor arrived in late 1999 with an offer the town couldn't refuse.

The newcomer was a marketing guru who worked for a start up dot com company out of Philadelphia by the name of Half.com. Half.com was an Amazon/eBay type of Internet service that catered to buyers and sellers of all sorts of items. The new company was looking for publicity, so the visionary marketing genius approached the city fathers of Halfway, and asked them to change the name of this home to 350 people to Half.com, Oregon. In return the community would get computers for the local school and cash for civic improvements.

After expressions of intense feelings on both sides of the issue, the name change was approved in early 2000. It wasn't the first time a city had changed its name to something out of the ordinary. After all, Hot Springs, New Mexico had changed its name to Truth or Consequences, the name of a popular television show, in 1950. More recently, the tiny town of Ismay, Montana (population 22) had changed its name to Joe, Montana, the name of the former quarterback. Just as the folks at Half.com had hoped, word of the town's new name spread quickly. Half.com, Oregon became the location of a live broadcast of the Today Show, and, in addition to *Time* and the *New York Times*, the town was featured in *USA TODAY*. We wondered if that day's edition made it to this part of Oregon, or if, "the guy that brings them around must have died or something." The people at Half.com presumably appreciated all of the relatively inexpensive publicity as the new company was sold to eBay in June of 2000 for $300 million in stock.

Our lunch in a small café included the wrong food order and change that was five dollars short, but that was okay. The somewhat flustered waitress was a pleasant young lady who sleepily told us, "The only thing for kids to do around here is go down to the swimmin' hole, and that's about it." Winters in the small town must be a real joy.

When the middle age man working in the kitchen overheard our discussion, he added, "If you don't hunt or fish there's not much to do. I've been married for 38 years, my wife owns this restaurant, and I've never cashed a paycheck in my life." In the years working outside the restaurant, he simply handed the check over to his wife who took care of all of the family's finances. "Working for her is no big deal. I've been working for her for 38 years anyhow," he added. Merj gave me a knowing glance and an affirmative nod. This guy was her hero.

Since the cook was obviously a long term resident of the area, it was impossible to resist asking him about the road to come, especially the part rising from Hells Canyon into Idaho. "It's not too bad because you'll just be followin' river grade," he described. Just following river grade was a description that brought a mixture of images to mind. After all, if one were to follow river grade up the Niagara River, a climb over Niagara Falls would be in the offing. Just following river grade was not a description that left us with a particularly confident feeling.

Since an early start was planned for the next day, Merj asked what time the café would be opening for breakfast. "I'll probably open at around eight or so depending on when I get out of bed," he told her rather matter-of-factly. A power bar breakfast and a splash of water along the road somewhere would have to suffice.

"THAT'S A LOTTA WORK, HOW 'BOUT A BEER INSTEAD."

The Stockman's Restaurant and Lounge became our choice for evening nourishment and conversation in Halfway or Half.com, or wherever we were. As we entered the restaurant, it was impossible not to notice that the walls were adorned with the large saws used by loggers. They were painted with colorful scenes representing eastern Oregon. Most of them were painted by local artists, and were very well done. Some of the prices ranged as high as $125.00.

The special of the day was a pork chop dinner for $7.95, so we decided to give it a try. When asked by the waitress to choose a beverage, the selection of chocolate milkshakes brought a facial expression that showed disappointment and maybe even outright disgust. "That's a lot of work. If you really want 'em I guess I can do it, but how 'bout a beer instead?" she asked. We quickly acquiesced and asked for two drafts. When instead two bottles of beer showed up at the table, we decided they were close enough. The husky voiced waitress, along with all of those saws hanging on the wall, had a certain intimidating effect. While sipping the beers and waiting for dinner to arrive, our friendly waitress walked to the blackboard that announced the day's specials and changed the price of the pork chops to $8.95. Our order was placed just in time to save a dollar.

The Hells Canyon Journal, the local weekly newspaper of choice, devoted a great amount of space to the upcoming Senior Pro Rodeo. Halfway was a stop on the Senior Pro Rodeo circuit, and the old guys would be in town during the upcoming weekend. The event was also publicized throughout the community with brightly colored posters on display in the windows of many of the local businesses. Merj expressed genuine disappointment that we would not be there to be part of the excitement. Being familiar with the Senior Golfer's Tour, we tried to visualize a guy in an Izod shirt and a pair of Foot Joys with chaps and spurs on top of a bucking bronco. Such musings made it obvious the day had been a long one; it was time to head back to the hotel for a good night's sleep.

Day 13 - 650 Miles Down, 3137 To Go

OLD GLORY

Leaving Halfway on the last morning in Oregon, we glanced back toward a sign at the edge of town that proudly announced

"Welcome to Half.com." It appeared that Half.com really was the name of this small town near the Idaho border. The seventeen-mile ride to Oxbow, the last vestige of Oregon, was pleasantly down hill through stands of pines. The last few miles in Oregon consisted of free and easy cycling above Pine Creek.

A few miles from Oxbow, a sight on the opposite side of the creek caused a quick stop and a search for the camera. On the other bank, about a hundred yards away, was a large dilapidated old house. A prominent feature on the old structure was a drooping front porch just a few feet off the edge of the rapidly moving water. The sagging, weather-beaten porch was covered with a collection of miscellaneous discarded artifacts. The setting of the old house, a flowing creek in front and a pine covered slope in the rear, was in itself an interesting photographic subject. What made it truly worthy of attention was the oversized American flag hanging across the front of the porch. The bright colors of the flag stood out in sharp contrast to the grays of the dwelling. The thoughts and feelings of September 11, 2001, although somewhat distant, were still fresh enough to send a tingle up my spine as I stared across the creek.

As I gazed down at the old house, its occupant came out to the corner of the porch and gave me a friendly wave. Fifty yards of rushing water prevented my joining him on the porch for what would have certainly been an enlightening discussion. The sight of this down-on-his-luck man standing under an oversized American flag waving up to a stranger on a bicycle remained with me for a long time.

Crossing the bridge over Pine Creek put us officially into Hells Canyon. On the other side of the creek something we had joked about back in McKenzie Pass came to be: A father and son, two cross country cyclists, approached from the opposite direction and stopped to chat. The father had started in Virginia and his son had joined him later some 2000 miles back. The son's bike was a yellow Cannondale T2000 just like ours, and it was good to hear of the dependable service it had given him across the country. We laughed as we compared our similar experiences and the people we had met.

They described an interesting fellow named Smokey waiting in that evening's destination of Cambridge. "You've got to meet this guy, he's a local legend," the father added. The positive, cheerful attitude they showed was comforting to see this late in their journey. The father's long held ambition to do the trip was also something we both shared. While getting ready to separate, we exchanged names and discovered that the father, Don, had named his son Skye. The triumvirate of Wind, River, and Skye was complete.

After leaving Don and Skye, and after a short climb and a bend or two, the wide, tranquil Snake River appeared on the left. This portion of the river, just upstream from Oxbow Dam, formed the boundary between Oregon and Idaho. To the right were the steep walls of Hells Canyon. We had been told that summer temperatures in the canyon can reach 110 degrees Fahrenheit. Such high temperatures were hard to believe as the cycling continued comfortably along the lightly traveled road under a clear blue, cloudless sky.

We decided to stop along the Snake River in the shadows of Brownlee Dam to take a break and eat the sandwiches that had been purchased in Halfway or Half.com. The river flowed slowly past the picnic spot with a gentle background sound that was interrupted by the occasional splash of a jumping fish. I found some suitable flat stones and deftly skipped them over the water surface reflecting back on another happy youthful memory. Stone skipping is an acquired skill, much like horseshoe pitching; once you had it, you never lost it. At least stone skipping was one talent that hadn't diminished over the passing years.

Crossing the Snake River on a narrow bridge directly in front of Brownlee Dam put us into Idaho. Brownlee Dam was an impressive earthen structure and the location of a power generating facility owned by Idaho Power. We would soon come upon the upstream pool of the dam, Brownlee Lake, but first things first. The sign welcoming visitors to Idaho was simple in its statement: "Entering Idaho." A couple of guys happened to be walking by, and one of them, Doug from Nebraska, took a ceremonial picture of the two of us by the sign. After 680 miles and thirteen days on the road, the first of eleven states had been successfully crossed.

idaho

"No problem 'cause I got a couple horses to break in the mornin' anyhow."

SMOKEY

While planning the trip no single source of information proved more helpful than Leo Hennessy from Idaho. Leo entered the picture during a winter phone call to the Idaho Department of Parks and Recreation. The receptionist who answered the phone forwarded the call to Leo, the alleged guy with the answers to bicycle touring questions. She was right. Leo was an avid cyclist who had toured much of the state. When told of our tentative route through Idaho, he enthusiastically endorsed our itinerary and described in detail what to expect along the way. Leo's information was presented in such detail that it felt as though we knew where to expect every pothole and watering hole in the state. His love of the state and his enthusiasm for what we were about to undertake was infectious. The picture he painted of Idaho was of energy sapping climbs, rewarded by beautiful scenery and gracious people. After a couple of talks with Leo, we couldn't wait to get there.

The euphoria of entering Leo's Idaho was temporarily put on hold by the start of a thirteen mile climb "up river grade" from Brownlee Dam. The leap frogged climb was interrupted by frequent checks of the GPS and glances back toward the dark blue of Brownlee Lake. The entire climb was under an increasingly hot sun with little or no shade for protection. The time of day even worked against us. Having entered the Mountain Time Zone when crossing into Idaho, it was now an hour later into the morning than it had been just moments before. Common sense said that the hour's gain didn't make a bit of difference, but psychologically it felt warmer.

The climbs were always a little deceiving. Looking ahead, the rise in the road was clearly evident, but upon stopping and looking back, the grades appeared steeper, and sometimes almost insurmountable. Maybe a set of blinders, the type worn by racehorses, would have been a worthwhile investment. On the other hand, looking back provided a sense of accomplishment and the rewarding feeling that somehow, that particular part of the climb had been conquered.

The higher elevation at the summit meant much cooler air and the need to put on more clothing for the ride down the other side. The initial drop was steep and created the much-anticipated rush that came with the speed and roar of wind that were part of flying down from a mountain pass. The ride into Cambridge for our first night in Idaho was a series of gradual drops and flat sections through unremarkable scenery. A small stream paralleled the road, and without watching the direction of the flowing water, it was impossible at times to tell whether the ride was slightly up or down grade.

The small high desert town of Cambridge, Idaho was much

like many of those we had previously visited. Situated at the base of Cuddy Mountain, Cambridge is the home to 375 people, and the oldest newspaper in Idaho. Agriculture is the major occupation in the area, more specifically dairy, cattle, and hay production. It was a cloudless, dry, 92 degrees when downtown Cambridge came into view.

The night in Cambridge was spent at Hunter's Inn. The brochure, mailed by the innkeeper during the winter, proudly displayed a long limousine parked in front. The limo served as a sort of beacon drawing guests to the establishment much as ants are attracted to a picnic lunch. Not that finding Hunter's Inn would have been difficult in Cambridge, but the sight of the limo led us straight to our home for the evening. A stretch limo in this part of Idaho was, well, a *stretch*, but closer examination showed that it fit quite well into the landscape. The mid-60's Chrysler was past its prime, but was big and beefy, reflecting the designs of its era and the nature of its current surroundings. It had been a while since a rock star, an athlete, an actor, or the Mayor of Cambridge had graced the inside of this white beauty.

After checking in, a short walk next door to Bucky's Café for a bowl of chili was met with another bit of déjà vu. Halfway through her chili, Merj bit down hard on something that obviously didn't belong. Close inspection revealed that a boulder, about three-eighths of an inch in diameter, had been mixed in with the chili beans. The waitress quickly replaced the chili with a bowl of complimentary soup. Fortunately the encounter wasn't cause for another visit to the dentist. It did cause one to wonder, though, why eating had become such a potentially dangerous dental experience. In spite of the problem with the chili, we learned that Smokey, the local legend described earlier in the day, frequented Bucky's on most late afternoons. We would be back later to try to make his acquaintance.

Meals usually turned out to be the non-cycling high point of the day. They offered a chance to reflect on the day's events, meet interesting people, learn about where we were; and find out about where we were going. The fact that we were gaining a better understanding of the people who lived in the high plains was due in large part to the people we met in restaurants. It was also a chance to impart a bit of good old Buckeye philosophy to new-found friends. Today's meals wouldn't disappoint.

Since there was a certain reluctance to return to Bucky's, a walk through downtown Cambridge showed few options for the evening meal save a bar not far from the Hunter's Inn. The bar was dark and nearly empty when we walked in and asked the bar owner if she served dinner. She responded, "Yeah, out back," and so that is where we headed. Out back, Richard, the owner's husband, waited under an awning shielding a grille and a couple of picnic tables. With spatula in hand he was ready to go to work. When we inquired about a menu, he politely informed us, "You can have either a hamburger or a cheeseburger." The good news was that the preparation of either selection could be observed right in front of a patron's eyes, and Richard handled the hamburgers with the skill of a surgeon.

While munching on the tasty burgers, three tough-looking boisterous couples sat down at the only other picnic table available. Their discussion was loud and profane, and there was no difficulty determining that they were motorcyclists just passing through town. An occasional glance our way gave us an impression that, to them, we were considered a couple of sniveling sissies. Soon, with the unsolicited help of Richard, they learned that, in fact, we shared membership with them in the exclusive club of two wheel travelers. The common bond the eight of us shared opened the door, and they soon brought us into their mellowing discussion.

Surprisingly the couples showed a great amount of interest in our adventure and provided information and advice of what to expect down the road. It was as if they were taking us under their wing, much as an older brother looks after his runny-nosed kid brother or, maybe more appropriately, a hog looks after its piglets. After a lively discussion, we bid good evening to Richard and our newfound friends. We had just experienced a classic example of why one should not judge a book by its cover. As we left the bar, I had a sudden urge to find a tattoo parlor and have CANNON-DALE tattooed across my forearm.

From the bar it was back to Bucky's for dessert and a chance encounter with Smokey. We sat at the counter and enjoyed a root-beer float, refreshingly free of stones or other unusual objects. At the end of the counter sat an elderly disheveled man with a long white beard who could have been Albert Einstein's long lost brother. The girl behind the counter gave an affirmative nod when asked if it was Smokey. There were few other people in the café so starting a conversation wasn't difficult. In fact, the others in the restaurant looked a little relieved when the attention of this talkative fellow was diverted our way.

Smokey was perched at what was evidently his usual counter spot, nursing a cup of coffee, and regaling the few people near him with his opinions. It didn't take long to get a conversation going, and he moved a few seats closer so as to accommodate our less than perfect hearing. Smokey quickly established his educational credibility. "I've got two master's degrees from the University of Wisconsin," he said. He talked of a former life that included a stint teaching high school chemistry, physics, and math. Maybe that Einstein look of his was for real. Before long he was informed that Merj was a retired teacher. That piece of information began the unique sharing of "war stories" that usually happens when teachers meet. There had to be a name for the shared phenomenon that took place when two teachers came into close proximity with each other. Named or not, it continued to be a source of wonder to the non-teacher in the three way conversation.

Smokey talked of having taught in a small Idaho town some years ago. "The school was in the town bar, and I taught those kids from the bandstand." With a twinkle in his eye Smokey explained, "I had many graduates of the bar, but hardly any of them became lawyers." He talked about his children and was clearly proud of the fact they were all well educated and most were teachers. This frail old man had obviously been an influence on those around him.

The conversation couldn't have continued without finding out how Smokey got his name. It didn't take much prompting to learn that, although he was a former teacher, most of his working life had been spent with the Forest Service during the 1940's and 1950's. "While I worked there," he said, "they used Smokey the Bear to teach folks about not startin' forest fires, and somehow I ended up with his name." Whether he was a smoker, liked honey, or slept through the winter in his younger days, we never found out exactly why the Smokey moniker had been picked for him.

Smokey was a charming old guy, the type of person it wasn't surprising to find in a small dusty town in western Idaho. He took a real liking to Merj and complimented her profusely. Merj, whose face displayed an "awe shucks" look while listening to Smokey's compliments, would have stayed and talked well into the evening, but it was time to walk back to Hunter's Inn and take care of the usual evening errands. Even though it was a very short walk, the thought crossed my mind that maybe we should call the limo. I had a feeling though that the old Chrysler would probably make a better planter than a working limousine.

With the daily routine completed, and as Merj drifted off to sleep, her wide awake companion decided to take a stroll around town to see what was going on. The town was small, so it didn't take long to find out that there really wasn't anything going on. Nearing the hotel room on the return trip, a chance encounter occurred with a young fellow by the name of Rick who was sitting outside his room next to an immaculately maintained motorcycle. I pulled up a chair and soon discovered that Rick and a buddy were taking an extended motorcycle tour of the west. In fact the bike had over 110,000 miles on it, so the motorcycle and Rick had spent a lot of time together.

Rick talked of having worked as a brewer for a small local western brewery. He unfortunately explained, "I had to get out of the beer business because I broke my back twice in motorcycle accidents." In spite of the misfortune, his sense of humor was still very much intact; we joked about what a shame it was to leave such a dream job. I admired his attitude, because I was pretty sure that if I had broken my back twice as a result of bicycle accidents, my two-wheeled transportation would have been on the curb with the garbage.

His knowledge of the West, gained by the many miles on the motorcycle, was helpful. Rick spoke of the beauty of the Sawtooth Mountains and of the area near Lowman. Both places were on our itinerary within the next week. On a scrap of paper, he scribbled the name of an old friend who lived east of Lowman, and asked if we would stop and say hello for him. As we headed for our respective rooms, I told him we would try to oblige his request.

Day 14 - 714 Miles Down, 3073 To Go

WHAT IF SOMEBODY COMES IN HERE?

The ride out of Cambridge was through miles of high desert and past occasional ranches. Signs, resembling branding irons, placed by the entrances identified the names of the ranches. The *Bonanza* feeling of a few days ago was back. The generally flat ride was interrupted by a moderate climb to an area named Mesa. A large sign at a pull-off told visitors that Mesa was once the home to the largest apple orchard under single management in the United States. Looking around at the high-desert landscape, it was amazing that any type of apples had ever grown there.

A stop in Council at the Sawtooth Café brought some mid-morning eggs, biscuits, and gravy; a tasty "low-cal" meal. The café was another of the husband and wife owned establishments that were becoming familiar. There was no attempt to hide who was in charge, though, as the male half of the ownership team often referred to his better-half as admiral. Merj found a pleasant lady at the neighboring booth and quickly struck up a conversation about quilting. She soon joined the lady and her husband in their booth to take a closer look at the woman's handiwork. It was not unusual to find a quilter in town, as there was a major gathering of quilt makers going on later in the day. As often happened, the local folks in the restaurant warned of a considerable hill a few miles outside of town. Even though prying Merj from her new-found quilting friend was fraught with a certain danger, the time had come to head out.

It hadn't taken many miles back in Oregon to discover that there were two road signs that sent a particular dread through our bodies. The first was PASSING LANE AHEAD, and the second was CHAIN PULL OFF AREA. Both signaled a significant hill. A chain pull-off sign predicted the day's first climb. As the bottom of the hill came into view, it started to rain lightly and the dive-bombing, ditch-living black birds had returned. The good news, though, was that the sore hip was starting to feel much better. That sports therapy waitress back in Sumpter obviously knew what she was talking about after all.

Like many of the previous climbs, the scenery on this one changed from high-desert browns to pine-forest green. Maybe it was the rain, but the morning pine smell of the forest seemed to be especially aromatic. Even the passing logging trucks, usually a wind buffeted exciting experience, were less threatening because of the pleasant odors left in their wake. The trucks, though, kicked up a spray that worsened the effect of the increasing rain. For the first time on the trip, I was soaked to the core and getting chilled. All of the high-tech weather gear was not living up to advertised expectations.

Fortunately at the top of the climb the tiny town of Tamarac provided improved weather and a chance to get out of the wet clothes. Though not even a one-stoplight town, Tamarac was home to a large logging operation. With no other options, the office of the logging company was the only available choice to change clothes, and hopefully, provide restrooms to deal with another urgent need exacerbated by the rain. I stood, dripping wet, at the reception desk and rang a bell on the counter that failed to produce a human of any form. The restrooms, however, were clearly visible off the reception area.

Considering the increasing urgency of the situation, an unannounced visit to one of them was in order. Being one who pretty much follows the rules, the fact that I was in the restroom of a private business without letting anyone know was troublesome. What if someone came in only to be surprised by a half-dressed bicycle rider? Would anyone believe the truth? I changed in record time; and no one entered the small restroom while the act was in progress. Feeling guilty, a stop by the reception desk on the way out to explain and thank them for use of the facilities was called for, but it remained unoccupied. Since Merj had not shared the same discomfort and had no reason to visit the office, she had patiently waited outside under a small awning. After explaining the angst caused by the restroom visit the concern and worry about my experience was evident on her face. At least I thought it was, until I detected a slight rolling of her eyes as we prepared to depart. Apparently it was one of those things, where you just had to be there.

Leaving Tamarac, the weather improved and arrival in the small town of New Meadow was met with an increasingly sunny sky. After an enjoyable lunch of soup and salad at the Sagebrush BBQ, it was back outside into a now comfortably warm afternoon.

While getting the wet gear repacked, a call that included our names came from across the street. Looking up, we were greeted by the wide smile of Andy, our National Guard friend from a few days ago. After a warm greeting, the traditional sharing of tales of the road began in earnest. The stories always left a feeling that our worries and feelings were pretty much the same as others, and that was comforting.

On this occasion, it felt great to hear Andy complain, "That rain was bad enough, but those trucks were a real pain." He continued, "On some of those long climbs, I find myself talking to the cows along he road." It was comforting to find that talking to cows was really no big deal after all as I too had occasionally found solace in directing mumbled commentary their way during a climb. It was also nice to hear that he too had single handedly downed an entire pizza the night before. I had done the same thing a couple nights ago myself. Ah, this group therapy was great! Since our itineraries would be diverging in New Meadow and not coming together again until Jackson, Wyoming, we figured this would most likely be our last encounter.

The night would be spent in the resort community of McCall. Although only about ten miles away, there was a significant climb a few miles out of town. Leaving New Meadow, it seemed that the effort required to pedal the bike was indicative of a mysterious upgrade that wasn't there. I stopped to check for brake drag or some sort of gearing problem, but none was evident. Since there seemed to be an odd low noise coming from the rear of the bike, and since the rest of the uphill day would not require heavy braking, I released the rear brakes just to make sure they weren't the cause. After continuing on for three miles or so, there was still no noticeable change in the effort or the noise. This time a dismount and closer inspection of the bike showed that one of the elastic straps that held the rear pack in place had not been replaced properly. It had been rubbing the rear wheel since New Meadow and was almost completely worn through. A knowing glance from Merj verified that her husband might not be the genius he would like to think he was. Not knowing a lot of Finnish made her utterance unintelligible, but some Scandinavian derivative of the word idiot may have softly crossed her lips.

The six-mile climb into McCall was a tough one with switch-backs, steep grades, heavy traffic, and sharp drop-offs that were unprotected by guardrails. The lush pine forest that bordered the road afforded some protection from the warm mid-afternoon sun. But even the occasional shade didn't keep the sweat caused by the effort of a steep climb from flowing profusely. It was hard to recall how chilly it had been just a few hours ago. After reaching the summit, the downhill ride into McCall was a pleasant one, on what was now a beautiful warm summer day.

The City of McCall, Idaho, a community of 2,000, is located on scenic Payette Lake and is one of Idaho's most popular resorts. Originally a timber town, the recreational roots of McCall go back to 1914 when the Northern Pacific Railroad arrived. The railroad allowed easy access to vacationing residents of the Boise Valley. Today McCall is only a two-hour drive along the Payette Scenic Byway from Boise, and is a year round destination for wintertime skiers and summertime swimming, fishing, boating, and hiking aficionados. In last winter's discussions with Leo, he had warned about being on the roads around McCall on Friday or Sunday afternoons when the folks from Boise would be making their pilgrimages to and from the resort area. My usual skillful planning had put us in McCall smack dab in the middle of a busy summer weekend.

The lodging in town was the appropriately named McCall Hotel. The second floor corner room provided a good look down the main street of McCall and a fabulous view out over the deep blue of Payette Lake. It was easy to make favorable comparisons with our favorite upstate New York town of Lake Placid. Since tomorrow would be a rest day, the bikes were taken to a local bike shop for a tune up and lubrication with the hope that a little oil would make them easier on the climbs.

McCall was a well-executed mix of modern retailing and the Old West. Summer visitors were numerous throughout the downtown stores and restaurants. Dinner was pasta outdoors at an excellent Italian restaurant with a beautiful evening view over Payette Lake. Dana, our 32-year-old waitress from Virginia, was typical of the outdoor loving people in this part of the country. She was a former smokejumper whose job as a firefighter was to parachute into forest fires. She had also led bicycle tours in Vermont, and that prompted a lengthy discussion of our adventure. Dana was now working at the restaurant to earn tuition money to study nursing. Based on her previous occupations, knowing a few nursing skills was probably a good idea. She was a very adventuresome young lady and was typical of many others around Idaho.

Day 15 - 770 Miles Down, 3017 To Go

THE OLDEST MAN IN IDAHO

A late wakeup and leisurely stroll to a recommended breakfast spot called Bev's Café began the second rest day of the trip. On the way to Bev's our directionally challenged twosome got lost and found it necessary to ask a passing gentleman for directions. The fellow appeared to be in his late 50's and wore a close cropped gray beard. He quickly gave directions to the café, only a hundred yards away from where we were standing. When asked if he was from McCall, he said he wasn't and was in town with his wife to celebrate their sixth wedding anniversary. He was a friendly person and conversation flowed freely. Before long we discovered that his name was Clark Heglar, and that he was an historian and native Idahoan. When told of our little adventure, he saw an opportunity to share a small amount of his lifetime-acquired storehouse of Idaho knowledge.

Clark stood with us in a parking lot and gave an informative thumbnail history of Idaho with special emphasis on the geological history of the state. As he talked, his enthusiasm grew with each new piece of information. I thought to myself how incredible it was that we had accidentally run across a source of so much Idaho history and information just by getting lost. If getting lost would be the key to learning about the country, we expected to be well educated by the time our front wheels found their way to the Atlantic.

Clark went on to explain that he talked to organizations throughout the state about its history and did so by playing the role of the "Oldest Man in Idaho." The role gave him the opportunity to talk about the state's history from a personal perspective, and speak from his "own" experiences. We half jokingly told him of our encounter with Denny back in Oregon and the definition we were given of a buckaroo. Quite honestly, although we thought the world of Denny and his family, the buckaroo description seemed a bit hard to believe.

Clark quickly corrected our thinking by agreeing with Denny's buckaroo philosophy, and then adding to it. He described the differences between buckaroos and cowboys, most of which are subtle but real. "Buckaroos consider themselves working ranchers and wear laced up working boots. Cowboys, on the other hand, pull on their boots." Clark also verified the buckaroo philosophy of life, "You gotta do what you gotta do." All of a sudden we felt bad about ever doubting Denny. It was comforting though to know that we too, like Denny, could be considered mobile buckaroos. After all, each morning began with lacing on a pair of biking shoes.

Clark asked about our proposed route through Idaho, and his enthusiasm began to spill forth anew. He described the unique geology and stark scenery of Craters of the Moon National Monument in eastern Idaho. He talked with energy of Redfish Lodge south of Stanley, an area that was part of the itinerary in a few days, and of the absolute necessity to stay there. Clark's knowledge and passionate love of Craters of the Moon and Redfish Lodge were largely due to his portrayal of Robert "Two Gun" Limbert. Old Two Gun was a colorful character from the early Twentieth Century who mapped and photographed a large portion of Craters of the Moon and built Redfish Lodge. It was easy to picture Clark in the garb of Two Gun.

Clark's detailed description of what lay ahead rivaled Leo's. A short walk to his nearby truck gave him the opportunity to supply information about his programs and pose for a picture with Merj. It was a recurring sense of amazement of what would come from chance meetings with people along the way. Meeting Clark in McCall was a classic case that left us feeling pleased about our good fortune.

NOT HERE, GERTA

A day of strolling around McCall included a stop in a small cloth-ing store that caught Merj's eye. While Merj was trying on clothes, an opportunity presented itself to chat with the lady who owned the store. It was clear from listening to this very neatly attired lady that she was no native of the area. After chatting for a while, I jokingly asked if she was from Mississippi. She laughed and responded, "Nope, Rhode Island." She told me her first name was Lenier and, "My husband and I moved here twelve years ago to take sales positions and liked the place. We decided to stay." It was a story shared by others.

Lenier opened the store three or so days a week and opined, "That's about enough, anything more would be too stressful." With a slight grin, she talked of a local elderly lady named Gerta who frequented the shop. Gerta was in her 80's and rode many miles on her bicycle by making laps around Payette Lake. She lapped the lake because, if anything happened, home wouldn't be far away. Gerta was a lot smarter than we were. Gerta enjoyed trying on clothes in Lenier's shop but didn't see the need for a dressing room. She apparently stripped down right in the store and tried on her selections. Lenier elaborated by saying, "She has a good body for a women in her 80's." It was way more information than necessary, but Lenier enjoyed telling the story.

Lenier was very easy to talk to and an excellent salesperson. Merj finally emerged from the changing room and Lenier immediately began a convincing sales pitch as to why certain items in the shop would be perfect for her. A pair of shorts, a blouse, a sweater, and $140.00 later we bid Lenier goodbye and headed back to the hotel. A carefully crafted questioning of Merj as to which bike would be carrying the newly purchased items produced an expected answer.

Day 16 - 770 Miles Down, 3017 To Go

WHICH WAY TO HELSINKI?

The young guys at the bike shop had done their job well. The bikes were in great shape after the tune up, and at twenty dollars apiece, the price was more than fair. Leaving the McCall shop, I had a strong desire to call the bike shop back home to share my feelings about their $79.00 a bike charge for the same service. Merj, however, convinced me to wait until we got home so we could *both* tell them face to face.

The ride out of McCall began with cool morning temperatures, a few drops of rain, and a passing of the Heikilla Funeral Home. As part of a Finnish family by marriage for thirty-two years, the funeral home owner's name was quickly recognized as Finnish. Finnish names usually have a recognizable combination of vowels and consonants that identify them rather easily. It brought to mind my father-in-law's conviction that the first name

of former Cleveland Indians' catcher Einar Diaz was actually
Einari and that he must be Finnish. After many attempts to convince him that there was a good chance that Mr. Diaz's knowledge
of Finland was probably minimal, it remained unclear as to
whether my efforts had successfully persuaded him.

To beat the heavy McCall area traffic, it was decided to take
the advice of the guys at the bike store and ride out of town on
a rural farm to market road named appropriately, Farm to
Market Road. It turned out to be a good choice, as the gentle
ups and downs on the lightly traveled road traversed green fields
with grazing milk cows and nearby snow capped mountains.

About ten miles from McCall another reference to Finland
presented itself in the form of a nicely manicured cemetery. A
neatly lettered white sign identified the cemetery as Finnish,
and a walk through it showed an assortment of Finnish names
on the well maintained head stones. Inside the cemetery two
flagpoles displayed the American flag and the blue and white
Finnish flag. Across from the cemetery on the other side of
Finn Church Road stood a gleaming white structure identified
as the Long Valley Finnish Church, founded in 1917. The
entire intersection was spotless and representative of the
Finnish culture. Pictures of Merj in front of the cemetery and
the church captured her pleasure at finding a part of her native
culture in rural Idaho.

A few miles down the road a sign announced entrance to
Finlandia Estates. The development was nestled off Farm to
Market Road. Surrounded by more green fields and dairy cattle,
the large modern houses projected a general feeling of affluence
compared to the variety of rural western housing that had been
the norm so far. Obviously the Finns around McCall were doing
quite well for themselves.

The fact that there was an enclave of Finns in remote Idaho
was fascinating because there just didn't seem to be enough of
them to go around. Finland, a relatively small country of 5.2 mil-

lion people, is about the size of Montana and is located in the northern Scandinavian portion of Europe. Finland is a land of 60,000 lakes, enough to make Minnesotans envious, with flat to rolling terrain and low hills. The quarter of the country that lies north of the Arctic Circle is referred to as Lapland. Finland was ruled by Sweden from the twelfth through the eighteenth centuries and by Russia from 1809 until the Finns won their independence in 1917. Today Finland is a modern industrialized nation on par with the countries of Western Europe.

The people of Finland are generally characterized by their fair skin, blue eyes, and blonde hair. The first Finnish immigrants to the United States settled in Delaware in 1638. Merj and her family came from the small town of Isojoki located about 200 miles northwest of the capital of Helsinki. In this country the Finns have a reputation as being hardworking, family oriented, skilled craftsmen. It was clear from her now rosy fair skin, flashing blue eyes, and bristling chemically enhanced blonde hair that Merj was excited about being in this part of Idaho.

The Farm to Market Road soon passed through the ghost town of Roseberry. Roseberry consisted of a church, an abandoned general store, a dilapidated leaning house, and a museum. We discovered that Roseberry was once made up of Finns that had fled oppressive Russian rule in the late nineteenth century. The question of why they chose to live in this part of Idaho was answered when we learned that the weather and landscape reminded the early settlers of their native Finland. Until the turn of the twentieth century, Roseberry was the largest town of Long Valley. When the railroad was constructed through nearby Donnelly, however, Roseberry essentially ceased to exist. The remaining general store and museum depicted Finnish life in the late nineteenth and early twentieth century. Unfortunately the museum and store were both closed; the history of Roseberry, this little ghost town, would remain a secret.

WIN ONE FOR THE GIPPER

We spent that evening in Cascade; a small community located in Long Valley about seventy-five miles north of Boise. The town of about one thousand people was situated between the North Fork of the Payette River and Cascade Lake. As in many other towns in the Northwest, the people of Cascade were employed in the logging, farming, and mining industries. The town was a destination for fishermen, hikers, campers and rafters during the summer, and snowmobilers and cross-country skiers in the winter. On this particular evening it would also be the destination for a couple of reinvigorated cross-country cyclists.

The chosen lodging in Cascade was The Pine Lodge Motel and RV Park. Although a sign out front advertised the motel for sale, it was currently owned by Paul and Audrey Parton. Audrey, a very accommodating older lady working behind the desk, cheerfully checked us in and then, with the help of her daughter, Jennifer, finished cleaning the room that would be our home for the night. At Audrey's suggestion, dinner consisted of a pizza in downtown Cascade. The steady diet of pizza since leaving the Oregon coast had caused some nutritional concern. There was always the hope, however, that during that same time period the federal government had decided to add pizza to the list of basic food groups. News traveled slowly in this part of the country so anything was possible. After dinner it was time to head back to the motel for conversation with the Partons.

Paul Parton, a dignified older gentleman, was an Air Force veteran who had become a charter jet pilot after leaving the service. Although now retired, over the years he had flown the Portland Trailblazers and the Seattle Supersonics professional basketball teams, along with a number of other celebrities. A framed autographed picture of Ronald Reagan hanging on the wall was reason enough to ask why it was there. Paul was an unassuming fellow, so it took a little prompting to get him to share his story. He talked of flying President Reagan after he had left office, and of the former President's kindness. Mr. Reagan had shown his appreciation by signing the photograph for Paul. Audrey added, "Most people who check into the motel like the picture, but one guy left when he saw it." She laughed and said, "Oh well, you can't please everybody." Audrey's political feelings were evident as she talked very favorably of President George W. Bush. When I brought up the impromptu opportunity I had had to run with former President Clinton on a beach at Hilton Head Island, her forehead wrinkled and she proceeded to express her less than complimentary opinions of Mr. Clinton. Steering clear of the political discussion, I did, however, share my view that he wasn't much of a runner.

Among others, Paul had also flown Arnold Schwartzenegger and his wife Maria Shriver prior to the actor's election as Governor of California, but he was most pleased with a bit of memorabilia from the comedian Red Skelton. The momento was an autographed sketch of a clown drawn on a small piece of notepaper. The clown face was drawn inside of a large letter R, apparently typical of the comedian's style. After expressing our admiration for Paul's flying experiences, he modestly said. "It's really no big deal. They were mostly like everyone else, just more well known."

Audrey and Paul were fascinated by the bike trip and asked many questions as we all sat in the small motel office and talked into the evening. In a short time everyone was on a first name basis. Paul, seeing my short haircut, asked, "Are you in the Army?" After telling him that it had been cut short enough to last for the three month bike trip, I shared with him the opinion that having a head of hair worthy of cutting was a plus at my age. As the discussion continued, Audrey mentioned that a fellow with an accent had called looking for Merj a short time earlier. Expecting to be joined by Merj's parents the next evening, there was little trouble guessing who had called. Audrey became fascinated by Merj's background, and insisted she say something in Finnish.

Merj complied with a short burst of unrecognizable verbiage, and then duly translated it for our hosts and me.

Over the years I had listened to long discussions in Finnish where occasionally my name would be mentioned and sometimes laughter would follow. At an appropriate pause in the conversation I usually inquired of Merj as to the content of the conversation. It was always amazing how she could condense a half-hour discussion into a thirty-second summary, no part of which sounded in the least bit laugh inducing. I wondered, when the U. S. Ambassador to the United Nations was speaking of some issue of world importance, did the representative from Tajikistan hear a summary of the day's baseball scores through his headphones? Not being prone to paranoia, I learned to shake such thoughts from my mind. As the evening wore on, Audrey found out that the next day would be Merj's birthday, and offered to buy her a bottle of wine from the downtown grocery. The evening was getting late so we politely declined.

The Partons represented the Americana that we had hoped to find on our trip; thoughtful, modest, hard working people with very interesting and meaningful life experiences. This elderly couple made anyone in their proximity feel comfortable within minutes. The Partons exhibited a spirit and work ethic that epitomized the good people of the rural West. Our biking experience had been enriched by their friendship.

The day also represented the last one for the rental support vehicle. Merj had remarkably juggled moving the vehicle and, more importantly, providing me company on her bike for substantial portions of the ride through Oregon; particularly the climbs. On some days, with all the doubling back required because of the vehicle, she may have ridden more miles than me. Her legs were considerably stronger and the pain that had proved difficult earlier was much diminished. We didn't know it at the time, but from here on out, Merj would ride every mile to the Atlantic Ocean.

Day 17 - 803 Miles Down, 2984 To Go

HEY BUDDY, HOW 'BOUT A RIDE

An early start to avoid the heavy traffic that Leo had warned about was a high priority. Heading south out of Cascade, a thin layer of fog hovered near the ground as the sun peaked over the distant mountains. A few miles out of town the fog thickened into a dense pea soup. The good news was that the fog had slowed traffic. The bad news was that drivers would have trouble seeing the bikes. There was initial comfort in knowing the blinking red taillight on the rear of the bikes provided visibility.

That comfort was quickly dashed when a rest stop showed they had quit working. Evidently the circuitry in the device didn't work well in moist conditions. The lights should have been equipped by the manufacturer with a warning label that said, "Check the weather forecast before depending on our product to provide even minimal safety benefit." Fortunately, the weather was improving and a bad taillight was not going to ruin the day.

The thick fog of the early morning soon lifted and the road began a long, sometimes steep descent through the Payette River Valley and the Boise National Forest. The ride along the river gorge was exhilarating, through thin pines rising from steep slopes on the right side, and sometimes severe rocky drops to the river on the left. An element of danger was present as many of the drops were unprotected by guardrails; a moment of inattention could result in serious injury.

The day had turned clear with an occasional area of wispy low fog. The ride through the valley became a delightful experience of high speeds down the winding road. On two occasions deer waited near the road around blind bends, and after being startled, bounded into the forest. The Payette River was at times calm only to be followed by stretches of fast flowing rapids.

A stop for breakfast along the river in the crossroads town of Banks, at the Banks Store and Café, allowed for a break and an opportunity to recollect the morning's ride through one of the most beautiful sections of the trip to date. The speeding bike, the rushing water, the tall slender pines, the morning sun over the mountain tops, the element of danger, and the wildlife had left a feeling that this trip was a worthwhile one. We lingered over a breakfast of eggs, biscuits, and gravy, and wondered why Idahoans didn't have a cardiac unit every couple of miles or so.

Before long it was time to head out of Banks "up river grade," along the South Fork of the Payette River toward Garden Valley. The morning warmed and the road rose to provide views of the rushing river a hundred feet below. A quick descent allowed for a close up view. The rise and fall cycle was repeated often on the road to Garden Valley.

We reached Garden Valley late in the morning and the hotel offered an opportunity to relax and watch TV. A brief look at the Weather Channel predicted 100 degree temperatures for nearby Boise tomorrow, so an idea began to form in two overactive minds. With Merj's parents arriving later in the evening, we decided to ride part-way into the next day's ride. The next morning, they could return us to our stopping point; by my logic we could reduce the suffering through much of the next day's predicted hot weather. The carefully thought out plan presented one problem; how would we get back from the stopping point to the hotel in Garden Valley? A decision was made to flag down a pick-up truck, throw the bikes into the bed, and ride back. The positive experience back in Oregon with Phil made the idea seem like no big deal. In retrospect it never ceased to amaze us how such apparently logical thinking could look so flawed when viewed from the perspective of common sense later on.

The early afternoon was warming significantly as we headed out of Garden Valley toward Lowman about twenty miles away. There was a feeling of confidence that there would be no problem finding someone in Lowman with a pickup truck who would be more than happy to take a couple of stranded Ohio cyclists back to Garden Valley. The ride toward Lowman was generally uphill through deep gorges along the South Fork of the Payette River. Looking way down to the fast flowing river below, an occasional kayak and larger rafts with eight to ten people could be seen challenging the rapids. The ride through the steep rocky cliffs was stark but beautiful, and the rushing river below offered a pleasantly noisy backdrop. The afternoon was now well into the mid ninety degree range, and it was clear by the increasing number of rest stops that Merj was struggling. Being a keen observer of the obvious and an extremely caring person, about fifteen miles into the ride I suggested that we stop right there and flag down a ride back to Garden Valley. There was no argument from the female half of the team.

One thing that had been troublesome during the last few miles was the absence of vehicles on the road. Traffic was extremely light and I worried about the lack of locals with pickup trucks to supply our now much-needed ride. The bikes were pulled off the road onto a wide shoulder and the location was marked by making an X on the guardrail with a sharp stone. Being a stickler for authenticity, I wanted to make sure that the bicycle trip was not compromised by our being transported back tomorrow morning to a point beyond where the day's ride had ended. I was an obsessive believer in the bicycle touring philosophy of EFI, " Every Friggin' Inch." Merj's facial expression indicated a philosophy that could have been best described as, "Forget the inches, a few miles one way or the other is close enough."

As Merj waited by the bikes, her knight in shining armor headed up the road to try to flag down a truck. After waiting for a considerable time, the first of what would eventually be three or four passing vehicle drivers smiled and waved politely at my unsuccessful motions for them to stop. I had to wonder what they thought I was doing out in the middle of nowhere waving my arms if it not to signify some need? While getting more and more discouraged, a leather clad Harley rider soon arrived on the scene and asked if there was a problem. After a brief discussion, he rode the short distance down the hill to Merj and waited for me to walk back.

Our new acquaintance offered to send someone back from Garden Valley, but we explained our desire to hitch a ride on a pickup and the lack of success to date. As another example of the two-wheel comraderie that is shared with motorcyclists, he confidently said, "I'm going to stand in the middle of the road, and I guarantee you no one with a truck will get by without stopping." We said fine, as if arguing would have made any difference. Almost on cue, a Dodge pickup rounded the bend. Not surprisingly, the driver stopped. To continue would have resulted in a charge of vehicular homicide. Our motorcycling buddy was true to his word and had taken up residence on the painted line in the middle of the road.

When asked, the couple in the truck quickly agreed to transport us back to Garden Valley. Since our comrade in leather had not moved from his fixed position in the road, the couple's choices were clearly limited. After thanking our new found motorcyclist friend, he roared off with a wave of the hand and quickly disappeared around a bend in the road.

Once the bikes were positioned in the truck bed, we climbed into the back seat of the air-conditioned pickup. The young parents in the front seat were on their way home to Boise after having delivered the oldest of their three children, a sixteen-year-old daughter, to a week long camp for diabetics in Stanley. The couple had become well educated about diabetes, and talked of ongoing research with an obvious hope that it would have a positive effect on their daughter's future. The usual questions of what lie ahead were answered with descriptions of long climbs but beautiful scenery on the road to Stanley.

The air-conditioned trip back to Garden Valley ended too soon; it was enjoyable to chat with the young couple in the

Dodge, and we were reluctant to get back out into the warm afternoon. At the hotel we unloaded the bikes, tried unsuccessfully to compensate the couple for their inconvenience, and bid them a fond goodbye. A short time later Merj's parents, John and Aili, arrived and joined us for a steak dinner in celebration of Merj's fifty-whatever-birthday. Any effort to gently comment on her advancing years was usually met with a not so subtle reminder that no matter how many birthdays she celebrated, she would always have to add two to her total to reach mine.

The small town of Garden Valley was originally named Upper Payette Valley but changed to its current name in 1875, when it became time to name the new post office. The name change to Garden Valley may have also been prompted by the unique ability to grow crops year round in the valley. The presence of naturally occurring geothermal hot water in the area made winter crop growing possible. The hot springs allowed immigrant Chinese growers to supply nearby gold miners throughout the year with fresh produce during the boom times of the 1870's. Today the hot waters heat homes and greenhouses. Many of the current residents of the Garden Valley area work in the logging, ranching, river sports, or service industries.

After dinner John and I walked out back of the hotel past a very large pile of logs into the Payette River Lumber Company. It was dusk and there was no one around as we inspected the small mill amidst the piles of logs. Mosquitoes had made the evening uncomfortable, and while heading back to the hotel a large pickup rolled up and the driver waved for us to approach. Since there was already some concern about being on private property, thoughts of spending the night in a Garden Valley correctional facility caused some fleeting anxiety.

Approaching the truck ready to apologize and also ready for a stern lecture, there was considerable relief in seeing the smiling person behind the wheel motion two trespassers to the driver's side window. It didn't take long to discover that the truck driver worked for the Payette Valley Lumber Company. He jokingly asked, "Are you guys in the market for some logs?" After assuring him we weren't, he went on to explain that the company bought logs, sorted and graded them, and then resold the logs to mills throughout the Northwest. "We use that mill back there," he explained, "to make custom timbers for specialized architectural needs."

While swatting at the swarming mosquitoes, the discussion moved to the closed lumber mills that were common throughout the Northwest and the effect it was having on the people and the towns along the route. When asked if environmental concerns, including the spotted owl issue, were contributing factors, he never really said but stated, "A lot of people are environmentalists because there's money to be made." In a tone that was free of bitterness he added, "It's America, and everybody's entitled to an opinion."

The mosquitoes finally got the best of us and it was time to bid our acquaintance a good evening. Walking the short distance back to the hotel, John and I agreed that the attitude of the Idaho logger regarding blame for the recent setbacks in his industry and his lack of anger or bitterness were really quite remarkable.

Day 18 - 865 Miles Down, 2922 To Go

DID YOU SAY WELL DONE?

The ride from outside Garden Valley through Stanley to Redfish Lake Lodge took two days and included an intermediate stop east of Lowman at the Sourdough Lodge. The early morning ride started at the "X" marked guardrail and continued through the gorge with rises well above the river followed by drops to the edge of the fast moving white water.

Just past Lowman the landscape changed considerably. Stands of green ponderosa pine were replaced by acres of burned trees. It was evident a significant fire had occurred there recently, so a stop at a small local grocery store to find out what had happened was in order. The establishment was identified by the catchy name of Burnt Pines General Store and was empty, save a thirty-something woman behind the counter. She was clearly not enjoying her day, so the prospect of conversation was limited at best. Regardless of her less than accommodating attitude, it didn't take long to discover that the fire had occurred in 1989 and had devastated a very large portion of the valley. Although it had been quite a while since the fire, the lack of green growth showed how long it took for an area destroyed by fire to show real signs of recovery.

Many of the same sort of hot springs that were part of the lore in Garden Valley appeared during another "up river grade" ride toward the Sourdough Lodge. They were evident by the wisps of white steam rising from small pockets of hot water along the banks of the river. Even though the sore hip was feeling pretty good, there was a temptation to try the therapeutic effect of the nearby hot water. The rising steam, however, gave reason to take pause before searing fragile body parts.

The Sourdough Lodge, located in the middle of a pine-forested nowhere, was composed of a restaurant, a few very nice log cabins, and a gas station. The lodge was owned by a mid-thirties couple, Pam and Jim, who seemed constantly busy with one chore or another. Our cabin was new and tidy and came equipped with a small kitchen and front porch. A screened in hot tub was located a few short steps from the front door and appeared much more inviting than the naturally occurring hot springs earlier in the day. The evening was spent sitting on the porch and relaxing in the hot tub with the pleasant smell of ponderosa pine always present.

Day 19 - 885 Miles Down, 2880 To Go

CAN'T A GUY GET A LITTLE SLEEP
AROUND HERE?

The cycling from the Sourdough Lodge to Stanley included a significant climb to Banner Summit. At 7,200 feet in elevation, Banner Summit represented the highest point of the trip to date. The slight headwind on the other side of the summit was offset by a gentle down hill ride through the high meadows covered with purple flowers, and the snow-capped Sawtooth Mountains in the distance. The ride was interrupted by numerous stops to take pictures of stunning views.

While enjoying the quiet serenity of the morning, a loud barking like noise and movement of two large animals about a hundred yards off the road caused a momentary bit of excitement. For an instant we thought the large brown critters were deer or elk, but quickly saw they were birds. It's hard to believe a bird could be mistaken for a deer, but it was another of those classic cases of "having to be there" to understand. It was clear by their strange, loud protestations that these odd birds were not happy to see two people on bicycles invade their space. A flapping of large wings and a short flight to the safety afforded by the nearby woods followed their display of displeasure.

A mid-morning stop at a roadside rest area allowed us the opportunity to take a break and chat with a friendly elderly couple acting as summer volunteers for the Park Service. While chatting, they pointed out a large herd of barely visible sheep near the base of a distant mountain range. The couple explained that sheep ranching was common in the Sawtooth area, and that border collies were often used to keep the herds in formation. They told us that a number of sheep and some of the herding dogs had been killed earlier in the summer by wolves. They also indicated that the winged noisemakers that had broken the silence of the early morning were sand hill cranes and identified the colorful flowers in the high meadows as lupines. The lupines formed a colorful carpet on the flat plateau between the distant mountain ranges on either side of the road.

The ride toward Stanley was through more colorful high meadows in the shadow of the snow capped Sawtooths. Stanley, the location of a satisfying lunch, was a nicely restored town of 100 people with an old western theme. The town was named for Captain John Stanley, a Civil War survivor who came upon the area in 1863 while leading a party of gold prospectors. A permanent settlement was not established until 1890. Today the town is the headquarters for float trip operators who take rafters down the Salmon River, as well as a destination for summer fishermen, winter snowmobilers, and cross-country skiers.

We spent the evening in a cabin at the Redfish Lake Lodge south of Stanley. The lodge and the surrounding cabins were located well off the main road, and the easy ride back to the lodge passed small streams and ponds. Located at the headwaters of the main fork of the Salmon River, Redfish Lake is a good sized body of water and a destination for boaters, fishermen, and hikers. A conversation with a young University of Utah graduate interning at the lodge offered an answer as to how the lake got its name. She explained that salmon were plentiful when settlers first arrived, and the name of the lake came from their reddish color. She went on to say the Fish and Wildlife Service had since purposely killed the native salmon so that the lake could be restocked with trout. The purposeful killing of the salmon sounded a little hard to believe, so we decided to find a second source of information to verify her claim.

Another young employee provided an alternative and more plausible answer. He explained that local environmentalists claimed that the sockeye salmon in the lake had disappeared because of the construction of dams on the Lower Snake River.

The dams had impeded the ability of the salmon to make their way upstream to Redfish Lake to spawn. A sighting of a sockeye in the lake was now a rare occurrence. The environmentalists' rationale sounded more reasonable, and, after a near unanimous vote of our travelling quartet, it was accepted as gospel.

The late afternoon was spent in a rocking chair looking out over the lake and casually drifting between sleep and consciousness. The presence of a number of families with small children, many of them speaking languages from various parts of the world, kept the activity nearby at a level that made prolonged sleep impossible. A German speaking father, playing soccer with his young children on the grass in front of the rocking chairs, supplied a diversion during the short periods between catnaps. A very brisk wind quickly came from nowhere and kicked up whitecaps on what had been a placid lake surface. Blowing sand interrupted the reprieve in the rocking chair and sent its groggy occupant scurrying back to the cabin. Almost as quickly as it began, the wind died and the calm of the evening returned.

Day 20 - 940 Miles Down, 2847 To Go

FOR WHOM THE BELLS TOLLS

During the winter discussions with Leo, he had waxed poetic about the beauty of the Sawtooth Mountains and of the ride into the Sun Valley region. He had also mentioned that a significant climb over Galena Summit awaited us on the road out of Redfish Lake toward Sun Valley. Since his earlier observations had been accurate, there was no reason to doubt his assessment of the Galena Summit climb. The early morning ride out of Redfish began in clear, cold air and required layers of warm-weather gear. As usual, the wind chill created by the moving bikes added to the cold. As the sun rose over the surrounding mountains, the morning warmed and the layers of warm clothing were soon shed.

The gentle up and down ride continued for a number of miles until reaching an oasis of civilization in the form of the small town of Smiley Creek. A break in a cafe provided our first look at the beginning of the Galena climb. Much ballyhooed mountain climbs were always met with a certain degree of apprehension, but the leapfrog climb to Galena Summit worked well, and stops along the way afforded an opportunity to take in the beautiful surroundings.

The views from a visitor center that was initially mistaken for the summit were spectacular. A number of other cyclists, all members of a local bicycle club, had assembled at the center after ascending the mountain from the other side. They were generally young, trim, fit, and decked out in colorful biking attire. Even though the contrast between this group of cycling hares and a couple of middle age tortoises was obvious to even a casual observer, they treated us as one of their own. Maybe we were mistaken; maybe we were better than mediocre cyclists. Maybe we were top-notch riders who wouldn't admit it to ourselves. Nah, the reality was that we really were just mediocre. Regardless, we were still "doin' what we had to do."

A volunteer couple from Dayton, Ohio manned the visitor's center, and it was enjoyable talking with them about life back East. There seemed to be a goodly number of Ohioans who had moved to the West. It was difficult to recall many native Idahoans back home. Even taking into account the fact that there were quite a few less Idahoans than Ohioans to begin with, there seemed to be a strong magnet that had attracted an inordinate number of Buckeyes to the western part of the country.

After a short ride from the visitor's center, we reached Galena Summit, along with a new highest elevation of 8,701 feet. Since the summit was obviously named after something or someone, natural human curiosity required finding the answer. Usually discovering information required that one of us be obnoxiously forward and ask someone familiar with the area to answer what was many times an inane question. Somehow Merj always seemed to busy herself when information became a need, so the task almost always fell to her inquisitive fellow traveler.

The whole exercise was a haunting reminder of more than a few car-buying experiences over the years. On those occasions Merj would, after long drawn out deliberation, select from the dealer's lot the vehicle and color of her choice. She would then disappear to the refuge of the family car as I went inside to take on the salesman. When later questioned about her timidity, she always explained that my negotiating technique made her tense. I tried to soothe her by telling her that my car negotiation techniques made *me* tense. Regardless of the psychological scars from the past, it was never difficult to approach people for information on this trip. They were almost always helpful and offered information or advice in a friendly, supportive manner.

It didn't take long to learn that Galena Summit was named after a mineral of the same name. Galena, or lead sulfide, is a principle ore used in the production of lead. Galena can also contain up to one percent silver. As a result, the large volume of galena used to produce lead has enough silver as a by-product to make it the leading ore of silver. Galena has a silver gray color and fractures into cubes making it an easily identified favorite of rock-hounds. It was also learned that the road over the summit was constructed in 1871 and was originally a toll road called Sawtooth Grade.

The trip down from Galena Summit to Ketchum and Sun Valley was an enjoyable twenty-six mile ride. The first portion was a twisting downhill road, which we covered at a quick pace. But speed is a relative thing; our high-speed, edge-of-control feelings were quickly put into proper perspective when a dozen or so members of the cycling club passed by as though we were moving in reverse. Still, our mood improved as we passed a number of cycle club members struggling up the hill toward the summit. They didn't look that much better than we had coming up the other side.

The miles passed quickly and before long the day's ride ended in the small resort town of Ketchum. Ketchum, a community of about 3,000 people, was located in the heart of the popular Sun Valley ski resort area. Large homes situated well back from the road and a nicely maintained downtown area with an abundance of shops and restaurants stood in contrast to the other rural Idaho towns that had proceeded it. There was a definite feeling of affluence in this small town.

The afternoon was spent in nearby Sun Valley, an upscale village that clearly catered to the winter sports crowd. Small shops and restaurants made up the ski oriented business area. The central area of Sun Valley is pedestrian only and is an easy place to stroll around or take a break on an available bench. It was strange to spend a lovely summer afternoon in a town that was essentially experiencing its off-season.

John and I did what we do best: attentively follow our wives into stores and express interest when asked for an opinion. There was always the fear of being caught daydreaming and not having a suitable answer when one was required — a situation not unfamiliar to most husbands. Be that as it may, the day was beautiful and soon a small bookstore on the edge of the shopping area offered suitable refuge.

The owner of the store was arranging books on the shelves and making conversation with her was easy in the lightly occupied store. She was a delightful lady who expressed a great amount of interest in the trip and encouraged us to write about it when we finished. She asked for an autographed copy of any future venture into literary excellence and copies of the masterpiece to sell in her store. Not wanting to disappoint this very accommodating lady by telling her a book was probably not going to happen, a promise was none the less made to send her the requested books. Guilt from the deceptive response caused a strong desire to buy something in the bookstore. Since an autographed book was probably a long shot, an autographed Master Card receipt would be the next best thing.

The bookstore owner went on to talk of the Ernest Hemmingway ties to the Sun Valley area. Between the storeowner and some further research it was revealed that Hemmingway, at forty and already a famous author, had come to the area in 1939. He finished his famous novel, *For Whom the Bell Tolls*, at the Sun Valley Lodge in Ketchum. An avid outdoorsman, he frequently hunted in the areas around Sun Valley. Though none of his fiction is set in Sun Valley, Hemmingway's characters, by their actions and knowledge of the outdoors, reflect his time there. European travels, extended stays in Cuba deep-sea fishing, and writing took him away from Idaho for long periods of time.

Hemmingway was a winner of a Pulitzer Prize in 1953 and the Nobel Prize for Literature in 1954. In 1959 he bought a house in Ketchum and returned to Idaho. Soon after returning, his health deteriorated, and the loss of several close friends along with financial problems caused him to suffer bouts of depression. Early on the morning of July 2, 1961, Hemingway died of a self-inflicted gunshot wound. He is buried in the Ketchum cemetery. Hemmingway's famous granddaughter, Mariel, still lives in the area with her two children.

While chatting with the storeowner, a young mother trying to corral her young children, overheard the conversation and joined in. She was a very personable woman who was in Sun Valley from Denver with her family for a legal conference. While her lawyer husband was attending meetings, she and her children were out enjoying a day of shopping. When she asked about my profession, her eyes lit up when I told her that I was an engineer. This was odd. Finding out one is an engineer usually provokes a comment like, "That's nice," and a quick change of the subject. The occasional exception was the person who asked about life in a locomotive.

Further conversation led this genial young mother to divulge, "My husband defends engineers in professional liability claims." Now *my* eyes lit up. Here in the middle of Idaho I had found somebody who was on my side. We all chatted for some time about the trip, things to do in Sun Valley, and the joys of raising children. As we began to leave the store, she asked, "Can you guys join us for dinner tomorrow night?" Since tomorrow would be another day on the road, it was necessary to decline. It was a shame because the dinner would have surely been an enjoyable one.

A beautiful summer evening in downtown Ketchum was spent at Rocco's Pizza devouring a loaded pizza in the outdoor seating area. On the way to the restaurant, we discovered that crossing the street in Ketchum was an occurrence unlike any other. At each crosswalk in the city, a number of red flags were stored in a holder on a light post adjacent to the curb. It was the responsibility of the person crossing the street to take one of the flags and carry it with him so as to warn oncoming drivers that a pedestrian was in the crosswalk. Upon reaching the other side, the flag was deposited in the holder for use of a pedestrian coming the other way. Although yellow safety vests, or flashing lights, or hard hats may have been equally successful, the red flags seemed to offer an effective means of preventing the unintended contact of steel and bone.

The evening meal provided an opportunity to learn that in 1880 the town of Ketchum was named after a trapper and guide named David Ketchum. Although originally part of one of the richest mining areas in the Northwest, the silver boom bottomed out in the late 1880's. Shortly after its demise, a new industry appeared when sheepherders began driving their herds through Ketchum on the way to summer grazing in the Sawtooth Mountains. It is hard to say quickly but, by 1920 Ketchum had become the largest sheep shipping station in the United States. This story was becoming familiar. A trapper or miner comes to town with a few guys searching for furs, gold, or silver. He stays long enough to have the town named for himself, and then he moves on to bigger and better things. After he leaves, the mine runs out and the town goes in a new direction. It was a story that had been repeated in many of the small towns of the West.

Sun Valley's resort origins go back to 1935 when a wealthy New Yorker named Avrell Harriman sent Austrian noble Count Felix Schaffgotsch to find a location to establish the country's first winter resort. The Count sent back a glowing report about the area and he and Harriman bought 4,300 acres in Sun Valley. Building soon started, and word spread quickly about the beautiful Idaho ski destination.

Apparently the Count wasn't much of a fur trader or miner because there was never a move to change the town name to Schaffgotsch. With the help of a newly constructed railroad, the celebrities of the day soon flocked to Sun Valley. Today, many present-day stars such as Jamie Lee Curtis, Arnold Schwartzenegger, and Bruce Willis call Sun Valley home. Many of the multi-million dollar houses in the area, including Bill Gates' 50,000 square foot home in nearby Elkhorn Village, are owned by some of the wealthiest people in the world.

Day 21 - 1000 Miles Down, 2787 To Go

PEEK-A-BOO

The ride out of Ketchum was slightly downhill on well-paved bike paths. The cycling was easy and, except for avoiding an occasional runner or fellow cyclist, side by side travel was possible for long periods of time. Riding along side each other was a rare and enjoyable treat as it allowed for sharing observations and chatting about the day's events. The bike path ended about twenty miles into the day in the small town of Bellevue.

Looking for a place to stop for a mid-morning snack and being somewhat confused about where to rejoin the highway, a middle age couple taking a morning walk helped us get straightened out. While making conversation, the man told us he was originally from Westlake, Ohio. Since Westlake is on the other side of Cleveland only about 40 miles or so from home, there was reason to continue the discussion. He had come to Idaho after his high school graduation in the early seventies with a buddy and reflected, "I only intended to stay a little while. That short stay ended up being thirty years." Yet another Ohioan had made that one way trip to Idaho never to return to his native state!

The couple turned out to have been pretty avid cyclists in their own right. They talked of a trip down the West Coast from Seattle to San Francisco that had been completed a few years earlier. The beauty of the Washington coastline and five flat tires in one day were their biggest memories of the trip. Our expertise at avoiding flat tires, although unsolicited, was eagerly shared with our new cyclist friends. The secret lay with an uncanny foresight to install liners inside the tires to protect the tubes from puncture. It would take a little while longer, but such tire cockiness would soon take a hit. After sharing more tales of the road, it was suggested that Glen's Grocery would be the place to find mid-morning snacks in Bellevue.

Glen's Grocery started it's life ninety years back as a bank. According to Glen, the older gentleman behind the counter, the building served as a bank for only the first fifteen years of its existence. Glen had purchased the grocery some years earlier and it had remained a food-providing staple of Bellvue since. When asked about a restroom, Glen said in a business like fashion, "It's back there, just past the meat counter." There is an indescribable feeling that comes over a person who, while utilizing a cramped restroom, hears the distinctive sounds of a butcher working not twenty feet away. Completing the business at hand takes on an urgency not present at typical restroom stops.

While leaving the store, we sensed that a purchase was expected for having used the meat department annex. After quickly selecting some drinks and nutrition bars and dutifully paying Glen, it was time to head back to the bikes.

The rest of the day was spent traversing farmland nestled between low hills. Much of the land was used to grow hay and barley and large rotary irrigation devices applied water to the fields. The hay and barley were made into large bales three or four feet high and six or eight feet long. Having worked on a farm during high school summers, the size of the bales created a certain curiosity. In younger days, a typical day during haying season consisted of hauling countless bales of hay into a hot dusty barn and stacking them to the rafters for later use. The hay bales in those days were eighteen inches or so high and about three feet long. Although a day of lifting bales was not exactly a day at the beach, the size of the bales made handling each one individually fairly easy. Four healthy sumo wrestlers could not have lifted these Idaho monstrosities without serious risk of hernias. Although we never saw how it was done, we assumed that some sort of a fork-lift device carried them to one of the large open sided barns that sheltered the bales from the elements. It would have been interesting seeing the machine that spat out those oversized bales.

The land not used for growing hay and barley was used for grazing by herds of cattle. On most occasions the nearby animals would look up from a morning meal and slowly swing their heads to follow the two passing interlopers. Their look of nonchalance usually gave us a chuckle and we greeted them with a friendly, "Good morning, ladies." On rare occasions, our passing would scare one or two of the cows munching near the road and a mini-stampede away from us would ensue. Realizing that a bovine obsession could be viewed by some as a character flaw, it must be remembered that on a typical day in the rural West one will see more cows than humans.

The late morning warmed considerably, as most of them usually did, and before long we rolled into the tiny crossroads town of Picabo, Idaho, which reminded me of a former Olympic skier by the name of Picabo (Peek-a-boo) Street. It was not surprising that the sign welcoming us to Picabo, also announced that this was the home of Ms. Street. I had a vague recollection that there was an interesting story behind her unique name. A question begged answering: Was Picabo named for this tiny town, or was it the other way around?

Local lore had it that Picabo's parents had wanted her to choose her own name, so they intended to leave her unnamed until she was old enough to make her own choice. For the first two years of life she was simply called "Little Girl" Street. When her mother took her young, unnamed daughter to get a passport for a visit to Mexico, the officer at the passport office refused to accept "Little Girl" as the two-year-old's name. He gave her mother two weeks to come back with a "real" name. Her parents, Stubby and Dee, came up with the name Picabo after the small Idaho town. When she was four, Picabo was given the option to change her name, but decided to keep it as it was. Picabo Street grew up in the small town of Triumph, near Ketchum, and went on to win an Olympic silver medal in the downhill in 1994 and the gold medal in the Super G in 1998.

The ride from Picabo to Carey, the stopping point for the day, was along a coast to coast highway designated as US Route 20, a roadway having special meaning to northeastern Ohioans. Route 20 runs in a west to east direction from Newport, Oregon to Boston and serves as the main street for many cities in northeastern Ohio. Cleveland's principal artery is Euclid Avenue, which is in fact US Route 20. Being on a familiar route was reason to joke about forgetting the planned itinerary and following Route 20 all the way to the East Coast. We feared, though, that spending a night in our own Ohio home may prove so inviting that our cross-country trip would end right there, some 800 miles short of the Atlantic Ocean.

Rolling into the town of Carey, a noticeable chagrin became obvious among the female contingent of our traveling party. Although we were always prepared to accept the fact that there would be a dearth of Ritz Carltons along the rural highways of America, the lodging in Carey was judged unacceptable even by our significantly lowered standards. The options were to continue another forty miles in the very warm afternoon sun to the next town, or with support now available, load the bikes on the car and seek shelter elsewhere. The car option was quickly chosen as the preferred one, and our small band of travelers backtracked to the town of Hailey. The rejected motel's parking lot in Carey would be tomorrow's point of departure. It was decided an X on the pavement would be a bit much, so a mental note of the day's stopping point would have to suffice.

Day 22 - 1041 Miles Down, 2746 To Go

I THINK I'LL HOLD IT

The discussions with Leo over the winter had painted a picture of the ride across Idaho being one of varying terrain and scenery. Unfortunately, he had also indicated that the least desirable part of the state was the area that we were about to cover over the next two days. According to Leo, the only exception to the bleak terrain was a national monument about halfway into the day's ride, Craters of the Moon.

The ride from the previous days stopping-point began through a tabletop, flat landscape and a definite high-desert feel. The road occasionally passed marsh-like areas that seemed out of place in the surrounding dry countryside. Low mountains were visible far to the northwest. The light traffic, the comfortably cool early morning weather, and the well-paved road made for a very enjoyable start to the day. Before long the surrounding scenery changed dramatically; fields of black and gray lava replaced the high-desert landscape. Soon the lava became the only visible ground cover for as far as the eye could see. We had come upon the outer fringes of Craters of the Moon.

Although the surroundings were impressive, the wide vistas and awe-inspiring starkness would have to wait. Merj had to go to the bathroom, and…NOW! Bathroom experiences had led to a string of interesting adventures. The long distances between centers of civilization had made for a certain amount of improvising and risk taking. Since most of the roads were lightly traveled, finding uninterrupted time to deal with the call of nature was not usually a problem. However, our travels also took us through miles and miles of countryside where the only thing providing any sort of cover was, well, nothing.

The usual routine was for me to deal with my needs rather quickly, and then take up an observation post along side the road. After carefully looking up and down the road, an "all clear!" declaration would be Merj's signal to head into the wide-open spaces. While hustling into the hinterlands, her instructions to me were always the same, "Don't turn around, and let me know if anyone is coming!" Those instructions were repeated many times, but never ceased to be a source of amazement. In the first place, the carefully positioned roadway observer had no reason or intention of turning around. In the second place, what exactly was supposed to happen if all of a sudden that same observer yelled out, "Here comes a logging truck!"

On this day, it was pretty much business as usual as I took my post along the side of the road, and Merj headed into the makeshift restroom strewn with lava rock. Dutifully, I did not look her way, and there was no one in sight for miles. The birds were chirping, the morning was beautiful, and life was good. It couldn't have been a more perfect time to deal with the little problems nature threw our way. As I mindlessly busied myself at the roadside, the calm of the morning was shattered by a blood-curdling scream from the lava field. Instantaneously Merj came flying out of the lava with eyes the size of the hubcaps on a '53 Buick.

There are two or three things in life that terrify Merj, and number one on the list is snakes. Number one had just made an appearance amid the rocks of Craters of the Moon. Merj deposited herself at my side, and in near hysterics, described her encounter with the snake, proving once again the law of physics that two objects cannot occupy the same place at the same time. As she described and redescribed the encounter, much like a fisherman describing his catch of the day, the length of the snake grew. Eventually, after much soothing and comforting sympathy from her traveling companion, she calmed down and the morning ride continued toward the park entrance. The experience was educational for me too; I now knew that if the occasion ever arose when it was appropriate to yell, "Here comes a logging truck," Merj could turn into a world class sprinter.

CRATERS OF THE MOON

Our arrival at Craters of the Moon was met with a near gale force wind that nearly blew us through the front doors of the visitor's center. After Merj's much delayed visit to the ladies room, and a leisurely picnic lunch, interrupted frequently by dashing after blowing picnic paraphernalia, it was time to explore this long anticipated national monument.

Craters of the Moon National Monument is part of the Snake River Plain, a volcanic terrain that forms a large part of southern Idaho. Lava eruptions for 15,000 years have formed a landscape that has given rise to a variety of flora and fauna adapted to the unusual conditions of the area. Geologic drilling operations have shown the lava to be up to 20,000 feet thick in certain spots. Craters of the Moon was formed by the most recent volcanic eruptions some 2,000 years ago. This comparatively recent volcanic activity has left the area with a moonscape appearance that visitors can't help but find starkly beautiful. One had to ponder what must have gone through the minds of the nineteenth century travelers when they came upon this formidable impediment to their progress. "The strangest 75 square miles on the North American continent," wrote one early settler. "An outdoor museum of volcanism," and, "a desolate and awful waste," recorded another.

The Craters of the Moon National Monument was created in 1924. The lava field covers 618 square miles, with 83 square miles preserved for the enjoyment of present and future generations. Craters of the Moon contains the largest young basaltic lava field in the lower 48 states. The Monument contains more than twenty-five volcanic cones including outstanding examples of spatter cones. Spatter cones are formed by small volcanic eruptions, when lava shoots into the air and then lands splattered on the sides of the cones. The spatter patterns were clearly visible. As a testament to the insulating capabilities of the porous rock, even on this very warm day there was snow visible ten or fifteen feet down at the bottom of the cone.

Our support car supplied the means to travel the seven mile paved loop through the park leisurely, and during frequent stops we ventured into the lava fields. The explorations included off road areas named Devil's Orchard, Big Cinder Butte, and Big Craters and Spatter Cones Area. A walk to the top of Infernal Cone—a very large cinder covered volcanic cone—was made more challenging by the continued strong winds. Although a reasonably full head of hair gave me no basis for knowing, I suspected the wind at the top was a toupee wearer's nightmare. While snapping photos of the surrounding area we had to lean into it sharply in order to stay standing.

The final stop in Craters of the Moon was at the Cave Area. A half-mile walk followed a path through a black and gray lunar landscape to caves named Dew Drop and Boy Scout. The cave floors and ceilings were made up of pointed sharp lava rock that a ranger had advised to regard with caution. To emphasize the point, she graphically warned, "People have left parts of their hair and scalp in there." Consideration of donning the bicycle helmets was soon dismissed as it was decided that the walk back to get them was too far. It was curious to think that, after riding bicycles for hundreds of miles, a few hundred-yard walk to protect one's scalp would be unanimously regarded as too strenuous, but such was the case. Although the day was very warm, the air temperature in the caves was cool. After short hikes into the cave entrances and numerous photographs, all with scalps fully intact, it was time to remount the bikes and get on with the day.

The visit to Craters of the Moon had been one of the most interesting experiences of the first three weeks on the road. The absolute desolation of the area, interrupted by snow capped mountains in the far distance, and occasional glimpses of small white flowers and foliage amid the rocky surface left an indelible impression. While looking at the white flowers from a low angle, it appeared the lava was covered with a thin layer of snow. We imagined the experiences of Two Gun Limbert as he photographed and mapped the park in the early twentieth century. The variety of scenery in Idaho continued to be a source of amazement.

We reluctantly left Craters of the Moon and headed toward the evening's destination of Arco, some eighteen miles away. The brisk winds of earlier in the day had not subsided, but had shifted so that they had now become a direct tail wind. The downhill road, in combination with the tail winds, allowed us to cover the distance at high speeds. The exhilarating ride was only interrupted by the blasts of air from the side, when tractor-trailers, loaded with the large bales of hay and barley we had seen the day before, blew by us.

Arriving at Arco was a bit of an eerie experience. Although it was a Saturday afternoon, Main Street was devoid of traffic and people. It would not have been surprising to see sagebrush blowing through this uninhabited downtown. There was a *Twilight Zone* feeling in this town of 1,000 in the middle of the Idaho desert.

The female twosome of our team checked out the two motels in Arco and pronounced one of them fit for a night of human habitation. At $35.00 a night, it also sounded acceptable to the male twosome. While the ladies were researching the accommodations, John and I sat in a swinging chair and chatted with a young woman who managed the motel that, alas, finished in second place. She was a local native who informed us, "Most of the people around here work at the Idaho National Environmental and Engineering Laboratory about twenty miles out of town."

The afternoon's wind was apparently not unusual, as blowing sand occasionally closed the town's main road. As the conversation continued, we learned that Arco was the first city in the country to be illuminated by nuclear power, and that the first submarine nuclear reactor was built here. Since Idaho Falls would be tomorrow's destination, we asked her for impressions of the city. "Idaho Falls is big time," she said. "It's got a Wal Mart."

The couple that owned the chosen motel suggested a local bar and restaurant as the only place in town to get a good supper. The meal choices at the recommended eatery, although limited, consisted of complete packages including soup, salad, entrée, and desert. The food was plentiful and reasonably priced which helped offset the surly attitude of the waitress. When it came time to pay, she bluntly informed us, "We don't take credit cards in here. You gotta pay with cash."

It was a scene typical of a Chevy Chase vacation movie. We emptied our pockets and wallets of all available coins and bills and spread the contents out on the table. The result was barely enough to cover the check. It was agreed that the waitress's attitude gave us little guilt about the small tip we left on the table. Guilt or no guilt, a speedy exit to avoid eye contact with the personality challenged, and now minimally tipped waitress, was deemed an appropriate course of action.

It was late evening and still warm upon return to the motel, so I decided to sit outside in front of the room to record the day's events. While pondering the significance of the day, two young ladies dressed in work clothing came out of their neighboring rooms and began rummaging around the back of a dirty Chevy Suburban adorned with U. S. Government license plates. Well! I certainly couldn't let this go unquestioned, so the interrogation began. The pleasant young women patiently explained that they were in the area doing plant surveys in Craters of the Moon. Niki, the boss, had degrees in botany, and Gina, her assistant, was a summer intern. The two verified that the flowers in the Sawtooth high plains were lupines and that the prior day's large bales were most likely alfalfa.

When told of our disappointment in not having yet seen any of Idaho's famous potatoes. Niki told me, "You'll see 'em when you get close to Idaho Falls." I shared Merj's bathroom adventure in the lava rocks in Craters of the Moon and asked if they had seen any snakes in their work. They acknowledged having seen a number of them and that rattlesnakes were not at all unusual in the park. For an instant I felt bad for making light of Merj's encounter, but the feeling quickly passed when I recalled those saucer-sized eyes.

Day 23 - 1086 Miles Down, 2701 To Go

THERE'S A CERTAIN GLOW ABOUT YOU

The day's ride had been a concern for some time. It would require negotiating 60 or 70 miles of generally uninhabited desert before reaching the developed outskirts of Idaho Falls. Since the day promised to be very warm, and with no prospect of shade, the ride began at sunrise under a crystal clear cloudless sky. Cycling through gentle ups and downs, it didn't take long to come upon a sign that announced entrance into the Idaho National Environmental Engineering Laboratory.

The Idaho National Environmental Engineering Laboratory (INEEL) was established in 1949 as the National Reactor Testing Station and was once the site of the world's largest concentration of nuclear reactors. Over the years fifty-two test reactors, many of them firsts of a kind, were built and operated at the facility. Three of the reactors are still in use. As the young lady at the motel back in Arco had informed us, the Navy's first nuclear propulsion plant was developed at the INEEL. As she had also said, the INEEL first used nuclear fission to produce a useable quantity of electricity in 1951. The location of that event, Experimental Breeder Reactor No. 1 (EBR-1), is now a registered national historic landmark open to the public. Today the INEEL consists of an 890-square mile reservation and employs 8,000 people at the facility and in offices in Idaho Falls.

The main entrance to the INEEL resembled a freeway interchange. Normally that would not be a big surprise, but in the middle of the barren landscape it was a bit odd to see such a complex intersection. It was obvious a significant number of people made their way into and out of the INEEL on a daily basis. The buildings of the INEEL were visible in the distance and resembled a college campus. Given the radioactive nature of activities at the facility, we joked that today would have been a good one to have worn lead lined biking shorts. (In the interest of accuracy, we never wore lead lined biking shorts. The bicycle seats were already uncomfortable enough. It would have been hard to imagine the added discomfort of a load of lead in the shorts.)

The road passed by the laboratory and an ocean of sagebrush. The only break in the flat terrain was an occasional butte rising high off the desert floor in the distance. The buttes, many of which are named, are impressive geological structures. They rise sharply from the desert to heights of 2,500 feet or more and resemble mountains with their tops truncated. We identified Big Butte and Three Buttes by signs along the road. Merj casually remarked, after following me for the better part of the morning, that she had already observed a particularly unattractive form of human Big Butte.

The day began to warm considerably, and the combination of heat and nothingness drove home the fact that we were unquestionably riding through a desert. The early start paid off as the outskirts of Idaho Falls appeared before the day became dangerously warm. Near Idaho Falls a strong cross wind began blowing and the surrounding vegetation offered absolutely nothing to stop it. At least the wind had a cooling effect.

With a few miles left in the day, a long anticipated event finally happened. On the west side of the road a very large crop of potatoes magically sprung forth from the rich soil. Cycling on, we passed rows and rows of perfectly aligned potato plants as far as the eye could see. We also noticed long, sod covered, triangular shaped structures that we assumed to be potato storage buildings. Although we had already covered most of the state, it was now that we felt we were officially in Idaho.

Approaching Idaho Falls, signs of civilization became more and more evident. At first an occasional farmhouse, including one with a pretty decent looking '57 DeSoto for sale in the front yard, broke up what had become an all too familiar desert landscape. Closer to town we passed Reid's Dairy where a sign promised home delivery and asked patrons to "Support Your Local Cow." A Burger King, followed by other staples of the fast food industry began to dot the landscape. Idaho Falls was going to be a lot more big time than just a Wal Mart.

"ALL THAT DOES IS TICK 'EM OFF."

Merj's fear of snakes had become evident in the lava rock of Craters of the Moon, but we had seen our first snake way back in

Oregon, smashed flatter than a flapjack along the shoulder of the road. That encounter prompted Merj to share her biggest snake fear. She was deathly afraid that an unexpected encounter would leave a snake caught in the spokes of her wheel only to bite her each time its head came around. Any strange noise Merj heard while cycling through the barren areas was cause for concern, since it was probably a snake bent on doing her no good. Even the dead snakes produced an audible squeal.

The earlier encounter had also caused Merj to change her normal roadside restroom routine. Before heading into a chosen off-road location, she would now take a handful of small stones and throw them ahead to scare away any lurking snake that may intend her harm. It was impossible to let her routine go by without some "good natured kidding," although I felt a certain twinge of concern about the possibility of the rattlesnakes Niki had told us about. With all of this in mind, I began looking for a knowledgeable local to verify the effectiveness of Merj's stone throwing defense. It didn't take long to find a grizzled old rancher to offer a concise, direct answer. After posing the question, he looked at me like I was some sort of citified moron and said, "All that does is tick 'em off." I quickly turned to Merj and said, "See, I told you so."

Her fear prompted a counting of the dead and mostly-dead snakes that would pass under the bike tires during our travels along the highway shoulders of America. The trip through the desert from Arco to Idaho Falls was a veritable gold mine of dead snakes. The poor critters would apparently seek the warm surface of the asphalt pavement and meet their quick demise under the wheels of a passing tractor-trailer. The day's ride added seven to the list and brought the total for the trip to twenty. The list would grow much longer before we reached South Carolina.

The snake encounters on the road were always memorialized into the handlebar-mounted recorder with a number designation, and sometimes an appropriate comment. Some of today's remarks were typical. *Dead Snake Number 13 - He was a definite goner...*

Number 14 - He was in bad shape... Number 15 - There's a lot of 'em out here... Number 16 - He wasn't dead by much. He was kind of intimidating... Number 17 - He was a flattened goner... Number 18 - I think it's 18? Sometimes it was easy to lose count, but count we did.

Day 24 - 1155 Miles Down, 2632 To Go

WHERE THE RED FERN GROWS

Idaho Falls, a community of a little over 50,000 people, was the location of a planned rest day. The history of modern Idaho Falls goes back to the early 1800's when the glowing accounts of Lewis and Clark led trappers and traders to Idaho. The real rush to Idaho, however, began in the 1860's with the discovery of gold.

In 1864, a man with the real name of Harry Rickets established a ferry to cross the Snake River north of current Idaho Falls. Shortly after, J. M. (Matt) Taylor, a pretty savvy nineteenth century entrepreneur, built a log toll bridge over the turbulent river near the city. The town was originally known as Taylor's Bridge, and later Eagle Rock, until the name change to Idaho Falls in 1891. As the gold veins played out, miners left the area and those who remained, many of them Mormons, irrigated the arid land and turned to farming. Today Idaho Falls is the processing and commercial hub for the surrounding farm, livestock, and dairy region as well as the home to industries that produce lumber, steel, and concrete.

Our day of rest in Idaho Falls began with a well-deserved, later-than-normal wakeup, and a leisurely morning taking care of errands, e-mails, and sight seeing. Lunch was enjoyed at a micro-brewery in a restored area a short walk from the falls. After an all too customary disregard for healthy eating habits, we headed to an area of quaint shops next to the brewery and stopped at a small gift shop. As the ladies shopped, John and I chatted with a classy older lady behind the counter by the name of Nellie.

Nellie was raised on a potato farm at the base of Taylor Mountain outside of Idaho Falls. Her grandfather, a fellow by the name of Abel Beasley, owned the farm. Abel had come to Idaho from Springfield, Illinois and worked as an assayer appraising the value of ores mined in the area. Not long after his arrival, he purchased the farmland where Nellie grew up and he began raising potatoes. Nellie told us, "My grandfather invented the russet potato."

Nellie talked of growing up on a farm where all of the children in the family helped out with the chores. "In the winter we all cut seed potatoes into pieces making sure there was an eye in each piece," she explained, "In the spring we all helped plant the seed potatoes and then weeded the fields by hand during the summer." When the potatoes were ready to be harvested, a machine dug them, and family members followed behind to pick up the potatoes and put them in baskets. Nellie verified that the long, triangular shaped, earthen covered structures that were a bit of a mystery the day before were, in fact, used to store potatoes. The earthen cover provided insulation, to keep the potatoes from freezing in the winter, and cool in the summer. When asked why potatoes were so prominent in Idaho, she described the rich volcanic soil, the cool nights, and the warm, sunny days as ideal conditions for raising potatoes.

Nellie and her husband, who had worked at the nearby INEEL facility, were now retired and spent part of the year volunteering at national parks. She strongly suggested a visit to the nearby Idaho Falls Library and a look at the sculpture of a young boy and his two dogs in front of the building. The sculpture represented characters from a book entitled *Where the Red Fern Grows* that was written by a local author named Wilson Rawls.

Merj had now joined the conversation, and upon hearing the name of the book, became an active participant in the discussion.

She read the book to her fifth-grade students each school year, and fondly recalled how much it had meant to her and them. There was real emotion in her voice as she recalled the book. As the enjoyable conversation came to an end, Nellie talked of having roomed with Rawls' wife before her marriage to the author. It was a very small world in eastern Idaho.

Although difficult to part with such a charming lady, it was time to leave Nellie and head to the library. "It's too bad you all won't be in town for the Fourth," she called in a manner that would have done the Chamber of Commerce proud, "We put on the largest fireworks display west of the Mississippi River." It was hard to imagine that that was the case, but it was equally difficult to doubt this nice lady.

The Idaho Falls Library was an impressive modern structure with the sculpture of the characters from *Where the Red Fern Grows* prominently displayed in front of the building. While assembled by the sculpture, Merj told us about the novel. It was obvious that she enjoyed sharing the story, and that the brief time in front of the library in Idaho Falls had been an important moment for her.

Day 24 - 1155 Miles Down, 2632 To Go

LITTLE RED CABOOSE

The cycling out of Idaho Falls was through green irrigated fields with snow capped mountains in the background. The scenery was much improved when compared to the sagebrush-dominated surroundings of two days earlier. The passing potato fields and the sod covered storage buildings gave occasions to stop and take pictures. As odd as it seemed, the long wait to see Idaho's famous potatoes caused a strange excitement with each passing spud. The odd thoughts of the day continued as the potatoes in Idaho triggered recollections of buckeye trees back in Ohio. Between our collective hundred or so years of living in the Buckeye State, we could only recall a few. Neither of us was much of a tree expert though, and it was possible that we could have been living in a stand of them for years and not have known it.

The musing brought back college era memories of working on a survey crew. One thing that was always important was to accurately record in a field book the size and type of trees that were located during a survey. In the summer, I could take a look at the leaves and have a fifty-fifty chance of getting the tree variety right. In the winter, with the leaves no longer on the trees, it was a nearly impossible to know one from the other. As a result, a tree that would have been recorded as a 24 inch maple in the summer was many times recorded as a 24 inch all-wood in the winter.

Potatoes and buckeyes, it was amazing the things that passed through one's mind when performing the mindless task of pedaling a bicycle across the country. Maybe it was the effect of the heat manifesting itself. Maybe it was a result of the extended time on the bikes resulting from the SLOW and STOP reminders on the front pack. Then again, maybe such thinking was just part of the process of "maturing" deeper into middle age.

The trip to Swan Valley, that night's destination, was one of gentle ups and downs into a fairly brisk head wind. Our ride had now taken us along the South Fork of the Snake River where numerous fishermen could be seen along and in the river. Seeing the many fishermen brought memories of a quote by Arnold Gingrich, "The fishing," he said, "is more important than the fish." A summary of the day's fishing efforts was well described in another memorable quote, "Bragging may not bring happiness, but no man having caught a large fish goes home through an alley."

The last evening in Idaho would be spent outside of Swan Valley at the Henson Silver Guest Ranch. A very polite Mrs. Henson gave us the sleeping options for the night: Either a modern cottage, or a room in a hundred-year-old barn that had been nicely restored and made into guestrooms. Since John and I were given the heavy responsibility of making the lodging choice, we opted for one of the rooms in the restored barn. The selection sounded good until Mrs. Henson casually let it be known that, "Some critter just died under the foundation, and the place sorta stinks." Knowing the olfactory sensitivity of the ladies in our travelling group, we quickly modified our choice to the cabin. It was a good choice, as the two-bedroom cabin was well appointed with an open beamed ceiling and a western theme.

The calories burned by the day's ride required immediate replacement lest the delicate biochemical balance of such finely conditioned bodies suffer degradation. Ice cream was thought to be the balance restorer of choice in Swan Valley. A trip back downtown soon put our quartet on the shores of Rainy Creek and then inside the Rainy Creek World Famous Square Ice Cream Store. The ice cream shop was a popular local attraction and the cheerful young lady behind the freezer worked furiously to keep up with demand. The ice cream cone was just as advertised, a cube of ice cream on a sugar cone. The delicious frozen treat was an excellent choice to restore caloric balance. The ice cream store provided a classic image of Americana, befitting the small eastern Idaho town of Swan Valley.

Back at the cabin, Bret Henson, Mrs. Henson's husband and business partner, provided a target for friendly interrogation. The questioning began by asking about a new looking home located a few hundred yards behind the cabin with a railroad caboose parked in the front yard. "I sold 'em the property a few years ago and they hauled the caboose in on a tractor-trailer." Bret said, "I have no idea why they decided to park it in the front yard."

It was hard to imagine having a neighbor back home with a caboose in the front yard and not knowing why it was there. It's possible that the members of the local zoning board may have slept through the meeting when the idea was proposed. It was typical though, of the "live and let live" nature of the people of the West.

Bret went on to say, "Most of the ranchers around here sold their property over the last few years because land prices have really gone up." He explained that land along the Snake River was being sold for $50,000 an acre, and it wasn't unusual for people, mostly Californians, to buy an acre of land, build an $800,000 home and then spend only three weeks a year there. Bret then described summer fly-fishing, especially for cutthroat trout, as the lifeblood of the local economy. In his opinion, "You gotta make it in the summer or you'll starve in the winter."

Bret and his wife were typical of the plainspoken folks we had grown accustomed to in the rural West. When asked for a key to the cabin, Bret handed it to us, but said, "You really don't need one." When we inquired about paying for the night, he said, "Hey, whenever you're ready to pay, come on over to the house." The morning meal was included in the lodging package, so Bret asked, "What time do you want me to cook up some pancakes and bacon for breakfast in the morning?" After cautiously giving him a time that was thought to be pretty early, he said, "No problem 'cause I got a couple horses to break in the mornin' anyhow." The *Bonanza* feeling returned once again.

The cabin had a roomy back porch that was fitted with comfortable chairs. John and I deposited ourselves in two of the chairs and talked of experiences to date and plans for tomorrow's ride. The air was dead calm and the warm day had given way to the cool of the evening. The sky was cloudless as the sun sat over the distant Snake River Mountains. It was hard to imagine a more picturesque setting. Soon darkness and a noticeable cool came over the porch and the sun disappeared behind the mountains. It was time to head inside for a good night's rest and end our last day in Idaho.

Day 26 - 1211 Miles Down, 2576 To Go

wyoming

"Next year I'm gonna try to stay sober during both days of summer."

HERE'S MUD IN YOUR EYE

It was the third of July when we rode out of Swan Valley through the tiny town of Irwin toward the Wyoming border. The upcoming Independence Day holiday was evident; American flags lined the main street of Irwin, and a large sign in the middle of town announced that a pig roast would be held on the Fourth. It was easy to picture all 157 inhabitants of Irwin gathering around the roasting pig, although it was somewhat of a mystery as to where the pig would come from. Many varieties of wildlife and livestock had been part of the scenery since leaving the Pacific coast, but it was impossible to recall seeing even a single pig. Perhaps a Honey Baked Ham on a skewer would supply the focal point for the Independence Day celebration in Irwin?

A flat road allowed easy cycling and a view of the occasional patches of snow on the distant Snake River Mountains. Only a red '61 Corvair sitting in front of a small wood frame home interrupted the bucolic scenery. The Corvair brought back memories of Merj's youth. When we first met, she was the proud driver of an early '60's vintage blue four-door model. In the days before Ralph Nadir's book *Unsafe at Any Speed* doomed the future of the car, two door Corvair coupes were sort of cool. Blue four door models, though, were never cool. That our relationship had continued then, and for many years after, was true testament to Merj's many other redeeming values. The single redeeming value, however, of not judging a car owner by her blue, four-door vehicle of choice could rightfully be attributed to the male half of the relationship.

After passing the Dam Store, probably named after the upcoming Palisades Dam, we soon entered the Targhee National Forest. The area was dominated by the mountains to the left, a caribou range to the right, and the large presence of Palisades Dam in front of us. The road rose considerably until reaching the top of the massive rock dam. A sign on the dam announced that visitors were entering the Calamity Recreation Area.

Targhee National Forest encompasses 1.8 million acres and abuts Grand Teton and Yellowstone National Parks. Targhee is part of the largest remaining block of relatively undisturbed plant and animal habitat in the contiguous United States. The Forest was established in 1908 by President Theodore Roosevelt and was named in honor of a Bannock Indian warrior. The Targhee includes areas of arid sagebrush covered land and timbered highlands with peaks of over 10,000 feet. The climate of the area ranges from summer temperatures of over 100 degrees Fahrenheit in the lower elevations, to winter temperatures of 40 degrees below or lower in the mountains.

The trip to Jackson, Wyoming from Swan Valley presented two options. The shortest by twenty miles was directly over Teton Pass, but involved a very steep climb. Leo had strongly advised consideration of the longer loop to the south as had Bret Henson, and in spite of Bret's warning of roadway construction, we decided to take our chances with the longer option.

The road along Palisades Lake was one of high climbs above the water surface and drops back down. The deep blue lake was situated between steeply rising mountain ranges and afforded many photographic opportunities. The occasional breaks were welcome, since Bret's early morning breakfast of pancakes and eggs still lay heavily in our stomachs. About twenty-five miles outside Swan Valley a sign welcomed us to Wyoming. It was strange; thirty percent of the total trip distance had been covered, but we had only crossed two states. The trip should have probably been planned through New England where a loop of 1,200 miles or so would have crossed eight or ten state lines. The states are big out west and a couple of the biggest ones were next on the itinerary. Regardless, it was time for well-deserved celebration at the Wyoming state line.

Shortly after entering Wyoming the route turned north along the scenic Snake River toward Jackson. A light rain started to fall, and a stop to quickly don rain gear was in order. Before long, Bret's prophecy of construction appeared. Traffic was limited to one lane through the lengthy construction zone, and after a patient wait in the rain, we, along with a long line of vehicles, were finally motioned through. The rain had made the construction site a muddy mess, and soon mud from the rough surface covered the bikes and us.

After three very muddy and difficult miles we were flagged down by a Wyoming Department of Transportation official and asked to pull to the side of the road. The state employee firmly, but politely, informed us that a truck was being sent to provide transportation to the end of the construction area. It was considered too dangerous for cyclists to ride through the area and no amount of arguing was going to change their edict. We were given no choice in the matter, so we awaited our ride.

Soon a battered muddy white Chevy pickup arrived and the driver motioned to load the bikes into the truck bed. The truck door had hardly closed before we discovered that the fellow in the truck worked as a flagger for the construction company that was rebuilding the road. He was in no particular hurry and talked non-stop from the time we climbed into the cab until we climbed out. He was unhappy with his $11.00 an hour, eighty hours a week job and ventured the opinion, "I can't go nowhere 'cause I don't play politics. Flaggers in Idaho," he said, "make $25.00 an hour." It was tempting to ask why he didn't travel just twenty or so miles to the west and pull down the big bucks, but I knew the answer wasn't really worth the explanation.

Even if the dedicated traffic control expert *did* work eighty hour weeks, a flagger's job didn't appear to be one of high-stress. It seemed that the only decisions to be made involved deciding when to turn the hand held sign from "slow" to "stop," but maybe there were job subtleties unapparent to the naked eye. An amateur geologist and mushroom expert, the flagger described rock for-mations in the area and of the joys of morel mushrooms. He was a friendly guy, and we were sure he was just trying to make con-versation and offer helpful information, but when we climbed out of the truck we felt a certain amount of relief.

My obsessive side took over as I tried to get an idea of how far we had been carried in the truck. By comparing the distance trav-eled by the support car with the bike odometers, it appeared that the truck ride was a little over two miles long. Unfortunately, most of the ride was downhill, so there was no benefit of the motorized assist. I comforted myself with the fact that the truck ride was not only downhill but much shorter than the miles that were added by getting lost back in Oregon. I still had bicycling miles in the bank. "You've go to be kidding me," Merj mumbled, speaking volumes. This unhealthy obsession had to end.

After leaving the construction site, the ride to Jackson contin-ued along busy roads with little or no shoulders. White water rafters rode the quick rapids in the Snake River below. More rain and some close calls with tractor-trailers made the bike path on the outskirts of Jackson a very welcome sight. It signaled the end of one of the most difficult days yet. The combination of rain, mud, construction, narrow shoulders, and traffic had combined to make us look forward to the evening's lodging.

COPPERTONE BABIES

Jackson, Wyoming was the first stop in a town that we had previously visited. The first of two visits was in the mid 1990's with an enjoyable, supported bicycle tour of the Tetons and Yellowstone that began and ended in Jackson. Tomorrow's first twenty-five miles or so north of Jackson would be on roads that were familiar. The second Jackson visit was in the late 90's as part of a car tour of the West. The second trip was considerably easier.

Jackson, Wyoming is part of a larger area known as Jackson Hole. Jackson Hole lies just west of the Continental Divide and encompasses 400 square miles of the Snake River Valley. American Indians including Crow, Shoshone, and Black Foot used the valley for hunting during the warm summer months until the first settlers arrived in the early 1800's. John Coulter, the first white man to see the area, explored much of the valley and attempted to trade with the native Indians. Jackson Hole became a major beaver trapping and fur trading area until the mid 1800's when interest in beaver adorned hats waned back East. Ranchers and farmers moved to the area in the late 1800's, and recreational fishermen, hunters, and visitors soon followed.

The city of Jackson is located at the south end of the Grand Teton Mountain Range. The town name originated from a local mountain man by the name of David Jackson. Mr. Jackson provided assistance to early trappers in the area, and like so many other western trappers, had a town named after him. Jackson officially became a city in 1901, and in the 1920's it became the first town in the nation governed by women. Today, Jackson is a stepping-off point for visitors to the Grand Teton and Yellowstone National Parks. Thousands of visitors come to the area for the winter skiing, snowmobiling, summer rafting, fly fishing, mountain biking, and climbing. The four arches formed from elk horns, erected at the corners of the downtown square, are well known landmarks.

Jackson was full of tourists for the Fourth of July holiday. We too were tourists, but figured that riding into town on bicycles somehow made us different. For example, nobody else had the unusually well defined tan lines created by the biking shorts and jersey. The real give away, though, was the untanned areas on the sides of our faces in the Y shape of the helmet straps. An equally telling characteristic was the tanned circular area on the back of our hands from the opening in the cycling gloves. Surprisingly, no one asked about our unusual tanning patterns.

Downtown Jackson is a combination of recreated Old West shops and contemporary businesses. Many of the locals bring their dogs to town, so well behaved Labradors and golden retrievers shared the downtown sidewalks. As the ladies shopped, John and I again did what we did best: show interest. Since wedding anniversary number thirty-two was only a week away, a jewelry purchase in a fashionable downtown store seemed appropriate. The saleswoman behind the counter was exceptionally good at her job and Merj and I left the store with more than we had come in with.

Day 27 - 1261 Miles Down, 2526 To Go

JUST LIKE BEING IN CHURCH

The Fourth of July dawned under cool sunny skies, and the ride out of Jackson toward the Grand Tetons was one of reminiscing about our earlier trip through the same area. Not far into the ride, the National Elk Refuge, framed by mountains to the east and west, spread over the wide grassy valley floor. The National Elk Refuge was created by the federal government in 1910 when several thousand acres were purchased to make an area available for the elk to graze during the winter and to keep them from eating feed intended for the rancher's cattle. We had not seen any elk during either of our previous trips through the refuge, but the area was huge, and they had to be out there somewhere. Like this one, both of those trips had been during the summer, and it was a winter feeding ground, which probably explains their absence. Our astute observations continued to be a source of wonder.

After only about five miles into the day, a large sign at a rest area announced entrance to Grand Teton National Park. The majestic snow capped Tetons provided the background for a photo opportunity in front of the sign. An older gentleman who appeared to be the patriarch of a large family piling out of a parked motor home offered to take a picture of the two of us together. He asked a few questions about the camera in a voice thick with an accent suggesting he was not from Massachusetts. After some good-natured joking, we discovered that this very charming fellow was from Arkansas. Like many others, he and his family were touring the Tetons and Yellowstone in a motorhome.

With their extended mirrors and wind buffeting, motorhomes were the bane of cyclists. They were everywhere in the Yellowstone area, and at times seemed to outnumber cars. Regardless, it wouldn't be right to hold the choice of transportation against our new friend. Although embarrassed not knowing what to call people from the state, it didn't stop our questioning why Arkansans or Arkansasians didn't seem to venture north. Our collective, although probably impaired, memories could recall meeting only one Arkansas native back home. The gentleman laughed and said, "I don't know why, but it sure is hot back home this summer." Since a later portion of the trip would traverse southern Missouri just north of Arkansas, it was not good news to hear of his weather woes. We could have spent the better part of the day talking to this friendly, gray haired gentleman, but the younger members of his travelling party were beckoning him back to the motorhome, and the Tetons were beckoning us.

Grand Teton National Park encompasses the Teton Mountain Range. The mountain range is forty miles long and seven to nine miles wide. The highest peak is Grand Teton at 13,770 feet, and the range includes twelve other peaks over 12,000 feet in elevation. The Snake River is the major waterway in the park and seven significant lakes dot the region, the largest being Jackson Lake. The National Park is home to numerous species of wildlife including, among others, black and grizzly bears, and over 300 species of birds. There are seven species of coniferous trees and over 900 species of flowering plants.

Our own observations were succinct and to the point: The Teton Mountains were absolutely awe-inspiring. They sprang from the valley floor as if some giant hand had thrust them toward the sky. The craggy gray peaks formed a jagged silhouette against the bright, crystal blue sky, and the clean white snow that filled the crevices and covered the peaks of the mountain range provided a bright contrast to the surrounding rock. Cycling along the valley floor a few miles from the base put us in constant sight of this magnificent natural phenomenon, and every mile thereafter brought more unforgettable views. It was difficult to put into words the humbling experience of being in the presence of the Teton Mountains. We felt as though we were cycling through a giant open aired cathedral.

Unfortunately, even in a majestic setting, people riding bicycles get hungry, and it was time to find a place for a mid-morning breakfast. Near the crossroads town of Moose, and with the Tetons in the background, a pleasant young Swedish exchange student served plenty of pancakes and eggs at picnic tables adjacent to the Original Moose Chuck Wagon. The owner of a small bike shop next to the restaurant suggested a detour to avoid construction that lay ahead on our planned route. Even though it would add nine miles to the day, after yesterday's construction difficulties we quickly chose the non-construction alternative.

The bright sunny day was warming, and it was soon time for Merj to peel off her cold weather leggings. Removal of the cool weather gear allowed an opportunity to show off her Independence Day attire. Out of her cycling shoes sprang red white and blue socks with white stars circling the top. She was one stylish patriot.

The day's ride continued in the shadow of the mountains and around pristine Jenny Lake. The lake and mountains dominated the scenery on our left, and a wide expanse of sagebrush and lupines spread out to our right as we headed north through Grand Teton National Park. Merj had decided to collect a small sample of soil from each state we crossed, so we stopped for the Wyoming sample. As we scooped up a handful of soil, cicadas chirped noisily in the background. They had evidently chosen this year to emerge from their seventeen-year slumber.

At about thirty miles into the day we reluctantly turned away from the Tetons and passed a yellow sign with a buffalo on it that warned, "Danger Do Not Approach Wildlife." We hoped the sign meant there would be an opportunity to see some of the natural inhabitants of the park. While cycling and scouring the surrounding area for wildlife, a large body of water appeared. The bright blue of Jackson Lake stood out in contrast to the gray, snow capped mountains. Unfortunately no wildlife was spotted.

A short time later, a stop near Moran Junction allowed an opportunity to take pictures back toward the Tetons. A wide expanse of yellow flowers directly in the foreground, along with the mountains in the distance, presented a striking photo opportunity. While snapping pictures of the beautiful view, a young family from Massachusetts pulled over with the same idea. The mother walked our way with a flower identification book in hand and a quizzical look on her face. If she was looking for us to provide answers, it didn't happen. Even with the book, the three of us weren't sure the flowers that surrounded us had been properly identified. Maybe the crossroads ahead should have been more properly designated "Moron Junction." It didn't matter; the wild flowers formed a colorful carpet on the valley floor.

WAS THAT A SOUFFLÉ YOU ORDERED?

Since that night would be spent off route, the stopping point for the day was variable. Once a decision was made to stop, our intention was to load the bikes on the support car and head back into Yellowstone to the Flagg Ranch. The road out of Moran Junction, really no more than the junction of two roads, toward Dubois included occasional short stretches of roadway construction. The attitude of some drivers, especially in construction zones, was always a source of bewilderment. We had a running contest for the "Idiot of the Day," and there was no problem finding plenty of candidates along this section of rural Wyoming highway.

Along that same stretch, we passed an occasional sign proclaiming "Grizzly Bear Area - Special Rules Apply." This made us wonder what exactly those rules were. We had received well-intentioned advice for dealing with bears from a number of sources; it included, be quiet, make noise, don't look at him, stare him in the eyes, jump up and down and play dead. It was common knowledge that a motivated grizzly could very likely catch a cyclist if he had a mind to. The hope was that if a test of motivation was forthcoming, two highly motivated fifty-something cyclists could muster enough speed to escape safely. I reminded Merj, however, that in reality it was only necessary to be the quicker of the two riders.

While taking a break along one of the construction zones, two cyclists approached from the same direction. The duo consisted of a young man and woman. When they pulled over to join us, we were surprised to find that the male was our trailer-pulling National Guard buddy Andy. Andy was last seen in western Idaho, and since we had taken very different routes the last two weeks, we hardly expected to meet him again.

Andy had met up with his female companion, Deena, in Montana, and the two had decided to ride together until they reached Colorado. He seemed to be happy to have her company. Andy shared an experience of being forced to ride in a pickup truck for eight miles through a construction zone in Montana. After sharing with him our similar two-mile experience of the day before, a feeling of satisfaction came over me. Our little assist was really nothing by comparison.

The day's ride ended at a small log cabin restaurant about eight miles from Moran Junction. Since the smell of food was in the air, a trip inside for a late lunch was in order. Before long our young server approached, asked for the food order, and informed us that he was working to save money for college. As the conversation continued, he indicated, "That road out front is all uphill until you get to the Continental Divide." He grew up in Port Angeles, Washington and told us that the city was also the hometown of John Elway, the former Denver Bronco quarterback. Although an exceptional quarterback, Elway was not anyone a Cleveland Browns history buff could cozy up to.

Flagg Ranch was located some distance back in Yellowstone. Lodging for the evening would be a comfortable cabin with a great view of the mountains. Our dinner waiter at the lodge was a young French student of international business who was working in this country to learn English. The young man was trying very hard to master English, so it was easy to overlook a number of linguistic mistakes he made. Even though he was struggling a little, he spoke English a lot better than we spoke French. In fact, in spite of two years of high school French and a recent refresher course, there were a number of bewildered looks when we had tried to communicate during the previous summer's bike tour of the French Loire Valley. Other restaurant staff members from Russia and Slovakia added to the international flavor of the lodge restaurant. Later, back in the cabin a local television newscaster announced that the largest fireworks show west of the Mississippi would be taking place that night in Idaho Falls, Idaho. Nellie, how could we have ever doubted you?

Yellowstone National Park had been the location of our first bicycle tour some eight years prior. Although this trip would not include much of the park, it was easy to remember this national treasure with fondness. Yellowstone, the country's first national park, encompasses nearly 3,500 square miles, mostly all within the northwest corner of Wyoming. The park is larger than Rhode Island and Delaware combined. Eighty percent of Yellowstone is forested and eighty percent of the forested area is covered with lodgepole pines. The remainder is covered with grassland (15%) and water (5%). The park includes an active volcano, more than 300 geysers, including Old Faithful, and experiences 2,000 earthquakes annually. Yellowstone contains the world's largest petrified forests and almost 300 waterfalls fifteen feet or higher. Every year nearly three million people from all over the world visit Yellowstone.

Day 28 - 1308 Miles Down, 2479 To Go

CRITTER NOSES

Immediately after leaving the previous day's restaurant stopping point, we commenced a climb to Togwotee Pass and our first crossing of the Continental Divide. Cold weather attire was quickly shed as the energy expended by the climb created a considerable amount of body heat. Eight miles into the climb, the appearance of an isolated restaurant supplied a welcome opportunity for rest and *another* hearty breakfast.

The long climb continued after breakfast, through rolling

meadows of yellow, blue, and white flowers. Mountains in the distance added to the beauty of the surrounding area. After eighteen
miles of rigorous climbing, we finally reached the summit at
Togwotee Pass, and our first encounter with the Continental
Divide.

The Continental Divide winds its way through the western
mountains and represents the dividing line between the Pacific
watershed to the west and the Atlantic watershed to the east. At elevation 9,658, Togwotee Pass represented the new highest point of
the trip. Since it was also the Continental Divide, theoretically it
should have been all down hill from here to the Mississippi River.
Unfortunately there were a number of other crossings of the
Continental Divide and more than a few hills east of the Mississippi
that had to be dealt with before the trip would be completed.

At the summit we were greeted by Andy and Erika, a young
couple last seen leaving the restaurant and a short time later Andy
and Deena joined the celebration by the Continental Divide sign.
Nearby patches of snow on the ground enhanced the high elevation feel of the area. Andy and Erika were crossing the country
from Seattle to Boston, and hoped to finish by Labor Day. They
were improvising as they went and discussed various routing
options for the remainder of the ride. A couple from Manitoba
touring the West on motorcycles approached and asked the
nature of our little adventure. Listening to us explain our trip,
they looked like people trying to talk someone down from a window ledge. Although supportive, they were convinced we were all
crazy. A consensus seemed to be building that suggested that very
conclusion.

Our climb up to Togwotee Pass was predicted on the maps we
carried with us on the bikes. Most of the maps were supplied by
the various states, and the ones supplied by the Wyoming
Department of Transportation had proven to be invaluable. The
maps were specially prepared for bicyclists and showed not only
highways, but also traffic volumes, road widths, and relative

grades. The back of the map showed road profiles for all of the major climbs. The cycling maps supplied by Oregon and upcoming Colorado were good, but Wyoming's were outstanding. Idaho didn't need extensive mapping; Idaho had Leo.

The ride down from Togwotee Pass was steep and, at times, allowed speeds of over forty miles per hour. The worries that go through one's mind when looking down at a bicycle's narrow, rapidly spinning, fenderless tires are many. Concerns about gravel on the road, a tire blowout, an unexpected side wind, and close calls from other vehicles are just some of the fears that came with a quick descent. If the road was straight the ride was fun. If sharp turns were part of the descent, the brakes got considerable use. To add to the experience, biking shorts were a constant reminder that a fall would put great amounts of exposed skin in harm's way. Experienced cyclists called it "road rash." The courage and skills of racing cyclists, such as those in the Tour d'France, was a source of great respect.

The quick ride offered a variety of scenery that changed around each bend; the road passed red and brown rocky cliffs and babbling brooks. The road soon flattened and we came upon Timberline Ranch. The ranch is the site of Miami (Ohio) University's geology field camp. Our oldest daughter had spent the better part of a summer at the camp as she worked toward a degree in geology. We stopped to take pictures of the camp for later proof of having actually been there. Our geologically trained daughter would have been of considerable value in explaining the varied terrain throughout the trip. Along with a geologist, it probably would have been a good idea to have included a physical therapist, a dentist, a bicycle mechanic, a meteorologist, a chef, and most appropriately, a psychiatrist. It wasn't difficult to visualize two lonely bicyclists trailed by a motor home full of "roadies."

It was 91 degrees when the day's ride ended in Dubois. For the first time in four or five nights the hotel had all the amenities, including air conditioning, telephone, and a television. Andy and

Deena soon showed up at the same hotel. Knowing they were on a tight budget, we were able to convince the lady behind the counter to let them use our AARP discount. Ah, the benefits of being over fifty!

Downtown Dubois is a restoration of an Old West town, including false fronts on many of the buildings and board side-walks. Suffice it to say the usual cast of explorers, trappers, and miners made their way through the town in the 1800's including the legendary outlaw, Butch Cassidy. Butch operated a horse ranch in Dubois, and it was alleged that he always seemed to sell more horses than he could raise.

Dubois was first settled in the 1870's and was originally known as "Never Sweat." Standing in the summer heat, it became clear that early settlers had arrived in the winter. When it came time to establish a post office, officials at the Postal Department in Washington determined the town would be named after Idaho Senator Fred Thomas Dubois, a member of the Postal Committee. Old Fred must have struck fear in the hearts of his comrades in the Senate; while chairman of another committee, he required that navy bean soup always be on the Senate menu. Afternoons in the Senate chamber must have been a real joy.

Dinner in downtown Dubois was eaten sitting at an outside table at the Really Wild Bunch Restaurant. It didn't take long to discover that Lou, the very affable young waitress, was originally from Mansfield, Ohio. We were beginning to wonder if anyone was still left back in Ohio! "I came out here looking for work," Lou explained, "found a guy and decided to stay." Her beau was a regular participant in the town's rodeo but was questionable for tonight's competition. Apparently, he had a bad experience with a bronco or bull or some other rodeo animal and was suffering with an assortment of sprains and breaks. Throughout supper we dis-cussed her boyfriend's chosen profession and her parents' accept-ance of this liaison. "They just came to town to meet him," she said happily, "and so far so good."

The evening was still young so there was no hurry consuming the usual fare of meat and potatoes. The leisurely pace also allowed an opportunity to chat a little longer with our vivacious server. Lou was a very talented waitress, but that was only one of her skills. When not at the Really Wild Bunch, she worked part-time for a local taxidermist. Working for a taxidermist in Wyoming wasn't all that unusual; the popularity of hunting and fishing in the area created a large customer base. What was unusual though, was the shop's specialty. Her employer specialized in noses. The noses must have been world class because Lou was proud of the fact that her work was shipped all over the country. At first we laughed and said, "You've got to be kidding me!" But she wasn't. Noses are apparently some of the most difficult parts of stuffed animals to get right, so good ones are in demand. Her company had the reputation of doing them right, so business was good enough to make them the largest supplier of artificial noses in the world.

Lou's parents arrived at the restaurant and sat down at the table next to ours. Lou provided introductions and the discussion quickly moved to Ohio and their daughter's bronco busting boyfriend. While we chatted with her parents, Lou told us she had earned a degree in biochemistry and wanted to become a veterinarian some day. In addition to her taxidermy skills, she had trained in the operation of farm machinery and was a certified backhoe operator. We wondered how, between the waitress, nose making, and backhoe operating jobs, she found time for her rodeo companion. Her parents were nice folks who were justifiably proud of their energetic, independent, twenty-four-year-old daughter.

As the evening wore on, a crusty looking old fellow set up his musical gear in preparation for serenading the assembled masses. While we chatted with "Red Dog," the entertainment for the evening, he put the final touches on his one-man orchestra, including adjustments to the harmonica propped in front of his mouth. Soon our newfound buddy began blasting out a steady stream of well-done Jimmy Buffet oldies. Red Dog was a talented songster who fit perfectly into the pleasant warm evening in western Wyoming.

Walking back to the motel, we passed the town's rodeo arena, which was filled with spectators and participants. The arena was a large oval-shape, with a fenced area and sections of bleachers around the perimeter. A loud public address system announced the events and the competitors. There were a few hundred spectators in the arena loudly supporting their favorites. Across the street in a bank parking lot, a number of rodeo fans were perched on the tops of pickup cabs to get a free view of the competition. The rodeo had the feeling of Friday night high school football back in Ohio. We wondered if Lou's boyfriend had patched himself up enough to be one of the participants.

Day 29 - 1355 Miles Down, 2432 To Go

A BICYCLE BUILT FOR FOUR

The ride out of Dubois was generally downhill with a tail wind along the Wind River. The morning cycling couldn't have been any better as we rode easily through areas of red cliffs and reddish brown soil. The colors of the surrounding terrain were spectacular and necessitated frequent stops to take pictures. Near the small town of Crowheart, twelve miles of brand new asphalt created a bicycle riding euphoria. Brisk riding down hill with the wind at one's back was reason to get a little cocky in the vast plains of Wyoming.

Outside of Crowheart a stop at a rest area near Crowheart Butte gave an opportunity to learn about the origin of the name. The name Crowheart evidently came from the actions of a Crow

Indian Chief by the name of Washakie. After a successful battle with one of his Crow rivals near the butte, Chief Washakie placed the heart of one of his vanquished foes on a lance while performing a traditional victory dance. It was clear that Chief Washakie was well thought of in the area because his name began appearing on an increasing number of landmarks.

About forty-five miles into the day's ride, the road entered the Wind River Indian Reservation. The reservation served as the home of the Eastern Shoshone and Northern Arapaho tribes. The tribes relocated to the 2.2 million-acre reservation during the 1860's and 1870's. The Wind River Reservation is the third largest in the country and the only reservation in the United States that occupies lands chosen by the tribe compelled to live there. Chief Washakie is buried in the reservation, as is Sacajewea, the young woman who served as a guide for Lewis and Clark.

The area was desolate for as far as the eye could see, and the eye could see a long way in this part of Wyoming. It made the high desert of Oregon and Idaho look almost lush by comparison. The day grew very warm and our earlier confidence began to evaporate as a head wind started to offer unwanted resistance. While still in the reservation, we stopped at a gas station/grocery in the small town of Ft. Washakie for drinks and a break. Fort Washakie is home to the reservation's tribal government and the only military fort in the U. S. to be named for an Indian chief. Native Americans from the surrounding reservation operated the store.

Leaving the store and heading toward Lander, it was impossible not to wonder about the difficulties faced by anyone trying to do something productive with this barren land. Neither Merj nor I were sufficiently versed in the history of western tribal resettlement to form a well-founded opinion. But, even though its occupants selected the land, it looked like a very tough place to try to make a go of it. We wondered what the unselected land must have looked like.

The last few miles into the evening destination of Lander

were through more hot arid landscape. At some distance to the southwest, smoke could be seen rising from a wooded area as helicopters dropped retardant on the site. Large, dark thunderclouds were building in the same direction. It appeared fire relief from nature would be on hand soon. Before long, a few drops of rain splashed off our helmets, and the pedaling quickened as the dark clouds approached.

Arriving hot and tired in Lander after a day's ride of almost eighty miles, rest and liquid replenishment were high on the list of things to do. Both were found at the appropriately named Lander Bar; a combination restaurant and bar near the motel. Restaurant-bars were the only eating options in many of the small Wyoming towns. They usually supplied local atmosphere, good food, and good conversation. The young woman behind the bar, although a native Landerite or Landerian, or whatever, had spent time working on Hilton Head Island, our ultimate destination. It was enjoyable sharing common experiences on the island, and more than a little unusual to find a person in the middle of these desert-like surroundings who even knew where it was. Hilton Head Island felt a long way away in more ways than one.

The discussion moved to the Indian reservation and our observations that it would be difficult to live there. "Teachers are paid a premium to teach at the reservation schools," she said. "Children on the reservation see so much at an early age that it makes them difficult to control in a classroom." Although there had been no evidence of oil, she explained that the reserves beneath the land were an income source. We talked of the problems with alcohol among Native Americans and again expressed our uneducated opinion that they seemed to have been given difficult conditions to live under. Although not disagreeing, she didn't exactly agree either. Somehow we wondered if the differences between the town folks and the people of the reservation were even greater than the stark differences in their surroundings.

Our newfound friend behind the bar spoke of a bicycling family that had passed through town a few days ago. She mentioned that there was an article in the local newspaper describing details of their trip. Leaving the restaurant, a stop at a sidewalk paper box supplied the most recent copy of the *Lander Journal*. The paper was three days old, but, nonetheless, the bicycling family was prominently displayed on the front page. The picture showed a family of four consisting of the mother, father, and two small boys. What made their trip unusual was that they were doing it on a custom made bicycle built for four. The family portrait of the four of them on the bike was quite impressive. The article went on to explain that the family was from New Hampshire and they were heading for California. The father was a civil engineer. That figured.

As Merj and I looked at the picture in the paper of the foursome on the bicycle, we were reminded of good friends from a previous tour. They were both accomplished cyclists who rode every mile of the tour on a tandem bike. Each day they would wear matching outfits and take their usual positions on the tandem; he in front, and she in the back. During the day's ride they would invariably pass with a choreographed machine-like cadence, accompanied by a nod and a wave.

Many evenings the long married duo would be peppered with questions about life on a tandem. Does the front rider know when the rear rider isn't pedaling? Yes, he does. Do you ever switch riding order? No, never. Does the scenery ever change for the occupant of the second seat? No, it doesn't. We tried unsuccessfully to imagine ourselves on a tandem bicycle. Changeless scenery would have made Merj a tad irritable, and the back of my neck would have likely been the target of her dissatisfaction.

Arriving back at the motel, it was impossible to miss a gleaming white '59 Edsel convertible parked in front of an adjacent room. Even though the Edsel is probably the most often cited example of automotive failure, restored ones are reasonably desirable collector cars. Before long, a young man and woman emerged and got into the car. Not trying to look too anxious, but not wanting to miss them either, I moved quickly to the car's side. The couple, Bill and Ruth, were in town for Bill's high school reunion. Bill grew up on the reservation, but attended Lander High School and had graduated twenty years ago. Wanting to do something special for the reunion, he borrowed the Edsel from his father who had purchased it a few years earlier.

Being the proud owner of a couple of classic cars myself, I quizzed Bill about specifics of the car and its history. My knowledge of Ford products was somewhat limited, but there are certain questions that apply to all classic cars, and Bill knew what he was talking about. The Edsel seemed to be mostly original and in good shape. Although outwardly cordial to the friendly Edsel driving, Lander natives, Merj's expressive face clearly exclaimed, "Oh boy, there he goes again."

Day 30 - 1433 Miles Down, 2354 To Go

EVEN A BROKEN CLOCK IS RIGHT TWICE A DAY

The ride from Lander to Jeffrey City was one of ups and downs with a six-mile climb thrown in for good measure. The area was generally barren with scenery much like the previous day. The cycling was peppered with occasional sightings of antelope among the sagebrush dotted landscape. The distances were long with no signs of civilization for many miles. The reliable support of Merj's parents in the form of water and snacks was much appreciated on this warm day.

Some days ago on the ride into Arco, Idaho there was a feeling of being in the *Twilight Zone*. The observations in Arco were appropriate then, but riding into Jeffrey City, Wyoming gave new meaning to that *Twilight Zone* feeling. We passed abandoned boarded up structures, overgrown yards, and few signs of human habitation. As we rode into town we both looked at each other and shared the same thought, "What in the world happened here?"

Nearly all of the western communities we had passed through shared similar trapping or mining origins that dated back to the 1800's. The story was pretty much the same in town after town. The history of Jeffrey City, Wyoming however, was very different.

The origin of Jeffrey City is fallout, so to speak, from the atomic bomb and goes back just a half century or so to the early 1950's. The time period following World War II produced a need for uranium for both nuclear weapons and nuclear power generating stations. The countryside around Jeffrey City provided a source for the uranium needed for both purposes. The mining of uranium brought thousands of people to the newly created town during the 1950's.

Thirty years later two events far removed from Jeffrey City sealed its fate. Within a short period of time in the early 1980's, the accidents at Three Mile Island in Pennsylvania and Chernobyl in the USSR effectively killed the construction of new nuclear power plants. No new power plants meant no need for uranium. No need for uranium meant no need for Jeffrey City. The death of this once booming town had become a foregone conclusion.

Prior to the nuclear power disasters, Jeffrey City had prospered and grew to a population of over 4,000 inhabitants. Large wooden dormitories were built to house many of the people working in the mines. Others lived in duplexes arranged along curbed, concrete streets. A modern, single story, kindergarten through twelfth grade school was built, and a huge multi-million dollar gymnasium was constructed on the northwestern edge of town. Along the only road in and out of town, the normal commercial businesses sprouted up to support the needs of the miners and their families. A motel, appropriately called the J C Motel, complete with a gas station in front, was built to provide lodging for visitors. In its prime, Jeffrey City had all the trappings of a prosperous, vibrant community.

It was impossible to visualize anything like that now. The dormitories stood weathered and boarded up. The duplexes on the criss-crossing streets were gone and all that remained were foundations and an occasional set of concrete steps leading nowhere. Weeds, sometimes reaching two feet in height, grew in the cracked concrete streets. Modern looking signs, marking street names such as Uranium Drive, stood alone helping lost visitors find their way to nothing. The downtown commercial area, save for a bar/café, was boarded up and the main street was absolutely empty. There were no vehicles or people to be seen anywhere.

The sight that was most indicative of the current state of Jeffrey City, however, was the school. The architectural features of the school were typical of the low modern looking structures that were built in many communities across the country during the last thirty years or so. The school was now totally abandoned and weeds had grown up to shroud many of the windows. A clock in the lobby stood frozen at 8:30.

The gymnasium, some distance from the school, stood in much the same condition. Like the school, it was in remarkably good shape but had clearly been unused for some time. Antelope wandered the grounds and occasionally peered inside. As they did, they saw a clock that also told the world that it was still 8:30 on some past day. The present school was across the street, a small home with a sign out front identifying it. There were a grand total of twelve students currently enrolled. The comparison of the two school buildings across the street from each other was a real indicator of what had happened to Jeffrey City, Wyoming.

Jeffrey City was surreal and unlike anything we had previously experienced. It was as if some greater power had reached down and taken its inhabitants off the face of the Earth. Walking around the abandoned city felt much like walking through a graveyard. We took pictures, and felt like trespassers in some empty movie studio lot. Jeffrey City could have been a real life subject of one of Rod Serling's classic television episodes.

"STOP BACK AT THE HOUSE AFTER DINNER, 'CAUSE I GOT SOMETHING I WANT TO SHOW YOU GUYS."

Jeffrey City was now home to maybe 200 people, and two of them owned the J C Motel. As we rolled into the parking lot of the motel, Merj looked at the weathered, wooden, one-story structure and immediately expressed concern. She insisted that one of the rooms be opened for her inspection. I didn't have the heart or courage to tell her that if the room wasn't up to standards it wouldn't much matter. There was no other lodging within sixty miles. Dutifully I knocked on the door of a house at the end of the parking lot that also served as the motel office. An elderly lady came to the door, and somewhat embarrassed, I asked her if we could see a room. On the short walk to the room, she told me that her name was Dorothy Coats and that she and her husband Bill owned the place. After checking the sheets and bathroom, Merj pronounce the room passable. The fact that it had a functioning air conditioner on this very hot day, a television, albeit black and white with only one channel, and would cost a mere $29.00 for the night was all I needed to know.

While John and I walked back to the office with Dorothy to pay for the rooms, we ran into Dorothy's husband Bill. Bill and Dorothy had just celebrated their wedding anniversary and a number of the family members had stayed at the motel to celebrate the event. Bill was loading a washing machine with yesterday's used linen, and being in no apparent hurry, he began to talk. "Before the town went bust, the gas station out front pumped over a million gallons of gasoline a year," Bill said. It had clearly been a while since anyone had filled his or her tank at the long abandoned station.

When asked why he chose to live in the middle of nowhere in a town that had definitely seen better days, Bill grinned, "Look around and tell me what you see," he asked. We told him we saw miles and miles of sagebrush. We told him we could see almost to the horizon, because there really wasn't much to get in the way. We told him we saw a town with nobody in it. When we finished, he told us, "You just found the reasons why I like it here." We were a little confused. We thought that our description had pretty much summarized why a person would *not* want to live in Jeffrey City. He laughed and said the wide-open spaces and the absence of other people were exactly why he stayed. This was starting to sound familiar; it was the same response given by our buckaroo buddy, Denny, back in Oregon.

Bill went on to explain that he had purchased the motel, gas station, and surrounding land in 1971 for $12,000. Even though Jeffrey City was clearly past its prime, Bill was pleased that his modest investment was worth more in the current real estate market. He talked of life during the cold windy winters in Wyoming and of his mountain lion hunting avocation. Bill noticed our quizzical look when he mentioned the mountain lions and said, "Stop back at the house after dinner, 'cause I got something I want to show you guys."

We bid a good afternoon to Bill and walked back to the room wondering what was in store for our after dinner visit. On the way, two other cyclists rolled into the parking lot. The father and daughter duo was crossing the country from east to west. The father was a 58-year-old finance professor from Gannon University in Erie, Pennsylvania, and his travelling companion was his twenty-something daughter, Sarah.

Sarah's mother had provided support for a portion of their trip much as John and Aili were doing for us. Having already covered territory that lay ahead, they afforded an opportunity to answer questions about what was in store. They described the friendly people of Kansas, but also the heat and winds. They talked of the climbs in Colorado and specifically the climb over Hoosier Pass, the highest point of the trip. They reflected on the heat and the Ozark Mountains of Missouri. To emphasize the point, they referred to the state as "Misery." Their tales of woe brought to mind the old saying, "Other than that Mrs. Lincoln, how did you like the play?"

"YOU GOTTA TALK TO JOE."

After due deliberation, a decision was made to have dinner in downtown Jeffrey City at the Split Rock Bar and Café. The usual weighing of dinner options was greatly simplified, as the Split Rock was the only eatery still in business. In fact, it was the only business still in business. A waitress greeted us at the door and showed the way to a table in the empty café side of the building. While being seated, she described her current condition as "dead tired from workin' day and night since the Fourth." Since it was now the seventh, her tired appearance was probably to be expected, but looking around the empty café, it was a mystery as to what exactly she had been doing for all that time.

Our bedraggled waitress plopped down in a chair at the end of the table and asked for our orders from the limited menu selections. After ordering the usual fare of hamburgers, French fries, and beers, the weary look in her eyes prompted our offer to give her a hand. She replied with a no thanks, pulled herself together and headed for the bar side of the building to get the beverages. After a tasty meal, we attempted to pry information from our fatigued waitress. "You gotta talk to Joe," she said.

Joe, a weathered fellow probably in his late 60's, happened to be holding court in the bar when he was summoned to our table. After asking the waitress to bring him a beer, the interrogation began. He started by explaining the uranium-based history of the town and the method of mining and processing the radioactive ore. According to Joe, the uranium was removed by open pit mining and then hauled to a mill where a Geiger counter was used to sort the ore by radioactivity and quality. The different ores were blended to make a material of specified radioactivity. They were then processed into a yellowish paste and shipped back East to be made into fuel rods.

Joe was a very talkative fellow with plenty of time on his hands. We too were in no hurry, so the gabfest continued for some time. Our fascination with the history of Jeffrey City led him to verify the negative effects the loss of the uranium market had on the town, and express a satisfaction with the current state of affairs in Jeffrey City. He, much like Bill Coats, didn't like a lot of people around.

Joe was a bit of a climatologist and regaled anyone in ear shot with tales of the local weather. He declared that warm weather in central Wyoming doesn't last long and claimed, "Next year I'm gonna try to stay sober for both days of summer." He talked of a winter in the late '70's where the temperature never got over minus forty for the whole month of December. According to Joe, it was so cold, "The ears and tails froze off some of my 200 pound calves." He talked of snows a few years later that were deep enough to cover trailers in the local mobile home park. Apparently after the storm, some fellows working on snow tractors were surprised to be greeted by one of the trailer owners. The owner had tunneled out of his home and politely asked the tractor operators to remove their vehicles from his roof. The stories had some believability, but it may have also been Joe's intent to have a little fun with his new found audience.

Since Joe was a veritable storehouse of local lore, we ordered him another beer and listened to more. He talked of the town's former name of Home on the Range, Wyoming. Having seen a sign with that same name on one of the abandoned downtown buildings, there was every reason to believe him. According to Joe, some years ago a doctor moved to town and said he would stay if the townsfolk changed the city's name to his. Having a doctor in town was obviously a very important need because it didn't take long to honor Dr. Jeffrey's request. The story had all the makings of a pairie legend, but had a certain charm, so it was accepted as unquestioned fact.

Joe wasn't done yet. He described reenactments of the Pony Express and wagon trains of the Oregon Trail that moved through town each summer. We expressed surprise and asked, "Why would anyone want to do something like that?" Joe looked at us with a slight grin, "Well you guys are riding bicycles across the country aren't you?" Craziness takes many forms. He also talked of groups of Mormons that had traveled near Jeffrey City in the mid-nineteenth century pulling their belongings in handcarts.

The handcarts were the vehicles of choice to transport Mormon families and their belongings to the Salt Lake Valley in Utah, and at about three feet by four feet in size, they were modeled after the ones used by street sweepers in larger cities. The carts could be pulled or pushed, carried up to 500 pounds, and were less expensive and moved faster than animal powered wagons. About 250 of the total of nearly 3,000 handcart immigrants died during the trip. In 1856 a group of 980 Mormons got a late start on their trip across the Plains and arrived in Wyoming much later than they should have. The result was the freezing death of 220 handcart-pulling travelers in a snowstorm near the Continental Divide. Many others suffered trailside amputation of fingers, toes, and limbs from frostbite. A museum and visitor center near the scene of the tragedy told their story.

Joe somehow sensed our doubt about the reenactments, and instructed his listeners to follow him to the next room to hear verification from the bar patrons. The five or six patrons assembled in the darkness of the bar pretty much represented the entire remaining male population of Jeffrey City. Joe made sure to first introduce us to the owner of the Sun Ranch, allegedly the largest ranch in Wyoming. The rancher stood out; he was the only man in a baseball cap amid the cowboy hatted assemblage.

Although we hoped he would keep his mouth shut, Joe was quick to inform his friends of our bike trip. The gathering of

Jeffrey City residents gave every indication that they could care less about a couple of people riding across the country on bicycles. It was likely that they looked at the trip as some sort of silly diversion by a couple of middle-aged dreamers from the wrong side of the Mississippi. Efforts to inch our way back to the café were unsuccessful. Joe wouldn't allow escape until many more bicycling questions were answered. Joe's buddies, however, did verify the Pony Express and Oregon Trail reenactment stories.

"A GUN AIN'T NO GOOD UNLESS IT'S LOADED."

Nearly all of the motels so far had allowed storage of the bicycles in the room over night. Dorothy Coats made it clear from the beginning that no such behavior would be tolerated in her establishment. Dorothy was a pleasant lady but left little doubt that her instructions should be followed. Back at the motel, the bicycles of cross-country riders filled the spots normally reserved for cars. Our support car was the only motorized vehicle in the lot. The odd feelings that had become the norm in Jeffrey City had not disappeared. Regardless, it was now time to have the much anticipated talk with Bill.

Dark clouds were building over the plains and lightning could be seen arcing through the distant skies. I tentatively knocked on the door of Bill and Dorothy's house with a hope that Bill hadn't forgotten about his earlier invitation. Dorothy answered the door and Bill followed close behind. After a brief exchange of pleasantries, Bill led me back to a bedroom at the rear of the small home where shelves filled with trophies lined one of the walls. Bill sat on the edge of the bed and began talking of his part-time job. He described the problems local ranchers had with mountain lions attacking and killing their livestock and that occasionally, one of them would hire Bill to kill the predator. "Once they hire me, my hound dogs do most of the hard work. When the dogs corner the mountain lion, I just shoot it." Championship hounds that Bill had either bred or trained had earned the many trophies on the shelves.

Bill reached under the bed and pulled out what appeared to be a rug. As he spread it out on the bed, it became obvious that the object was a large mountain lion pelt with its ferocious looking head still attached. He explained that this particular animal had been the first of fifty or so mountain lions he had killed during his career. "This one killed one of my dogs," he explained. Having lost a prize hound was probably a reason why Bill decided to make the mountain lion into a rug.

It was clear Bill was a strong supporter of killing troublesome mountain lions in order to protect rancher's herds. He believed animal rights advocates who oppose killing the animals under any circumstances were badly misinformed. Bill was particularly upset with a "Save the Mountain Lion" television campaign that former *Bonanza* patriarch Lorne Greene had done a few years ago. In the pitch, Greene contended that mountain lions killed only what they needed for food. Bill went on to talk of a Utah rancher who had called him a few years ago to deal with a mountain lion that had killed eighty sheep and ewes. Bill bristled, "I don't know any mountain lion that can eat eighty sheep and ewes." It was Bill's way of saying that the mountain lion's natural instinct is to kill other creatures. He was clearly fed up with the "city slicker attitude" of people who he felt didn't know what they were talking about.

Bill displayed a photo album showing winter scenes in Wyoming. A number of the photos pictured him on a snowmobile accompanied by his hounds on the trail of a mountain lion. He also showed pictures of bears he had killed while stalking his main prey. When asked what he used to kill the mountain lions, he explained that a .22 caliber pistol was his usual weapon of choice. Although not a weapons expert, I knew a .22 wasn't all that powerful a gun. Bill explained, "Well, if you use something stronger like a .357 it just gets the mountain lion upset and it will kill one of your dogs." He said his objective with the smaller pistol was to hit the mountain lion in its lung and then he explained, "The animal just staggers and goes down." I pretended to nod knowingly as Bill explained the hunting process. He was a pretty sharp old man, though, and I was sure Bill knew that he could have told me that a slingshot was the best way to kill a mountain lion and I would have believed him.

As we headed back to the front door, Bill reached up to the top shelf of a closet, pulled out a pistol and handed it to me. Not knowing what was in my hand, he soon informed me that it was a .357. While examining the heavy pistol, Bill warned, "Be careful, that thing is loaded." Afraid that a finger twitch on my part may have caused a portion of the Coats' interior décor to disappear, I quickly handed the gun back. Bill took it and said, matter-of-factly, "What good is a gun if it ain't loaded?"

The worsening weather turned the walk back to the room into a mad dash. The dark clouds from earlier had opened, and a wind driven rain swept over the Wyoming plains. The remaining members of our entourage were waiting in the room to learn of Bill's adventures. After sharing my discussion with Bill, we all talked of the day's experiences in Jeffrey City. From the initial ride into town, until leaving the Coats' house, the whole day was filled with one eye-opening revelation after another. Even though Jeffrey City was a modern day ghost town, we agreed it was the most intriguing stop of our first month on the road.

Day 31 - 1493 Miles Down, 2294 To Go

MOMMA TOLD US THERE'D BE DAYS LIKE THIS

Jeffrey City and its colorful inhabitants were left behind with a certain amount of reluctance. The town was such a departure from the usual, that it was difficult to get it out of our minds. The day promised to be a warm one, so to beat the heat, a pre-sunrise departure was in order. The ride out of Jeffrey City began into headwinds with threatening clouds hanging over mountains to the east. Three antelope watched us pass and then jogged along side at a short distance off the side of the road. A short time later, three full-grown horses and two young colts silhouetted themselves against the sunrise and created a need to hurriedly stop and snap pictures before our presence disturbed them.

The worrisome clouds moved away to the east, but the heat and headwinds picked up. The winds had become the most difficult of the trip, and there was absolutely nothing to stop them. Twenty or so miles into the day we arrived at the crossroads town of Muddy Gap which consisted of mostly abandoned buildings and a lot of discarded junk. The Mormon museum and monument to the handcart travelers that Joe had described in Jeffrey City was located a few miles from the intersection. Muddy Gap, however, did have one redeeming value. It was the place where our route turned and the headwinds came around more from the side and back. A glorious ride of five or six miles soon ended as the road again turned into the wind.

The increasingly warm and difficult ride included a second crossing of the Continental Divide. In fact the area was called the Continental Basin and consisted of a generally flat area that was circled by the Continental Divide. A lunch break was planned for the town of Lamont, the only location for miles that showed any hint of a place to eat. Lamont consisted of a few abandoned and run-down buildings and Grandma's Café. The waitress at Grandma's was a native of Marion, Ohio. We began to hope that someone would build a wall around Ohio soon. If this exodus continued, the state was going to become a larger version of Jeffrey City.

Why people moved to these stark surroundings was always a source of wonder. Although the question was never asked, we assumed that much like others we spoke to, the waitress in Grandma's didn't like being crowded. Crowding in Lamont would not be a problem. While eating lunch, Andy and Deena arrived at the otherwise empty restaurant and sat down in a neighboring booth. The two of them provided a welcome opportunity to share complaints about the heat and wind of the morning's ride. Our vigorous and animated complaining caught the attention of the waitress. "Today's wind ain't nothin'," she told us casually, "It gets a lot worse than this." The look on Merj's face clearly indicated that such comparisons had no relevance. To her, today's wind was somethin', and three other now satiated cyclists offered the same opinion.

While eating lunch, the day had grown warmer. The road from Grandma's turned back into the wind toward the night's destination of Rawlins some thirty miles away. It didn't take long to realize there was absolutely nothing for miles to block the wind or break up the starkness of the landscape. The combination of heat, wind, desolate scenery, and heavy truck traffic was making this day the most forgettable so far. Oddly, though, the barren surroundings created a feeling of openness, and we stopped every so often to photographically record it. In reality the pictures were all pretty much the same; a pose of one of us standing in front of nothingness as far as the eye could see.

Before an upcoming climb we took a break in a place designated as a raptor area. According to a sign along the road, eagles and hawks nested there from March to July. It was comforting to know that at least there was some redeeming value to the land around us. Merj's worried look exhibited a fear that snakes might be lurking among the raptors, and she suggested the rest stop be a brief one.

The climb began just like many of the others. About a third of the way into it, however, my bike started to handle strangely. It didn't take long to determine that the front tire was going flat. Within a quarter mile or so the tire had lost all its air and it was time to dismount and deal with the problem. The support team had already set up camp a few hundred yards ahead, so the bike was pushed to the car and John and I sprung into action.

The tire changing instructions that had been given before

leaving home proved invaluable. In about ten minutes the tube was changed, refilled from a compressed gas cylinder, and remounted. We were a team worthy of a NASCAR pit stop. Close inspection of the old tube showed that a wire-like sliver of steel had pierced both the tire liner and the tube. Evidently the tire liners were not as invincible as we had been led to believe. We guessed the steel shard might have come from one of the many shredded truck tires that were common along the road shoulders.

The hot climb ended in a mile or two with another crossing of the Continental Divide. At a little over sixty miles into the day, while stopped for a water break, a few drops of rain fell from the sky. Merj laughed and said sarcastically, "Well, we've had everything to deal with today except snow." As we drank from the water bottles, tumbleweed blew across the highway, and we noticed a few more dead snakes and a dead fox to add to the list of critters that had met their demise along the hot stretch of highway in south central Wyoming. It was symbolic of the day.

MAKE SURE THOSE ARE PICKLES IN THERE BEFORE YOU REACH INTO THAT BARREL

The sign welcoming visitors to Rawlins was a long awaited and welcome sight. With about a mile and a half to the hotel, the day's ride turned into a ferocious headwind. A bank sign proclaimed the time of day as 3:07 and the temperature, 95 degrees.

Not seeing our motel and not wanting to pedal any farther than necessary, it was decided to stop at a gas station and ask directions. While coming back to the bikes, Andy, also lost, rolled in. He looked sunburned and tired, so we asked how he was doing. His response was short but descriptive. "I'm gassed," he said. Since we were old enough to have a son Andy's age, we felt a little better about our own "gassed" condition.

Back in Dubois, while complaining to a local about the desert ride from Arco to Idaho Falls he told us, "That was nothing. Wait 'till you ride from Lamar to Rawlins." He was right on target. This seventy-mile day was not going to give up without a fight. In a mile or so the hotel sign finally appeared over a rise in the busy street. After a very difficult day on the road, our lodging for the evening in Rawlins was like an oasis in the Wyoming desert.

The City of Rawlins traces its beginning to 1868 as a railroad town and the departure point for prospectors heading to the gold fields. The town was named after General John Rawlins. The General, whose troops were protecting the railroad survey crews in the area, discovered a spring at what is the current town location. In 1901 the Wyoming State Prison was built in Rawlins. Today Rawlins is home to nearly 9,000 people who earn their living from sheep ranching and the nearby coal and natural gas resources.

Like many of the towns of the Old West, Rawlins had been home to more than a few unusual characters over the years. One of the more intriguing stories related to the city's most famous outlaw, Big Nose George Parrot. In 1878, after a failed attempt to rob a payroll train, Parrot eluded capture for a while but killed two posse members in the process. He was captured, convicted and sentenced to hang, but escaped before the sentence could be carried out. Old Big Nose was captured soon after his escape, and his sentence was carried out by a lynch mob.

So far so good, but the story took a bizarre turn. A physician in town, Dr. John E. Osborne, took possession of the body and made a death mask of Parrot's well-known and apparently large-nosed profile. He gave the mask to his female assistant as a gift and she used it as a doorstop for years after. The doctor wasn't finished, though; he proceeded to saw Parrot's skull open to observe the outlaw's brain, and then skinned him, tanned his hide, and made shoes from the leather. The good doctor then pickled what was left of Parrot in a whiskey barrel. The death mask, shoes, and pickle barrel were still on display at the Carbon County Museum. Residents of Wyoming were truly a different breed. We weren't surprised to discover that Dr. Osborne's career actually flourished after his strange handling of the remains of Big Nose Parrott. About ten years later he was elected governor and also served for a while in the Senate.

Day 32 - 1563 Miles Down, 2224 To Go

GET YOUR HOT DOGS HERE

It was decided that a late wakeup in Rawlins was a deserved reward for the previous day's long ride. After relatively leisurely preparations and anxiously checking the wind direction, the bikes headed east out of Rawlins at 7:30 AM. The road was flat and paralleled Interstate 80 for the first few miles. About eight miles into the day, we came to the small community of Sinclair, a town of 500 inhabitants that included a small square with a well-restored Union Pacific caboose prominently displayed. On the outskirts of Sinclair stood a large oil refinery operated by the Sinclair Oil Company. The origin of the town name had now became obvious to even the most intellectually challenged member of our cycling duo. The refinery seemed to be prospering, but downtown Sinclair had seen better days.

The repeating pattern of these small, ghostly towns was starting to become a trend. There was a bit of mystery as to what had happened to the people of these formerly thriving communities and what they now did to earn a living. It was a disquieting feeling that we often shared rolling through one town after another. In most cases it seemed a local resource had dried up or a major industry had pulled up stakes and moved. Although similar situations had occurred in towns back home, their frequency in the West was none the less getting tougher to deal with.

A short time later, at a truck stop near an entrance ramp to I-80, Andy and Deena arrived. This would be Deena's last day with

Andy. She intended to hitch a ride to Cheyenne, and then fly back to her home in Seattle. Andy had obviously learned a lot about Deena, as he talked of her having spent a year and a half in Antarctica and that she was heading home to compete in a triathlon. He described Deena's cycling skills as better than his and that he had become stronger by keeping up with her. I thought to myself that if Merj kept adding dirt samples to my bike with each passing state, I too would become much stronger keeping up with *her*. Merj, being an astute observer of the human condition, remarked that Andy and Deena seemed to have "bonded." She also observed that Andy seemed sad to be losing his companion. Not being prone to disturb the delicate balance that had been forged in our cross-country tandem, I trusted Merj's observation. I also kept my mouth shut about the dirt samples.

Today's ride would include a thirteen-mile stretch of I-80. Wyoming is one of the few states that allow bicycles on Interstates, and although there were certain apprehensions about riding on a freeway, no other option existed. The first few miles were surprisingly comfortable as the gradual grades and wide shoulders associated with Interstate highway design made the cycling comparatively easy. The easy freeway ride ended though, when construction directed all of the traffic onto the two eastbound lanes. The last ten miles were a harrowing experience of wind buffeting by speeding trucks and motor homes, as well as the occasional trip onto the grass to avoid getting decapitated by a wide load or side mounted mirror. It was with more than a little relief when the view from the crest of a hill showed the exit ramp ahead.

The ride south from I-80 continued through more of the sagebrush covered landscape of the previous day. The lack of traffic and headwinds, and the gradual rises and falls, however, made the cycling much more enjoyable. A mid-morning break was enhanced by a staring contest with an antelope some hundred feet or so away. It was difficult to imagine the thoughts going through the mind of our four-legged adversary as he easily outlasted his human counterparts. Forty miles into the day splashes of green vegetation began to appear. The welcome sightings of life were evidence of entry into the North Platte River Valley. We soon arrived in the small town of Saratoga where the support team awaited at a picnic table next to the appropriately named "Hot Dog Stand."

The ride into Saratoga, Wyoming was much different than most of the others we'd experienced over the last few weeks. This town of 1,900 people was situated along the North Platte River and looked to be vibrant and relatively prosperous. Part of Saratoga's apparent prosperity was due to the natural hot springs located near downtown. Since the mid 1800's, the hot springs had been a draw for those seeking the healing and relaxation offered by the warm waters. The green growth in Saratoga and its functioning business area lifted our spirits as we sat down to sip Pepsis next to the hot dog stand.

As we rested, Ellie, an apron clad woman working at the hot dog stand, came out of her small trailer and quickly refilled the Pepsis. Ellie was a very friendly early middle age lady who owned the stand, and usually opened it for business from April to November. She was a full time resident of Saratoga and asked many questions about the trip. Although not all that unusual among the people of the West, her energetic and optimistic outlook on life was nonetheless refreshing.

At a nearby picnic table, a young family consisting of two young boys and their parents enjoyed an ice cream dessert. The energetic boys provided entertainment while the grown-ups chatted. It was not surprising that the boys' parents were high school sweethearts who had grown up together in Saratoga. Such relationships seemed appropriate in a community like Saratoga. Both talked of the benefits of living in the small town and suggested a visit to the nearby hot springs. The boys became intrigued with our bicycling equipment, and soon donned helmets, sunglasses, and cycling gloves to become the objects of a photo session.

We explained to the boy's father that we were considering spending the night in Saratoga rather than continuing eighteen more miles to our original destination of Riverside. The day was getting warm, and a commitment to Merj had been made after yesterday's difficult ride to divide the next two planned days into three. After forty plus days on the road the maker of such a commitment had every intention of fulfilling it. However, the young father explained, "The road to Riverside's not bad. You guys outta give it a try."

The decision was totally Merj's and after more questions about the road ahead and due deliberation, she decided the day would end in Riverside. The fact that the day's ride, other than the freeway portion, was much better than the day before was a factor in her decision. Another reason was the uplifting experience with the good folks of Saratoga.

JIM FOR MAYOR

The ride out of Saratoga traversed gentle rolling terrain with sagebrush to the right and the green grasses and trees along the North Platte River to the left. It was as if the road bisected two entirely different worlds. The trees were a welcome addition to the day, as was the slight tail wind. A few miles from Riverside, we stopped to enjoy the shade of a roadside tree. It had been a while since experiencing such simple contentment.

Although the day's ride was only six miles less than yesterday's, there was still plenty of gas in the tank when the day ended. The difference made by the absence of headwinds was never more apparent. Riverside, previously known as Dogget, was located on the banks of the Encampment River and took its current name around 1900. The town originally consisted of a store and a few cabins and was never intended to be more than a stop over on the way to the nearby, more important, copper mining town of Encampment. When copper prices fell, Riverside declined to its current state which consisted of a motel/RV park, a small general store, a garage, The Mangy Moose Saloon and eighty five inhabitants.

The evening in Riverside would be spent at the Lazy Acres Motel and RV Park. A low ceiling building served as the office where Larry and Judy, the husband and wife owners, seemed to be waiting for us when we walked in. The motel was on a route frequented by cyclists, so they asked visitors to sign a book that was filled with the names of other riders who had stayed at their establishment over the years. Larry told us he had recently driven the Colorado route that lay ahead, "The road conditions are good, the fires aren't a problem, the air's clean, things are under control." It was refreshing to hear a positive road report for a change.

The room for the evening was part of a four unit wooden structure that stood on stilts some three or four feet off the ground. It was surmised that lifting the building off the ground might have been done to accommodate potential flooding from the nearby Encampment River. Regardless, the room was clean and had a television and air conditioning, so all was well.

After a tasty dinner of sandwiches and potato salad at a picnic table next to our room, John and I decided to explore the nearby town of Encampment. Encampment was a prime example of the effect of the boom or bust economies of the West. At the turn of the last century, Encampment was home to a booming copper industry. The Rudefeha Copper Mine in the Sierra Madres, about sixteen miles from town, supplied ore by an aerial tramway to a smelter in town where it was processed. The catchy mine name came from its four partners: *Ru*msey, *De*al, *Fe*rris, and *Ha*ggarty. When the price of copper fell, the mine was no longer profitable to operate, and Encampment went bust.

The mine name set me wondering about other partnerships that could have described different aspects of our trip. The business combination of *Le*onard, *Ap*pleton, *Fr*ench and *Og*den described our hill climbing technique, and *We*st, *Re*dmond, *Lo*gan and *St*rong described a thought that often crossed our minds. A reference by new acquaintances to either of us could be described by the foursome of *C*restwood, *A*zcue, *Y*oung and *N*ewman. Since Merj had already pointed out a number of obsessive behaviors, I decided to keep the mental exercise of assembling four-name lists to myself.

Among other things, the town museum displays a two-story outhouse that was frequently used during the boom times. The second story was added to allow use of the building when deep snows prevented access to the first floor. While marveling at the creativity of the early residents of Encampment, we wondered if there may have been times when a patron using the first floor of the outhouse was surprised to find that the second floor was also in use.

Today Encampment is home to 400 people and resembled most of the other western towns that had seen better times. Downtown had a bit of an Old West feeling with three or four saloons, a small library, and other assorted buildings. It was not unusual to find that even the most down trodden towns seemed to have modern educational facilities. Encampment was no exception; a nice school complex occupied a section of downtown. On the outskirts of town, a hand-lettered sign proclaiming "Jim for Mayor" hung from the raised scoop of a front-end loader. It stood in sharp contrast to the slick political campaigns that were the custom back home. To win the plumb job of Encampment mayor, Old Jim probably only needed to get eighty or ninety votes. The strategic placement of the loader on the main road into town probably assured his success. Besides, there was no other political advertising anywhere else in town.

A white Chevy truck with Police Department prominently displayed on its side sat in a small parking area next to Jim's sign. Inside sat a bored looking police officer who soon became a source for local information. While entering Encampment a few abandoned permanent structures resembling teepees had been seen not far off the road. When asked of their use, the friendly officer explained that they had been used as kilns to dry lumber and burn scraps and sawdust from a nearby abandoned lumber-yard. Questions about mayoral candidate Jim brought laughter and the opinion, "He'll probably be elected."

The police officer talked of coming to Encampment to get away from the stress of police duty in Saratoga. Having just come from Saratoga, and having been impressed by the serenity of the community, it was a bit of a mystery as to how much stress could be associated with being a police officer in that seemingly sleepy town. He planned five more years on the Encampment police force and then intended to retire and spend his days fishing on a nearby lake. The casual atmosphere, customary in most of these small western towns, seemed to indicate that many of the residents were already retired.

Back at the motel, it was impossible not to notice some weathered log buildings with cacti growing on their flat roofs. The buildings were so low that standing inside one of them would have required the occupant to bend over to keep from hitting his head. Judy happened to be walking through the area and explained a couple of theories as to what purpose the buildings had served. The first was that the men who came to the area at the turn of the last century to fell trees and cut them into railroad ties used the squatty structures as winter barracks. The second theory held that they were used as barracks by the copper miners who worked in the local mines about the same time. Judy guessed that the original roof was probably covered with sod rather than the current cacti. It was difficult to imagine spending a winter in one of the strange looking structures with a bunch of log splitters or copper miners. Throwing open the front door on the first warm day of spring had to have been met with a certain joy.

We spent our last night in Wyoming sitting at the picnic table next to our motel room talking about the prior week. Wyoming was a state of extreme contrasts. Back near Jackson Hole we had been surrounded by forested mountains and the rushing Snake River. The city of Jackson was a modern thriving resort area. Our ride along the splendid Grand Tetons was a near religious experience, and was followed by an eerie feeling of desolation through the sagebrush covered, arid landscape of the rest of the state. Other than Jackson, and to a lesser extent Dubois, Lamar, Rawlins, and Saratoga, our route took us through one small ghost town, or near ghost town, after another. We spent many hours on the bicycle seat pondering what had happened to the people who had lived in those dusty crossroad collections of abandoned buildings. The images of Jeffrey City, like those of the Teton Mountains, would always remain with us, albeit it for entirely different reasons.

In some ways the arid landscape of Wyoming was so different from what we had grown up around and become accustomed to that it held its own strange beauty. One significant natural resource of the state, however, was its people. Almost without exception the free spirited, friendly folks who inhabited Wyoming took great pains to patiently deal with our problems and many questions. It was with a certain amount of regret that we left Wyoming. Nonetheless, we anticipated Colorado with a sense of new adventure much like our feelings entering the first three states of the trip.

Day 43 - 1626 Miles Down, 2161 To Go

colorado

"I'm wrong, that's a tough climb."

GET ALONG LITTLE DOGGIE

Like so many other occasions, the stay in Riverside brought back youthful memories. In this case, the recollections were of our high school days many years before at Riverside High School in Painesville, Ohio. The school, situated along the Grand River, derived its name from its location. The river theme was carried forth in the selection of the beaver as the school mascot. Eventually, the football field was officially designated the Beaver Bowl, and the yearbook, the *Beaver's Tale*. It is difficult to describe the emotional scars Merj and I carried from the derisive comments from others about our bucked tooth, dam building mascot. Regardless of a long wounded psyche, it was time to leave Riverside, Wyoming and head into Colorado.

About halfway to the Colorado border, a significant climb

slowed the morning's progress. A sign at the summit indicated that the just completed grade was a seven percenter. Bicycle tracks in the soft gravel near the sign gave evidence that others had been there before. The GPS unit showed an elevation of 8,127 and the views of the surrounding mountains were spectacular. Past the summit, the landscape turned into a green valley, home to the Big Creek Ranch. The ranch sat well off the road and consisted of well-maintained white buildings with bright red roofs. It's bright colors made it markedly different in appearance than the many other ranches we had already passed. A group of sleek horses grazed in a fenced area near the road.

The morning's traffic was light as were the winds, and a wide shoulder made the riding safe. With the luxury of the wide shoulder, however, came another bane to cyclists in the form of rumble strips. These were particularly annoying. Rumble strips usually consist of closely spaced grooves, one to two inches deep and twelve to eighteen inches long. The groves are normally cut into the pavement just off the traveled portion of the road, alerting drivers that they had ventured off the roadway.

In most cases, the rumble strips were close enough to the roadway so that a fair amount of room remained on the right to allow comfortable cycling. In some cases, though, the strips occupied most of the shoulder. If traffic was light, it was possible to ride on the road surface and avoid the strips. On busy roads, they were a pain, not only in the neck, but in a number of other sensitive body parts. To a cyclist, rumble strips can only be described as noisy, teeth jarring, equipment rattling experiences to be avoided whenever possible.

At mid-morning a sign announcing the Colorado state line appeared along with the support team waiting to photograph the crossing into our fourth new state. The bikes were parked and we posed under the Colorado sign. The surrounding terrain had the high-plains feel that had been present for much of the trip. Another nearby sign announced that the state line was also the county line for Jackson County. The "o" in County was obliterated by a number of bullet holes; apparently that part of the sign served as a bull's eye for local marksmen.

As we stood for our photograph, we heard the sound of large animals approaching from behind a low hill in the distance. Although they were still not visible, the sounds from beyond were unmistakably those of a bovine nature. Soon two cowboys on horseback preceded a large herd of cattle into the open prairie. In a short time, four or five cowboys appeared with an even larger number of steers, and moved slowly toward the road. There was a real old-fashion cattle drive right there in front of us.

Since it was assumed that the herd would cross the road some hundred yards to the rear and then proceed east down a barely visible dirt road toward the nearby low hills, we decided to record the event with photographs. Unfortunately as the herd approached the road it made a right angle turn directly toward us. At first it was expected that the steers would simply pass by, but a fence about fifteen yards off the road's edge confined the herd to a fairly narrow path. These very large animals were going to occupy the same real estate that we occupied if we didn't move fast.

Merj's panic was obvious as she clamored to get the helmet situated on her head and move out. And move out we did. Joining the support team a safe distance up the road, we collected our thoughts. The noise, dust, and ground vibrations created by a great number of large animals moving as a group was imposing. The cowboys were skilled in rounding up the occasional stragglers and directing the mass of cattle, and it was likely that they enjoyed the panicked departure of a couple of bicycle riders. There didn't seem to be much else around to provide them entertainment.

IS THAT UNLEADED YOU'RE WEARING?

The warm afternoon ride generally consisted of repeated ups and downs through the high plains. In the distance an occasional large herd of antelope watched with the usual nonchalance. As the afternoon wore on, much smaller four-legged creatures in the form of neurotic prairie dogs provided accompaniment. When approached, the small animals scurried into one of the many holes along the side of the road. It was entertaining to watch them scoot along the ground and suddenly disappear into their subterranean homes.

The prairie dogs were a source of curiosity and there was a need to learn more about them. It was discovered that prairie dogs are the most social members of the squirrel family, and like squirrels they are rodents. Even though our newfound friends were smaller, most prairie dogs are eleven to thirteen inches long and the chubby little critters weigh between one and a half to three pounds.

Prairie dogs have a high-pitched, bark-like call that many believe represents one of the most sophisticated of all natural animal languages. The bark caused early settlers to call them dogs or sod poodles. Their main predators include hawks, owls, eagles, ravens, coyotes, badgers, ferrets, and snakes. Although prairie dogs can run from their predators at 35 miles per hour for short distances, their best defense is a quick dash into a hole. With many potential enemies attacking from the ground and the air, disappearing into a hole seemed like an excellent idea.

Notwithstanding an occasional arrangement with a friend or neighbor, prairie dogs dig their own burrows. The tunnels normally have three to four inch diameter funnel-shaped entrances. They lead down steeply on a slant for fifteen feet or so and then level off for another twenty to fifty feet. Chambers constructed off the main corridors are used for storage and nesting and for escape from invading predators and floodwaters. Some of the underground complexes, called "towns," can extend up to a hundred feet. That being the case, the prairie dog towns were bigger than many of the human towns we had passed. In 1900 a prairie dog town in the high plains of Texas extended 100 miles in one direction and 250 miles in the other. It was estimated that 400 million prairie dogs lived in that far-reaching Texas town. One couldn't help but wonder what lucky census taker had innocently walked into his office one morning and been assigned the job of prairie dog counting.

Since prairie dogs are vegetarian, their diet usually consists of crops grown by farmers and ranchers. Decades of eradication by governmental agencies, poisoning, disease, and recreational shooting reduced the area inhabited by prairie dogs to only about two percent of their peak occupied area. The little critters were a pleasant and humorous diversion as they darted over the ground alerting each other to the two oncoming "predators" on strange looking yellow vehicles.

Leaving the prairie dogs, the cycling continued through the high-plains toward Walden. Outside Walden, the road bisected the small almost ghost town of Cowdrey, which now consisted of the Cowdrey General Store and a few other buildings. Nearing town, we were joined by the support team. They had performed motel reconnaissance in Walden and explained that there were two possible places to spend the evening.

In a short time we arrived at the motel judged to be the more preferable and found a note on the office door. The note indicated that the owner had gone shopping for the day in Cheyenne and would return later. Since this motel was the clear preference of the two available, it was decided to go to a local pub, have a leisurely lunch, and come back later. Our post lunch return to the motel, however, showed no change from the earlier visit. A combination of the afternoon getting late and a desire to insure a place to stay for the evening prompted a decision to take two rooms in the second choice.

Motel number two was unfortunately the low point of lodging on the trip so far. Merj's look of dismay upon entering our "suite" was obvious. Although my standards were considerably lower, I too shared her opinion. There was dirty carpeting, beat up furnishings, a less than attractive bathroom/shower, and no air conditioning. The mud of Fort Knox, thirty years back, all of a sudden had a certain homey feeling to it. Unfortunately there was no other option available in this town of 734 people.

After opening the door and windows to cool the warm room, a strong odor of gasoline from fueling operations at a nearby upwind gas station wafted through. The odors were intense enough to cause a return to the office to request a room relocation. Unfortunately the locked office door had a sign taped to it stating, "Office closed, gone to Little League baseball game."

During the unproductive walk to the motel office, a motorcyclist had perched on a chair in front of the room next to ours and proceeded to light up a cigarette. An instantaneous image of a giant gasoline vapor induced fireball flashed in our minds. Unfortunately he didn't look the type who would take kindly to any suggestion to stash his smoke. Deciding to avoid conflict, we returned to the pub. The pub offered protection from the impending firestorm and an opportunity to spend as much time as possible away from our humble lodgings. Fortunately, the winds had shifted and the smell of gasoline had much diminished when we returned later on. It would, however, be one of those nights when we would both sleep on top of the sheets with our socks on.

Day 34 - 1676 Miles Down, 2111 To Go

REAL COWBOYS WEAR LEVIS

After a restless sleep, an early departure through cool predawn air allowed an opportunity to bid goodbye to Walden, Colorado. Today was our thirty-second wedding anniversary and the intent was to spend it off route in the luxury of Steamboat Springs. After the previous night's motel, an Afghan cave would have been considered a luxury.

The cool morning ride was one of more gentle ups and downs through a wide plain surrounded by low mountains in the foreground and craggy peaks in the distance. A large sign proclaiming "Real Cowboys Wear Levis" provided a backdrop for a mid-morning rest stop. It was a good bet that relatively few of them would be caught dead in biking shorts. We wondered about the trouser choice of real buckaroos.

As the comparatively easy cycling continued, a small trailer appeared at a pull off area along side the road. A sign on the trailer indicated that it was a rest stop for Cycle America. Two cordial ladies occupying the trailer offered some of the free refreshments they were dispensing. We declined but asked them what was going on. They told us Cycle America was an organized cross-country bicycle tour, but unlike RAAM, it was not a race. After leaving the trailer, and for the next eight or ten miles, about a dozen touring cyclists passed going the opposite direction. The entourage included three tandem bikes.

The ride to Muddy Pass, the high point of the day, was a bit deceiving, as it was difficult to tell that the road was rising. The pass represented the fourth crossing of the Continental Divide and was situated amid refreshingly green stands of large pine trees. Heading downhill from Muddy Pass, the landscape returned to the more barren looking feel of the last few days except that we were surrounded by mountains. The road shoulders were narrow, the road was twisting, and the traffic was heavy making for a harrowing, but quick ride down from the pass. The last six miles into Kremmling was an enjoyable downhill, wind aided ride. At a centrally located downtown park in Kremmling, the bikes were loaded on the support vehicle and we headed fifty-seven miles off route to Steamboat Springs. My maturation over the course of the trip was obvious; I did not mark the end point of the day's ride with an "X" or any other designation. Maybe the obsession was easing a bit.

Day 35 - 1739 Miles Down, 2048 To Go

STEAMBOATIN'

Steamboat Springs, Colorado is known throughout the world by its copyrighted name of Ski Town USA. Although now a world class ski destination, the area around Steamboat Springs was once the summer home for the Ute Indians. The Utes came to the area for its abundant fish and wildlife, mild climate, and numerous mineral springs. Not surprisingly trappers traveling through the area in the mid 1800's played a role in the naming of the town. The trappers discovered a spring that made a chugging noise which sounded like a steamboat, hence the town name. We guessed that any other steam related moniker, such as Locomotive Springs or Steam Shovel Springs, might have changed the course of the town's history.

Soon after the turn of the last century, skiing became the economic backbone of the community. Since then Steamboat Springs has produced more Winter Olympic athletes than any other town in the United States. The total now stands at an impressive thirty-five. Billy Kidd, one of the town's Olympic medallists, is Steamboat's director of skiing and conducts a daily run down the mountain with lucky visiting skiers. There would likely be no run on this 90 plus degree day.

Steamboat Springs was a welcome respite and would be the location of a planned rest day. The selected hotel was situated on a hillside next to a chair lift, and was luxurious by most standards, but five star compared to much of the lodging of the last few weeks. After a quick shower it was time to head downtown to celebrate a wedding anniversary.

Downtown Steamboat Springs is a mixture of Old West and modern ski resort much like Jackson, Wyoming and Sun Valley Idaho. Shops and restaurants lined the main street, and never failing to disappoint, it didn't take long for the female contingent of our group to find a section of high-end shops. John and I didn't even attempt our usual show of interest, but instead, took up residence on a bench to watch life pass by. While resting, two other bleary-eyed husbands with the same intent joined us. One of the middle age fellows was an avid cyclist from Oklahoma and his buddy was from Kansas. Having been concerned for some time about the upcoming winds of Kansas, this chance encounter became an opportunity to question our two new acquaintances.

The Oklahoman had completed cycling tours across Kansas. With confidence he said, "The summer winds in Kansas ain't that bad." The decision to cross the country from west to east was, to a large degree, based on what a native Kansan had told us about the prevailing southwesterly winds in Kansas. "The wind will probably be a crosswind from the south," our new acquaintances opined, "It'll be important to get early morning starts, 'cause the winds get worse in the afternoon." All four wives soon appeared, and the conversation came to an abrupt conclusion. It was time for John and I to resume our well-practiced shopping support role. Regardless, there was a little better feeling about what awaited in Kansas.

Our anniversary dinner was enjoyed at a French restaurant located a block off the beaten path. Sitting at an outside table along a small creek flowing through town, we marveled at the difference a day made. Although the many rural towns that had been the norm to date had supplied innumerable memorable experiences, it was refreshing on occasion to spend time in a larger community. Had we been married a day earlier, the celebratory experience would have been spent in Walden with a beer on a chair next to a motel parking lot with the smell of unleaded gasoline added for effect.

DO YOU SPEAK COLORADISH?

Rest day in Steamboat Springs began with a leisurely wakeup that was purposely without benefit of an alarm clock. Before breakfast a trip to a small park on the banks of the Yanpa River provided an opportunity for an early morning run. The park offered a chance for cyclists, rollerbladers, walkers, and runners to exercise using the asphalt path bordering the river. I hadn't had many occasions to run since leaving Oregon, so I wasn't sure how I'd feel in the high elevation of Steamboat Springs.

I proceeded along the trail, until the regular routine of running was pleasantly interrupted be a number of hot air balloons that slowly ascended from an open area close by. The brightly colored balloons stood out in sharp contrast to the magnificent blue of the early morning sky. The distinctive whoosh sound of the propane burner atop the hanging basket announced that a climb was soon to follow.

As it turned out, the run proved to be very much like similar duration workouts back home. Although no world records were endangered, the cycling had evidently maintained a decent cardiovascular fitness level. It had also allowed acclimation to the high elevations. A weigh-in on a scale at the hotel had also shown about a six-pound weight loss over the month on the road. Considering the nature and quantity of food we consumed, the weight loss was a bit of a surprise. If the same eating habits continued after completing the trip, we would likely become circus sideshow attractions.

A short walk after breakfast led to discovery of a gift shop filled with all sorts of Scandinavian related paraphernalia. The woman working in the store was of Norwegian descent and in a very short time she and Merj became engaged in lively conversation. Upon learning of her Finnish heritage, the clerk directed Merj to a number of Finnish oriented goods in the store. The usual show of interest by the male contingent of the group kicked into gear as the store's contents were searched and researched by the female contingent in pursuit of the ultimate Scandinavian artifact. Such purposeful effort went unrewarded, but while leaving the establishment with nothing in hand, the owner told us of a young Finnish woman who worked in a local eye glass store.

We quickly located the store after a short drive to a shopping center. There were two young ladies inside and as one approached it was clear by her distinctive characteristics that she was the native Finlander. It must have been obvious to the other three members of our group too, because a steady barrage of Finnish soon greeted the clerk. After an initial look of surprise, a large smile spread over her face and she responded in a likewise manner. Since the other young lady was a native Coloradan, I busied myself chatting with her in Coloradish as the four Finnish natives continued what appeared to be a pleasant conversation. While taking pictures of our new Finnish acquaintance standing next to a noisy, brightly colored parrot in front of the store, she talked of having recently married a local American lad. It would have been interesting to have spent an hour or so with the young man comparing notes and giving him advice gained over many years.

The day had warmed to 96 degrees, but, regardless of the warm temperatures, the winter resort nature of Steamboat Springs was evident throughout the town. There had been a number of signs along the road advertising the E. M. Light and Sons general store, so it was decided to pay a visit. The store was located in the middle of the original section of town and claimed to be the oldest in Steamboat Springs. The interior was filled with a collection of everything from clothing to jewelry to humorous trinkets. As the ladies shopped, John and I talked to the young people adorned in E. M. Light tee shirts who offered helpful assistance to the store patrons.

As was becoming the norm, we walked out of the store with absolutely nothing in hand. A large fiberglass horse on the sidewalk in front of the store provided a chance for some contrived photographic memories. Hopefully, the inventor of fiberglass had bigger things in mind for his life's work than this hollow memorial to equines.

Days 36 - 1739 Miles Down, 2048 To Go

"HOOSIER PASS IS NO BIG DEAL."

After an enjoyable day off the bikes, it was time to get back in the saddle in the park in Kremmling. The day began with a general rise along a road with minimal shoulders and a fair amount of traffic. Although it was probably psychological, it seemed to take a while to get back into the groove after having taken a day off. Another psychological factor that was beginning to occupy precious neurons in our overactive minds, was the looming climb to Hoosier Pass in two more days. At an elevation of 11,600 feet, Hoosier Pass represented the highest point of the entire trip and had been a source of discussion with cyclists riding the other way. Merj was already mulling over strategies to conquer the climb and a certain degree of tension seemed to be building inside her.

The day's scenery was a mixture of sagebrush and, as the road rose, more and more pine trees. While passing the Green Mountain Reservoir about fifteen miles from Kremmling, it was impossible not to notice the very low lake levels. A great portion of the West had been experiencing a long drought and the lake reflected the lack of precipitation in the area. The continued rise in elevation was apparent as more and more of the landscape became covered in pine. The day's ride included six miles of difficult and dusty riding through a construction area that made us feel fortunate to have opted for heavier touring bikes rather than lighter road bikes. Although not admitting it to Merj, the rough ride through the construction zone had a bit of a mountain bike feel to it and was, in some respects, an enjoyable diversion. It was pretty obvious that she would not have shared the same feeling. The last few miles of the ride into Dillon included a smooth bike path through the town of Silverthorne and into areas showing a growing level of affluence. Near town, while observing a large nest high on an abandoned power pole, an osprey looked down as if we were, at best, a minor curiosity.

The Town of Dillon began as a stage stop and trading post and was incorporated in 1883. The town has relocated three times since its original incorporation. The first move was to be closer to a railroad; the second was to locate between the Snake, Blue, and Ten Mile Rivers. The final move began in 1956, when the people of the town were told by the Denver Water Board to sell their property and be gone by 1961. The reason for the forced exodus was the pending construction of the Dillon Reservoir. The town's current location on the banks of the reservoir is home to about 750 permanent residents and 4,000 during the ski season. The location of Dillon in Summit County put it amid such famous ski resorts as Keystone, Breckenridge, Copper Mountain, and Vail.

Nearing the hotel, the Dillon Reservoir, dotted with sailboats, came into view. Picturesquely situated amid the pine covered mountains, the reservoir water level was clearly low, and reflective of the lack of precipitation in the Dillon area. The evening's lodging was located on a hill and the view of the lake and surrounding mountains was stunning. Part of a relaxing afternoon was spent collecting colorful stones while walking along a beach made much wider by the low water level. Smooth flat stones for skipping were plentiful and getting multiple skips from each throw was easy. Even though the practice of marking X's at stopping points had become less of an obsession, trying to recreate memorable, youthful experiences had replaced it; but who cared? A big reason for making the trip was to do just that.

Leaving the beach and heading to the Dillon Dam Brewery afforded an opportunity to enjoy a memorable dining experience at an outdoor table with a great view of the surrounding mountains. While eating dinner, quick conversation was made with a middle age married couple at an adjoining table. The couple was vacationing in Dillon from their home in Denver. Both were retired teachers, so that unnamed phenomenon that occurs when more than two teachers come together began anew. Merj and our new friends soon solved the nation's educational woes.

Since they were long-time Colorado residents, Merj succumbed to her growing Hoosierphobia and asked what they knew about the pass. The husband quickly responded, "Hoosier pass is no big deal." An audible sigh could be heard by all at the table, as Merj's relief was clearly evident. But after a minute the wife seemed convinced that her husband had confused his passes. After careful reconsideration, the affable Colorado native's forehead wrinkled and he restated his previous information, "I'm wrong," he apologized, "that's a tough climb." An ashen look on Merj's face indicated an immediate departure of the blood in her head toward her toes. A middle of the night wide eyed Hoosier Pass awakening could unfortunately be in the offing.

As the evening turned to dusk, a short walk from the hotel led to a fairly large open aired amphitheater that had been carved out of the reservoir bank. The theater consisted of semi-circular seating rising above a stage enclosed by a concrete shell. A group singing Cajun music supplied the night's entertainment. Not having knowledge of Cajun music, and wondering how it had made its way to this part of the country didn't stop enjoyment of the experience as dusk fell on a beautiful evening in the mountains of Colorado.

Day 37 - 1779 Miles Down, 2008 To Go

WILL SOMEBODY PLEASE STOP THAT RINGING IN MY HEAD?

The ride from Dillon to the ski resort area of Breckenridge was short, but involved a significant elevation gain on the way to the next day's climb over Hoosier Pass. The cycling was comfortable as the ride followed a bike path around Dillon Lake and into the lush green forested mountains. Because of the local drought, the south end of the lake could have been more accurately described as a mud flat; the low water levels had exposed great amounts of the lake bottom. The outdoor orientation of the people of the area was evident that Sunday morning. Rollerbladers, runners, walkers, and other cyclists joined us on the path.

A father running along the path accompanied by his young bicycle riding daughter brought back very fond memories of earlier times when my own daughters offered encouragement from their bikes on Sunday morning runs. A pleasant babbling brook was a companion for a portion of the ride and an occasional wooden bridge over the quick flowing stream added to the picturesque morning ride. After passing the small town of Frisco, the road headed along the Blue River toward Breckenridge. The river with its occasional small rapids and waterfalls was the chosen spot for a few early morning fishermen. Two tail wagging Labrador Retrievers splashed toward us, and we waved to their smiling owner as the gentle upgrade ride continued.

After about fifteen miles a decorative sign welcomed visitors to Breckenridge. The sign was the most elaborate of the many welcome signs previously encountered and was indicative of the prosperous nature of downtown Breckenridge. Many very nicely maintained shops, restaurants, and hotels lined the main street.

Breckenridge was not always the ski resort destination that it is today. The town was founded in 1859 as a gold and silver mining community and in 1860, hoping it would help get a post office, took the name of Vice President John Cabell Breckinridge. After the Civil War broke out, the pro Union citizenry of Breckinridge became upset when the V. P. sided with the South and decided to protest his Confederate sympathies by changing the town's name. The simple solution was to change the original *i* to an *e*, and it has been Breckenridge ever since.

Like many other western towns, Breckenridge was a town

with a bawdy past and a cast of colorful characters. One of them was John Lewis Dyer, a circuit riding Methodist minister from Minnesota. Father Dyer became a legendary western figure whose exploits included walking on to Denver when his horse faltered in Omaha. Upon his arrival in Breckenridge, Father Dyer preached against the drinking, gambling, and prostitution that were prevalent at the time. He took his calling seriously and refused to stop ringing his church's bell until the rowdy townsfolk saw the light. One morning the hungover residents of Breckenridge took offense to Father Dyer's tactics and used dynamite mining caps to blow up his church steeple. The church bell never rang again. John Dyer's larger than life reputation lived on when he was later selected as one of the Sixteen Founders of Colorado that were honored in stained glass windows in the State Capitol Dome. The Father Dyer Methodist Church still exists in Breckenridge and has continuously ministered since 1880.

In 1887, a resident by the name of Tom Groves found the largest gold nugget ever discovered in North America. The nugget could have been more aptly described as a boulder. It weighed in at 151 ounces and was about the size of a human head. Groves frequently paraded his find around town like a newborn child, so the nugget was soon dubbed "Tom's Baby." One of the unsolved mysteries of Breckenridge is the mysterious disappearance of Tom Groves' "baby."

The cycling day ended five miles outside of Breckenridge at the south corporation limit of the rural community of Blue River. The stopping point, which was duly noted by the obsessive member of the cycling team, was about six miles from and 1,300 feet below Hoosier Pass. The support vehicle provided transportation back to Breckenridge where we enjoyed lunch outdoors, directly in front of an impressive ski slope. Patches of snow resembled neatly manicured golf bunkers, and we joked with our waiter about the "sand traps" near the top of the mountain. Although he chuckled politely, our attempt at humor was probably viewed as pretty lame.

The shops of Breckenridge, like those in most of the other resort towns beckoned shoppers inside. This time, though, there was one that even John and I enjoyed. The store was filled with interesting photographs and artwork from the area. After a short time, a unique wooden picture puzzle was selected for purchase from the large collection. The puzzle, tucked under one arm, became my silent companion as the ladies continued to shop and the male shopper's mind went into its usual trance.

Unfortunately the trance was still very much present while walking out of the store with the yet unpurchased puzzle in hand. A hundred yards or so outside the door, a realization of what had happened required a sheepish return to the store. Fortunately the folks behind the counter forgave the momentary, and unintentional, lapse of honesty and offered no more than good-natured teasing.

The early evening was spent using the support vehicle to drive some thirty five miles or so to the old mining town of Leadville. The ride passed through beautiful scenery consisting of high pine covered mountains and craggy peaks and a number of less beautiful molybdenum mining operations. During the Second World War the molybdenum mines bustled with activity as the mineral was used as a steel additive to increase its strength. At its peak the Climax Mining Company employed many folks in the area, but current low prices for molybdenum had been the reason for a much-reduced workforce. No matter how much we tried, mastery of the word "molybdenum" was never satisfactorily accomplished.

Leadville is North America's highest incorporated city at elevation 10,430 feet, and once had a population of over 30,000. Horace Austin Warner (H. A. W.) Tabor, known as the Silver King, was one of the first to develop mines in the area and was instrumental in the creation of Leadville. Tabor became extremely wealthy from his silver mining operations and in 1880 married his second wife, a much younger woman known as "Baby Doe." The couple lived a very lavish lifestyle until the silver market crash at the turn of the century left them living a life of poverty.

On his deathbed a penniless Taylor told Baby Doe to hang onto the mining property called the Matchless, "Because some day it will make millions again."

Over the next thirty-six years, an impoverished Baby Doe traveled the streets of Leadville with her feet wrapped in burlap to protect them from the cold. This once extravagantly wealthy and still proud woman refused to take food and clothing from those wanting to help her. Remaining true to the promise she made to her dying husband, Baby Doe died in a small log cabin next to the mineshaft in 1935.

Day 38 - 1801 Miles Down, 1986 To Go

THE STRONG SILENT TYPE

An absolutely beautiful, high-mountain morning greeted us, as did contemplation of the long anticipated crossing of Hoosier Pass. Merj's clenched jaw showed an unmistakable resolve to get to the top one way or the other. The steep climb started very shortly after beginning the day's cycling and before long the leap frogging technique was adapted. The narrow road and the fairly heavy traffic didn't detract from the beauty of the morning on the lush, pine covered mountainside. Even though the morning air was cool, the energy expended by the climb caused reason to quickly peel off the cold weather gear. We had been concerned about an ability to breathe efficiently in the high elevations, but fortunately, that worry was dispelled rather quickly as no particular difficulty in breathing was encountered. Weeks of cycling through the mountains had apparently provided proper acclimation to the altitude.

The last portion of the grade included sharp switchbacks that nearly put us back on ourselves as the summit finally came into view a short distance away. The support team was waiting with cameras when we finally rolled up to the sign designating Hoosier Pass. The sign also represented the fifth and final crossing of the Continental Divide. It was now officially downhill to the Misssissippi River. The view of the surrounding mountains from the prominent peak, as would be expected, was spectacular. Feeling somewhat giddy, John and I used a couple of traffic cones as megaphones to imitate the Swiss guy in the Ricola television commercial. Maybe there was something to that thin air worry after all. The ladies humored us by recording the moment in photographs. There was blissful unconcern that in ten years or so a yet to be born grandchild might possibly look at the photos and rightfully ask what was wrong with grandpa and great grandpa.

At an elevation of 11,542 feet, Hoosier Pass got its name from Hoosier Gulch, an area discovered by a group of Indiana Hoosiers in 1816. As with the previous passes, the ride down from Hoosier Pass was a fast and enjoyable one through the high, pine covered landscape. Approaching the town of Alma about seven miles from the pass, the search began for an alleged bike path that would continue on to Fairplay. When we couldn't find it, it became necessary to find someone from the area to ask for directions.

A police car parked a short distance away with an officer on duty behind the wheel appeared to solve the problem. As I rather articulately described the need for directions, the officer made no effort to acknowledge my presence and continued to stare straight ahead. Finding his lack of response odd, a look inside the police car showed that, no matter the question, there would be no answer from this particular officer of the law. The clean-shaven, nattily uniformed policeman was in fact a mannequin. Feeling a little embarrassed at having been duped, I called John over to join the "discussion." It felt a little better when John, falling for the ruse, began a conversation of his own with our silent friend. As with other similar situations, the first reaction was to look around to see if anyone saw us. There was a bit of a fear that the little incident could become a future *Candid Camera* episode. We could only guess that the town fathers might have decided to place the mannequin in the police car to slow down potential speeders.

FIVE HUNDRED DOLLARS AND A BOTTLE OF WHISKEY

The bike path out of Alma was downhill and the easy cycling and ability to ride side by side made it an enjoyable ride. After cycling through the small town of Fairplay, the route headed into a landscape that was much less green than that of Hoosier Pass. As had first become evident back in the Cascades, it again seemed that the western side of the mountain range received much more precipitation than the eastern. Large ranches with grazing herds of cattle became fairly frequent. Low red hills in the distance spotted with occasional pine trees formed a backdrop as the ride continued past corrals filled with horses into a slight headwind.

During a break, Merj tossed her snake warning stones into the intended restroom area, and I took up my usual observation post along the road. Scouting the half of the landscape that avoided a view of the makeshift restroom, it was hard not to be impressed by the beauty of the stark environment. The general high-plains feel of the area was nicely complimented by the low red hills in the distance. When Merj returned, it was safe to confirm that the other half of the terrain shared much the same beauty. Sometimes circumstances dictated that our beautiful surroundings be absorbed half at a time.

A short time later three large bison watched the slow passage of two cyclists as they grazed a hundred or so yards off the road. Their relative nonchalance was welcomed, as the large animals represented a potential for real damage had they decided a threat was present. A short time later a herd of fifty or sixty of the impressive creatures could be seen grazing some distance away. The bison, spread out on the wide plain with the red hills in the background, was reason enough to scramble for the camera.

After many miles of cycling on road shoulders, road kill had become an all to frequent occurrance. The variety of road kill was a regular topic of discussion while cycling through the remote areas of the West. Many birds, an occasional deer or antelope, numerous small critters, and over thirty snakes had "greeted" us on the highways of America. Today, however, we added the first porcupine to the list. The fat fellow had gone "paws up" after encountering a fast moving vehicle in the high plains of Colorado.

The cycling day ended south of the crossroads town of Hartsel at a Colorado Department of Transportation garage. The bikes were loaded on the support vehicle and a fifty mile trek to the evening's destination of Cripple Creek was completed an hour or so later. Cripple Creek is allegedly named in honor of a cow that fell in the creek and broke her leg. It's origins go back to the 1880's, when Robert "Crazy Bob" Wormack discovered gold in the area. By 1891 the last of the great gold rushes in the Continental U. S. was on. In 1890 there were less than 500 people living in Cripple Creek, but by 1900, 25,000 people in search of instant riches lived in the booming Colorado town.

Local lore had it that Crazy Bob's passion for liquor overcame him and he sold his claim, the El Paso Lode, for $500 and a bottle of whiskey. In the following years gold valued at over five million dollars was mined from the El Paso Lode. In 1909 Bob Wormach died a poor and lonely man in Colorado Springs. Since gold was first discovered, over $600 million worth of the precious ore has been removed from the area around Cripple Creek.

Today Cripple Creek benefits from being one of the historic Colorado mining areas allowed by the state legislature to become a gaming center. After getting cleaned up, it was decided to take a shuttle van the short distance downtown to try our luck at one of over twenty-five casinos operating in Cripple Creek. On the way, the driver explained that gold was still mined in the area by the open strip mining method. He explained further that the gold was separated from the ore by a process utilizing arsenic and cyanide. "I'll bet the guys working there don't live to a ripe old age," I joked, but it wasn't clear from his reaction if he recognized a clumsy Midwestern attempt at humor or not.

Day 39 - 1845 Miles Down, 1942 To Go

ROYAL GORGE WAR

After unloading the bikes at the Colorado Department of Transportation garage, the start of the day was delayed a few minutes to enjoy a glimpse toward the early morning sun lighting the low hills and the distant high peaks. The cycling day began with an eight-mile gradual climb to Currant Creek Pass. The fire hazard presented by the drought in the West was evident by the surrounding dry grasses and a Smokey the Bear sign that showed "Extreme Fire Danger." At elevation 9,404, Currant Creek Pass represented a drop of over 2,000 feet from yesterday's high point at Hoosier Pass. The ride down from Currant Pass was one of the most delightful of the trip. The combination of light winds, low traffic, and elevation drop allowed covering a great portion of the highway at thirty miles per hour or more. The morning was magnificent, the riding was fast and nearly effortless. Merj and I were almost giddy as we enjoyed the mid-summer morning in central Colorado.

About twenty miles into the day the downhill ride was effectively ended by a series of short, but fairly steep climbs. The day remained beautiful, however, and complaining was generally muted as we continued through scenic pine covered river valleys. Not long after, however, a few three or four mile climbs and a slight headwind began to create a bit of amnesia about the earlier ride down from Currant Pass. About eight miles from the evening's stopping point of Canon City (pronounced Canyon) a turn onto a major highway presented wide shoulders but heavy traffic. The remainder of the ride into Canon City passed a number of impressive red rocked canyon walls and reason to snap pictures of the interesting geology of the area. A sign announcing the location of Royal Gorge offered enough information to provoke a visit later on in the support vehicle.

Royal Gorge is a very impressive deep vertical walled canyon that has been carved out of solid granite by the Arkansas River over a period of three million years. The usual cast of traders and trappers visited the area in the 1700's, and in 1806, Lt. Zebulon Montgomery Pike, the person for whom Pike's Peak was named, sent a party to explore the canyon. In 1877 silver was discovered along the Arkansas River and the Santa Fe and the Rio Grande Railroads competed to build a railroad to haul ore from the mines. The disagreement escalated to the dynamiting of competitor's equipment and exchange of gunshots. The open conflict resulted in a six-month battle in the courts ultimately resulting in the Rio Grande's victory. The Santa Fe took offense to the outcome and hired the legendary gun fighter Bat Masterson and a portion of his gang. Not to be outdone, the Rio Grand assembled a 200 man posse and eventually prevailed.

Spanning Royal Gorge is the world's highest suspension bridge. The bridge stands 1,053 feet above the roaring Arkansas River below. We stayed a safe distance from the unprotected edge of the viewpoint and gazed out to the bridge and way down toward the floor of the gorge. A train carrying sightseers, presumably following the old tracks of the victorious Rio Grande, slowly passed on the narrow strip between the river and the base of the canyon wall. It was a very long way down to the train.

"THE ONLY THING TO STOP THE WIND IN KANSAS IS A BARB WIRE FENCE."

After fifty miles on the road a sign announced our entrance into

Canon City, elevation 5,332. During the day's ride over four thousand feet of elevation had been lost, and in the space of two days we had dropped over six thousand feet. Canon City's past and present are both very closely tied to lawbreakers. An early prison, The Colorado Territorial Penitentiary, opened its doors in Canon City in 1871. Once known as one of the "Hell Holes" of the Old West, the penitentiary has carried out seventy-eight executions. Showing their versatility and willingness to try new ideas, forty-five were executed by hanging, thirty-two died in the prison's gas chamber and one was killed by lethal injection. In 1988, the Museum of Colorado Prisons opened in what was once the old prison for women, just outside the east wall of the Territorial Penitentiary. Today there are 800 prisoners incarcerated in the medium security prison.

Since the penitentiary was such a big part of the community, it was decided to visit the prison museum. The old gas chamber stood outside the entrance as visitors walked up the steps of the old brick building. Inside there were thirty-two cells containing photographs and artifacts of life in the prison. Artifacts included the hangman's noose from the last hanging, prisoner's weapons, stories of the exploits of past wardens, news clippings about uprisings and escapes, and a reconstructed mess hall. It was an impressive display of reasons to avoid incarceration.

While sitting outside the motel room in the pleasant, warm evening, I was joined by a couple staying in the room next to ours. J. B. and Darlene carried heavy accents that undoubtedly placed them somewhere south of the Mason-Dixon Line. After further conversation J. B. revealed, "We're from Deep East Texas, about a half mile from the Arkansas border." I realized that in five weeks on the road there had been a tripling of the number of Arkansans and near-Arkansans that had made our acquaintance.

Interestingly, it was the second marriage for both. Darlene's first husband had died a few years ago while in church playing Santa Claus. "He just died right there on the spot," Darlene said.

About six months later, J. B.'s wife died in her sleep. The two couples had been friends for many years so most of the folks in their small Texarkana town actively encouraged them to get together. As J. B. added, "And the worst one of them all was the preacher." They finally did get together and the match-making preacher had asked them as they exchanged vows, "Is that your final answer?" Apparently the once popular television show *Who Wants to be a Millionaire?* was one of the reverend's favorites.

J. B. and Darlene were probably in their early seventies and clearly enjoyed each other's company. Since they were heading out the next day over the same roads that had been part of our last few days, we asked them to think of us as they drove over Hoosier Pass. In a very pleasant manner Darlene asked, "Why in the world would anybody want to ride a bicycle across the country, and how did you talk your wife into it?" Since Merj was within easy earshot, I quietly told them that I too had been surprised. I asked J. B. about the winds of Kansas. "Well, the prevailing wind is from the southwest, but you never can tell because sometimes it blows 35 miles per hour all night and all day," he said. "The only thing to stop the wind in Kansas is a barb wire fence." That bit of information was not good news.

The couple lived about forty miles from Hope, Arkansas, so a question about their feelings about former President Clinton was in order. "The best thing to happen to the people of Arkansas was that he left and went to Washington," J. B. quickly told us. He spread his dislike for office holders to both parties, though, and voiced his less than enthusiastic feelings about President Bush. "No politicians are honest, and the best of them is a damn liar." I had learned a long time ago that arguing about politics or religion is an exercise in futility. Expressing one's viewpoint about either subject would not change the opinion of the other participant in the discussion. Such advice served me well as I kept my mouth shut and enjoyed the couple's company.

We were better for having spent time with J. B. and Darlene.

This happy couple was indicative of many of the people of their generation. They still had a basic belief in what was right and lived their lives through their church and friends. It was refreshing to talk to these rock solid folks from east Texas. In many ways they represented what was still right with the great majority of the people of the country.

Day 40 - 1896 Miles Down, 1891 To Go

WHICH WAY FROM HERE ZEBULON?

The road toward Pueblo proved to be one of transition from the Rocky Mountains into the beginnings of the Great Plains. The morning ride passed through dry brown terrain with the mountains slowly disappearing in our rearview mirrors. The landscape was becoming flatter with wide expanses occasionally dotted with trees. The cycling was generally easy, but the predicted temperature for the day, 104 degrees, made it imperative to get most of the riding done as early as possible.

While stopped at a gas station for snacks and a restroom break during the already warm morning, two Colorado Department of Transportation workers approached with a look of urgency. One of them appeared to be ill and the other, in an effort to seek aid, approached me with a syringe and said, "Stick this thing in his arm, he's real sick." Although usually willing to accommodate, jabbing a needle in the old guy's arm was well beyond my limited medical skills. I politely responded, "No way!" Upon hearing my response, the "healthy" member of the duo took measures into his own hands and stuck his fellow employee with the needle.

Suddenly, the two began to laugh in a manner that clearly indicated they had pulled something over on us. The needle-wielding member of the twosome proceeded to show us that his "syringe" was in fact a ballpoint pen that resembled the medical device. Apparently we weren't the first people they had pulled their little scam on. Sometimes, though, it did feel like someone had put a "kick me" sign on our backs. The fellows who work for the Colorado Department of Transportation were friendly, fun loving guys, but obviously had way too much time on their hands.

The City of Pueblo, with a population of 103,000, represented the largest city on the trip so far. Pueblo is situated at the base of the Rockies along the Arkansas River. The well known Pikes Peak, named after Zebulon Pike, is located about 45 miles from Pueblo and, at 14,410 feet in elevation, can be seen from downtown.

Zebulon Pike spent time camped in Pueblo on his ill-fated trek to conquer the peak that would later bear his name. Even though Pike never made it to the summit, as the discoverer of the peak, it was given his name. After leaving the Pueblo area, Zebulon Pike headed south from Colorado and was stopped by Spanish officials and charged with illegal entry into Spanish held territory. The officials confiscated all of his exploration notes and records and escorted him and his party to Louisiana. When Pike published his memorized recollections of the trip, it spurred businessmen and politicians into expanding into Texas. Unfortunately he also helped enhance the myth of the Great American Desert. Describing the Great Plains, Pike wrote, "These vast plains of the western hemisphere may become in time equally celebrated as the sandy deserts of Africa..." His descriptions of relative desolation were a contributing factor in delaying settlement of the Great Plains.

We wondered about the luck of Old Zebulon. Here was a guy who on one of his earlier expeditions incorrectly identified the headwaters of the Mississippi. On his trip through Pueblo, he failed to reach to top of a peak that was, regardless, later named after him. He then proceeded to get captured by the Spanish who took all of his records and escorted him out of Texas. The federal government funded his voyages of discovery, and considering what it got in return, Zebulon Pike was like a Nineteenth Century version of a $600 hammer or $1,500 toilet seat; a grossly over-priced governmental purchase.

A MODERN DAY CHUCK WAGON

Pueblo was also the end of an early cattle-driving trail called the Goodnight-Loving Trail. The trail began in Texas, and passed through eastern New Mexico into Colorado. It was named for Texas cattleman Charles Goodnight. Goodnight's place in history, however, will best be remembered as the inventor of the chuck wagon. In 1866 he and his partner Oliver Loving purchased a government wagon as part of their preparation for taking a herd of 2,000 longhorn cattle to Colorado. Before leaving, he had the wagon completely rebuilt to his specifications. The distinguishing characteristic of the revamped wagon was a sloping box with a hinged cover that would fold out to serve as a cook's table. The box extended the entire width of the wagon and held shelves and drawers for stowing food and utensils. The cowboys referred to food as "chuck," so the box became known as the chuck box and the wagon as the chuck wagon.

The chuck wagon was usually the mobile headquarters of the cattle drive. It served as the social and recreational spot for the cow-boys as they used it as a gathering point for telling stories of the day's ride. If the chuck wagon was the cattle driver's home, the cook was its king. Since the cook played such a large role in the morale of the men and the smooth functioning of the camp, his authority was absolutely unquestioned. It has been said that even the cattle drive boss walked softly in the vicinity of the chuck wagon cook.

The atmosphere around a chuck wagon has been described by some as being "pleasantly barbaric." The language was colorful and profane, as would be expected from a group of men spending long tough days on the range. No cowboy, however, dared serve himself or touch any of the cook's utensils. After being served they never used the cook's table to eat on, but rather, sat on the ground to eat their meal. Meals consisting of meat were the norm with fried steak being the most common menu entrée. If the cook was feeling extra good, he might make a fruit pie for desert for his boys. When not preparing or serving food the cook was the barber, banker, dentist, priest, and counselor. As the most valuable member of the cattle drive, he was often paid twice or more what the cowboys earned.

We began to see parallels between historical events in eastern Colorado and our trip. Just like Zebulon Pike, we too occasionally got lost and had to be "escorted" back to our intended route. We too misidentified waterways along the way and were probably overly descriptive of the desert-like landscape we passed. In many ways, Merj's bike served as the chuck wagon; she carried most of the snacks and daily supplies. Even though the discussions were usually neither colorful nor profane, most were held around her bike. Meals were eaten off the bikes and most consisted of some sort of beef with maybe a pie for desert if her "cowboy" had been good. It was also preferable on some occasions to "tread lightly" around Merj's two wheeled chuck wagon. Merj's role as counselor, doctor, and banker were also uncanny parallels. It was surprising how the passage of a couple of hundred years had not really changed the basic factors affecting travel through the Rocky Mountains and Great Plains.

While in Pueblo, I took the unaccustomed position behind the wheel of the support vehicle from the motel to a late lunch and noticed that it had developed a perceptible loss of power and a gear-shifting problem. John and I soon found a local dealership and cooled our heels for a couple of hours talking about cars with the staff and looking through brochures while the mechanics inspected the vehicle.

After due deliberation, they informed us everything was

fine and that somehow the car had sensed that someone else had been driving it. The modern automobile is a marvel of technology, but knowing that someone different had been in the driver's seat seemed a bit of a stretch. Furthermore, deciding that it didn't like the new driver and was going to send him a message by acting up was even more of a reach. Not knowing enough about the current state of automotive electronics to question the finding, we decided to just let it go. There was a strong suspicion that the dealer really wanted to tell us that the car had sensed a problem in the driver's head.

The evening dinner allowed conversation with Jessica, a young restaurant manager who had been raised on a 1,600 acre ranch near our future destination of Lamar. She wore a large shiny belt buckle of the kind that cowboys had proudly displayed at previous stops. The buckle attracted attention and some good-natured kidding. Jessica talked about her love of growing up on the ranch, but of a reluctance to take up ranching as a career. Her trepidation was clear, "I watched my father struggle through forty-two years at the whim of weather and other things out of his control."

She had recently taken her boyfriend out to the ranch to meet her parents and, while there, ended up helping her dad with chores. As her boyfriend watched, Jessica herded cattle into fenced areas for branding and neutering and lassoed stragglers. Questions soon followed as to whether the young man still chose to be her boyfriend after watching her in action, especially the neutering part? She laughed and assured us the two of them were still a happy pair. Merj took the opportunity to ask her standard question about the risk of snakes. "It's not just the rattlesnakes you gotta worry about, there's badgers out there too." Off road restroom breaks were now going to be a real joy.

Day 41 - 1948 Miles Down, 1839 To Go

HONEY, DID YOU TAKE YOUR BOOTS OFF AT THE DOOR?

Once past the commercial development and the municipal airport, the ride east of Pueblo became an enjoyable one along flat roads with good wide shoulders. The early morning start and the flat terrain allowed a beautiful view of the bright orange sunrise over the distant horizon. The ride continued along the Arkansas River and included the first sighting of a large field of corn. Soon after, we passed fields of melons being harvested in the green river valley. The workers in the fields had a well choreographed system; they would throw the melons up to a buddy on the back of a farm wagon, where they were then neatly stacked. It had the look of a quarterback pitching out to his tailback for a run around the right side.

Further east, large feed lots full of cattle being fattened for shipping to market began making regular appearances. The odors from a particularly large lot announced its presence some time before it was reached. Knowing the ultimate fate of the cattle, there was always a sense of sadness when passing the cramped feed lots. The sadness, however, never translated into a change in eating habits. Hamburgers and steak continued to be consumed as if there was nothing else on the menu.

The feed lots were the first of many that would follow in the days to come. We learned that feed lots were the final stop for cattle before being shipped to a slaughterhouse for processing. When cattle reach a certain age they are sold at auction and then shipped by truck to feed lots. Cattle trucks, with their recognizable fragrance, had become increasingly frequent companions on the roads as we cycled toward Kansas.

While at the feed lots, cattle are fed a diet of grains and may be given growth hormones to enhance weight gain. Large feed storage structures are usually a prominent feature of any lot. The cattle's stay in a feed lot can last two months or so and result in a weight gain of 200 pounds or more. The cattle generally leave the feed lots to a second auction and then to slaughterhouses. There are about forty million cows raised each year for human or other consumption.

It was natural, or so we thought, to wonder about the people who work in feed lots and if they got up in the morning anxious to get to work. Again having a lot of time to think about such things, we discovered that a troublesome problem faced by the workers is proper protection of their feet. Those that wear heavy leather boots need to replace them every couple of months because of the high acid content of the cattle waste on the ground. If they wear rubber boots, the heat of the manure raises the temperature in the boots to an uncomfortable level and can cause infections or athlete's foot. Many have opted for treating their leather boots with oils to waterproof them and extend their life. It was always fascinating to discover the special problems that make any job unique. We guessed that foot problems would be just one of a number of unique obstacles that one would have to overcome to get through the workday at a feed lot. The nightly question of, "How did your day go today, dear?" must have had a certain monotony as the response was probably pretty much predictable.

The crosswinds picked up as the cycling continued past a herd of pygmy goats and through the town of Fowler. A local resident had printed a large sign on the side of an abandoned semi-trailer warning, "Watch Your Speed-Speed Trap Ahead." Outside of Fowler it was necessary to apply the brakes quickly to keep from running into a large deer that darted across the road as the ride continued along the Burlington Santa Fe Railroad toward the small town of Swink. Swink was an agricultural working town that served the ranchers and farmers of the area. A water tower with SWINK proudly displayed on the side provided the only photo opportunity of the day.

In LaJunta, the evening's destination, a bank sign told us the temperature; a warm 90 degrees. LaJunta was obviously a big time community as a large Wal Mart occupied a good-sized chunk of real estate along the roadway. After checking into the motel, it was time to head to The Hog's Breath Saloon, a restaurant suggested by the friendly female cattle branding and neutering restaurant manager from the previous night.

The large restaurant was decorated in a typical western motif with a menu keeping with the theme. The waitress was all business; she went about her job in a workman like fashion with no more conversation than absolutely necessary. The usual charm that had successfully started many a conversation with waitresses over the last two thousand miles was met with uncharacteristic indifference. "Never say die" efforts to get conversation started with our sphinx-like waitress produced brisk kicks under the table from Merj, accompanied by a furrowed brow and that unmistakable look that said, "cool it."

Day 42-1998 Miles Down, 1789 To Go

IT MAY BE CRAP TO YOU, BUT IT'S OUR BREAD AND BUTTER

A 5:45 am start was in order leaving LaJunta to avoid most of the heat from another predicted warm day. A brilliant red sunrise greeted us on the outskirts of town and afforded an opportunity to snap a picture of Merj's darkened silhouette riding toward it. The sunrises on the flat plains were already becoming a much-anticipated daily event. Merj's day brightened even more as an honest to goodness rest area with an honest to goodness water flushing restroom appeared at the perfect time. There would be no rock-throwing announcement or sentry posted at the roadside for this morning's restroom experience.

The morning's ride paralleled the Burlington Santa Fe and was a continuation of the flat riding that had become the recent norm. It was hard to imagine that just a few days ago we had been cycling in the high elevations of the Rockies. The only climbs of this day were occasional manmade overpasses crossing the railroad. One such overpass appeared just outside the small town of Las Animas and gave a panoramic view of a good-sized rodeo arena. Rodeo arenas continued to pop up in the small western towns much like Little League baseball fields back home.

Las Animas was also the location of another announced speed trap with a police cruiser parked off the side of the road. This one was empty. Obviously the people of Las Animas were a lot harder to fool than those gullible folks back in Alma. Outside of Las Animas we crossed over an Arkansas River, reduced to a mere trickle by the drought plaguing the West. Each contact with the Arkansas River served as a reminder: People on the plains pronounced the river's name as Ark-kansas rather than the customary pronunciation of Ark-kan-saw.

The morning's terrain was close to table-top flat with low brown sand hills visible far to the south. Small sand mounds like wind driven sand dunes occasionally interrupted the nearby landscape. We planned a modest celebration about thirty-five miles outside La Junta, since a rough calculation had showed that location to be the halfway point of the trip. The "celebration" came unexpectedly in the form of a flat rear tire on my bike. Pomp and circumstance would have to be replaced by grease and more mumbles of impure thoughts. Ironically we would later realize that the actual half-way point had been reached two days earlier, west of Pueblo.

The tiny town of Hasty provided a chance for a break and some energy restoring snacks at a small store. Across from the store stood a weathered, wooden building that housed the Post

Office on the first floor, and an Army Navy store on the second floor. An American flag stood horizontally in the brisk wind blowing from the south. The wind also brought forth the unmistakable odor of nearby cows. The cow smell in this part of Colorado was a sign of relative prosperity, much like the smoke belching from a factory stack during the boom times of the industrial rust-belt. I was reminded of a time worn saying of environmental engineers, "It may be crap to you, but it's our bread and butter."

The sign at the entrance into the night's destination of Lamar announced that it was "A Historic Town on the Santa Fe Trail." Between 1821 and 1880, the Santa Fe Trail was a major commercial highway connecting Missouri and Santa Fe, New Mexico. The trail was used for transporting supplies to military forts in the Southwest, as a stagecoach line, and a route for gold seekers, trappers, and emigrants. Textiles and hardware were traded west while silver and mules were traded east. The trail essentially ceased to exist when the railroad reached Santa Fe in 1880. The day's ride had paralleled the same Santa Fe Railroad for much of the way. Much like the barbwire in nearby Kansas, the railroad had done little to stop the strong headwinds that made the day a bit of a challenge.

The town of Lamar, population 8,900, was named after Lucius Quitus Cincinnatus Lamar, a former Secretary of the Interior and U. S. Supreme Court Justice. It made one wonder if Lucius may have also stopped in Cincinnati and lent his name to that city on his way out to Colorado. Lamar could best be described as a well-maintained community with small parks and modern governmental buildings. A nicely restored steam locomotive and a train depot that had been converted to a visitor's center and Chamber of Commerce office were the focal points of a small park in the central part of the city. A sign at the park informed visitors that during World War II a number of Japanese Americans were relocated to the area after the bombing of Pearl Harbor in 1941.

The relocation of Japanese Americans during World War II remains one of the darker moments in American History. The internment camp near Lamar was located a few miles east in Granada. The camp opened in August 1942 and closed in October 1945. It peaked at a population of 7,318 Japanese Americans, most of whom were relocated from California. Thirty-one members of the camp lost their lives fighting as American soldiers in World War II, and 120 died while interned there.

In 1942 over 120,000 Americans of Japanese ancestry living in California, Oregon, and Washington were relocated to camps throughout the West. The internees were given one week to dispose of their household goods and were permitted to take just what they could carry to the camp. Many of the camps were located in unpopulated, barren regions of the country and were hastily built with a minimum of conveniences. Families existed in small rooms with little or no privacy or furnishings. The time in camp was spent behind barbed wire while guards patrolled the perimeter.

By mid-1943 the federal government encouraged the evacuees to relocate to the Midwest and some did. In 1980, the federal government established the Commission on Wartime Relocation and Internment of Civilians. The commission determined that the internees were victims of discrimination by the federal government. In 1988, President Reagan signed the Civil Liberties Act that granted a presidential apology and payment of $20,000 to the internees and persons of Japanese ancestry who lost liberty or property because of the discriminatory practices of the federal government during World War II.

The night in Lamar was spent at the Best Western Cow Palace. Although the name was appropriate for the prime business of the area, the image of a "cow palace" conflicted with the very nice lodgings the hotel offered. Hamburgers at the hotel's bar gave us an opportunity to get lodging recommendations for the next evening from an accommodating waitress. The pleasant lady enjoyed offering help to a couple of wayward cyclists, and even called a friend to make sure her recommendation was accurate. Since this would be the last night in Colorado, it was decided to enjoy a leisurely meal and celebrate another successful state crossing in the air-conditioned comfort of the restaurant.

Day 43 - 2055 Miles Down, 1732 To Go

kansas

"If the wind ain't a blowin', there's a storm a brewin'."

YOU'VE GOT TO BE KIDDING, HILLS IN KANSAS?

The last day in Colorado began at 5:12 am with an early morning temperature that had already reached 74 degrees. The unmistakable wakeup call of a rooster greeted the day, as did another brilliant red sunrise. Occasional breaks in the flat terrain were supplied by manmade crossings over a railroad that paralleled the roadway. Not long into the day, near the small town of Holly, it became necessary to dodge numerous small hard packed cubes lying along the road. We later learned that the cubes were compressed grain used for livestock feed. The unappetizing looking morsels were apparently the cow version of granola bars. A stop at a mini-mart for human refreshment involved negotiating a parking lot filled with pickup trucks. The well-used pickups were clearly not for show, but served the basic utilitarian needs of the local ranchers. Someone wanting to sell cars for a living in eastern Colorado would likely starve to death.

About two miles from the Kansas border the first "natural" hill of the day sprouted out of the flat, eastern Colorado landscape. Soon after descending from the short climb, John and Aili waited at the Kansas border for the usual state line crossing ritual. This particular crossing had none of the excitement of Colorado, no rushing herd of cattle charged us as we posed under the WELCOME TO KANSAS sign, but entering a Midwestern state was another comforting indication that eastward progress was slowly being made. Although it was only 9:30 in the morning, the temperature at the state line had already reached 86 degrees.

A sign just inside Kansas informed travelers that they were traversing the Santa Fe Trail Mountain Route. Reference to a mountain route seemed a bit out of place. There wasn't a mountain in sight, and in fact, none had been visible since leaving Pueblo two days earlier. It did make one wonder about the existence of a Santa Fe Trail Plains Route, and if there was one, how flat it must have been. Rumor had it that mountains would probably be very infrequent in the Sunflower State.

Much of western Kansas consisted of low sand hills and occasional fields of maize. A large low warehouse sat some distance to the north, atop one of the sand hills. The building housed a dairy; surprising since we had not seen any dairy cows for some time. An Amtrak train made up of passenger and freight cars thundered past us a few feet off the wide shouldered highway. The engineer's friendly wave was a pleasant diversion on a warm Kansas morning. Soon after, grain elevators became visible on the eastern horizon. Surprisingly, the grain elevators would end up being six miles away and located in Syracuse across the street from the evening's motel.

The origins of the small town of Syracuse go back to the late 1800's when a group from Syracuse, New York learned of business and agricultural opportunities in the western part of Kansas. The group decided to send a small exploratory party to see if the area was as advertised. When they arrived in 1872, the town was called Hollidaysburg and was only a whistle stop, with a sidetrack and water tower. The New Yorkers decided to stay and named their new home Syracuse in honor of their hometown.

The lodging in Syracuse was generally forgettable, but alternatives were just about non-existent. A young man charged with the responsibility of registering patrons insisted on calling everyone he came into contact with Bud. When asked what was stored in the huge elevators across the street, he stated in a matter of fact fashion, "I have no idea, Bud." Our Bud calling acquaintance had worked at the motel for three years. How he had come to work every day for three years and not known what was inside the massive structures casting a shadow over the motel was hard to imagine. His lack of inquisitiveness probably insured a long career behind the front desk.

While getting organized in the motel room, it was hard to miss the fact that there were electrical outlets in the ceiling. After much thought, John, who had spent more than thirty years of his career dealing with electricity, could not come up with any reason why there would be electrical outlets in a motel ceiling. It was a question that would have to go unanswered, asking the fellow behind the front desk would be a waste of time. Next to the motel was a short section of railroad track with a passenger car sitting on it. The railroad car was available for a night's lodging should someone desire to recreate the experience of rolling across the Great Plains in a Pullman Sleeper. It wouldn't have been surprising to find that the prerecorded clickety-clack sounds of travel by rail were available on request.

A short walk for lunch to an air-conditioned restaurant next to the motel was a welcome respite from the 96 degree heat. The eyes of the patrons already inside followed us from the time we entered until we were seated. It was obvious that in this town everyone knew everyone else, and no one in the restaurant knew us. Regardless, the hostess provided escort to a seat near the kitchen and a conversation ensued with two ladies at the next table. Edith, the owner of the restaurant, sat with her friend, Martha, and neither looked as though they were in a hurry to get outside to the oppressive afternoon heat.

Merj took the opportunity to use the obvious sources of local information to her advantage. Next to snakes, her biggest cycling concern was hills. She glanced at me and as my mystified face looked back, she asked our new friends if there were any hills to worry about east of Syracuse. Embarrassed for her, I whispered softly in her ear, "Why are you asking that question, we're in Kansas for goodness sakes." Edith, very much to my surprise, responded, "There's some pretty good ones a few miles east of town." Martha verified her story and even elaborated some as to their difficulty. Merj's jaw tightened and her appetite left her. Serenity returned a few minutes later, however, when some of the previously antagonistic looking locals in the restaurant, having heard Edith's hill descriptions, discreetly suggested that they might have been slightly exaggerated.

Edith also owned a restaurant called Frank's in Lakin, a small town on tomorrow's ride. Her daughter worked there, and she asked us to stop in and tell her how we did on the hills. She went on to explain that the huge grain elevators across the street were filled with wheat. The pleasant company and the relief provided by the air-conditioned restaurant made it difficult to return to the motel, but there were clothes to wash and e-mails to deal with. As we walked the short distance across the sweltering parking lot back to the motel, the early afternoon temperature had reached 101 degrees.

The evening meal was eaten at a supper club attached to the back of Edith's restaurant. Supper clubs in Kansas were set up to deal with local restrictions placed on the sale of alcoholic beverages in many of the small rural towns. Our waitress tried to explain how they worked and even enlisted the help of her husband, but we still didn't understood their purpose. Regardless of our inability to understand such complex concepts, we enjoyed a good steak dinner and pleasant conversation with a husband and wife dining at an adjacent table.

The couple were well-known in the supper club and seemed to be prominent members of the community. The fact that the husband was a wheat farmer who owned about 8,000 acres of land near town likely contributed to their local notoriety. His wife joined the conversation and told of helping on the ranch by performing various tasks from the cab of an air-conditioned tractor. My wandering heat affected mind silently wondered that if air conditioned tractors had become reality, could air conditioned bicycles be far behind? "Most of the ranchers live in town and drive out to their ranches in the morning," the wife continued, "Really, they're just like commuters driving to work." Apparently the Kansas version of an office cubicle was the cab of a tractor.

The rancher indicated that his primary crop was winter wheat. "We plant winter wheat in the fall, it goes dormant over the winter, and then we harvest it in the summer," the rancher explained. He also talked of leasing part of his land to a company that would be constructing windmills for generating electricity. The innocent reference to windmills caused a renewed stir in the female member of our tandem. After all, didn't windmills require wind to be of any productive use? A wind worry began to inch closer to an already well-established hill worry on Merj's list of concerns.

I asked the rancher about the grain elevator across the street. "A lot of the local ranchers sell their wheat to the elevator owner, who in turn sells it to a processor." He had chosen a second option, "I store my wheat in there at three cents a month per bushel," He went on to say that the wheat in the large elevator was intended for human consumption. Since it was still early on a Saturday night, we asked him what there was to do in Syracuse. He laughed and said, "You're doin' it."

The rancher and his wife asked a number of questions about the bike trip and after patiently listening offered the straightforward comment, "You guys are nuts." We didn't disagree, and the conversation quickly changed to the ever-present winds of Kansas—the same ones that would be powering those windmills. He tried to dispel our wind-related concerns. "Don't worry about it, the summer winds usually blow from the south or southwest." Although reassuring to hear, we were never quite sure whether we were getting the whole truth. There was always a suspicion that upon seeing the worried look on our faces, the locals simply decided to tell us something they thought we *wanted* to hear.

While chatting with the few other people in the supper club, there was a sense that most of the old time residents were more comfortable with life in days gone by. This small town of 1,300 in western Kansas was now about half populated by foreign workers, many of whom worked at local dairy operations. Although not necessarily hostile toward their new neighbors, a feeling that the few people remaining in the supper club had not yet adjusted to the changing demographics of their community was somewhat apparent.

Day 44 - 2106 Miles Down, 1681 To Go

KANSAS CATHEDRALS

We left the shadows of the grain elevators at 4:45 am to avoid what was predicted to be a very warm day. The bank downtown already showed a temperature of 75 degrees as the day began with yet another beautiful red sunrise over the distant sand hills. The road was generally flat with light winds coming from the south. The hills that had been promised by Edith, while not insignificant, were met with relative ease. A little over twelve miles into the day a sign announced entrance into the Central Time Zone.

New time zones were, in some ways, more of a cause for celebration than state lines. After all, the journey would cross eleven states but only four time zones.

For years a mental image of Kansas had formed in my mind, resembling a real life version of the old *Green Acres* television show. Flat terrain with fields of corn or wheat extending as far as the eye could see was the anticipated landscape. I expected the only interruptions to be narrow ribbons of lightly traveled roadways running east and west, or north and south with no natural physical barriers to change their direction. The picturesque portion of the Kansas image, though included a well maintained white farmhouse accompanied by a large red barn and scattered small out buildings every once in a while. Adding a windmill, a swing set, and a few chickens made the image complete. The trip through Kansas was in search of those images.

While still only a relatively short distance into the first full day of Kansas, reality had a look much like the high plains of Oregon, rather than the imaginary one that had formed over the years. There was a sagebrush-covered look that included little in the way of corn, white farmhouses or chickens. In their absence were occasional grazing cattle and oil wells. Western Kansas was suffering from an extended drought that was evident as parched land and dry river and creek beds were prevalent for miles. Local old timers described the conditions as being worse than those of the 1930's Dust Bowl. In some areas, newspapers reported that the sand and soil blowing across the roads had drifted much like snow. The drifts had become a big enough problem that road graders had to be used to clear a path.

The other image of Kansas was the one portrayed in the *Wizard of Oz*. On more than one occasion it appeared that, when viewed from afar, the tall grain elevators resembled the magical city on the hill from the movie. The grain elevators were the prominent features of the small Kansas towns and were visible for miles. As we cycled along the flat roads, the sight of grain elevators would give us reason to anticipate a well-deserved break. It didn't take long to learn that a grain elevator sighting usually meant a six or seven mile ride before reaching the town. Judging distances on the flat plains was very deceiving.

The huge cylindrical grain elevators first appeared along the newly constructed railways that crossed the Midwest in the 1800's. They were first constructed of wood, then tile, steel, and, more recently, concrete. The structures are complex arrangement of elevators, conveyor belts, chutes, and silos that move and store the grain. Roman Hruska, called by many "the stupidest person in Congress," once interrupted a Senate Defense Appropriations Committee discussion about funding for missile silos with the blunt comment, "If you're going to talk about silos, you should go talk to the Agriculture Committee."

A worrisome fear for the elevator operators and the people that live near them was the possibility of explosion of the highly explosive grain dust. Although quite rare, the explosions were devastating when they occurred. The truly impressive structures, sometimes referred to as Kansas's cathedrals, announced the upcoming hamlets of Kansas from miles away, much like the downtown skyscrapers of a large city.

A stop in the small town of Lincoln at a mini-mart afforded an opportunity for yet another mid-morning restroom break. The stop was unremarkable, save for a cockroach or two in the rest-room and the lady who worked behind the counter. The large woman had decided to take a break and stepped outside to light up a cigarette and ask about the bike trip. While chatting with her, the occasion arose to again express fears of the headwinds of Kansas. Upon hearing our concern, she rolled her head back, laughed, and informed anyone within ear shot, "In Kansas, if the wind ain't a blowin' there's a storm a brewin'." Her eloquence was succinct yet clearly understood.

It didn't take long to finally begin to see the corn and maize that was part of my preconceived Kansas imagery. While cycling through the fields, an occasional smell would announce the upcoming presence of some type of livestock. The smell of cattle was one that had become customary and was not a particular cause for more than a casual look when reaching the source of the odor. Today however, an unrecognizable smell wafted over the corn tassels; the source turned out to be a herd of lambs. It was strange to see a large group of the fluffy four-legged critters amid the ranches of Kansas. The lambs brought laughter and agreement that they were dead ringers for Merj's dog Ditto.

Ditto was a Bedlington Terrier whose name was Max when he arrived as a puppy. Since a Labrador Retriever named Max already had taken up residence in our home, a new name was needed for Max II. After due deliberation, the name Ditto was chosen for our second canine acquisition. Those familiar with the Bedlington Terrier breed have reason to believe they have lamb in their heritage. Soon after passing the lambs another distinct livestock odor wafted through the warm morning. This one emanated from a group, or bevy, or herd of pigs. There was no dog at home that resembled a pig.

The approach to Garden City required a turn due south into a brisk wind that made the last few miles a real challenge. After getting situated in the motel room, the local weather channel informed viewers that the winds had been twenty to twenty-five mph with gusts of thirty-five mph. If the winds of the last few miles had been there all day, it would have been a very difficult day on the bikes. The wind paranoia was back and might be more than paranoia after all. The television also reported that tomorrow's temperatures would "only" be in the mid 90's.

By western Kansas standards, Garden City was a large community. Its 26,000 residents had all the amenities needed for modern life including a signature of approval from the Wal Mart Corporation. Much of the town's development began in the late 1800's when the William D. Fulton family moved in. Mr. Fulton played a significant role in its growth including convincing the

Santa Fe Railroad to make the community a regular stop. Garden City was eventually named after Mrs. Fulton's beautiful garden. Garden City provided an opportunity to eat at familiar chain restaurants and catch-up on shopping in air conditioned comfort. It was strange how the simple pleasures of life had become so magnified after weeks of visiting the small towns of America.

Day 45 - 2162 Miles Down, 1625 To Go

HONEST TOM

Clouds hid the usual bright red sunrise during an early morning departure from Garden City. The cloud cover screened the hot, direct sun and made the ride much more comfortable than those of the last few days. A turn to the southeast made the ride even more enjoyable as it provided the benefit of a fairly brisk tail wind from the north. Unfortunately the earlier wide shoulder had all but disappeared and an increasing number of large cattle trucks were competing for a share of the road surface.

The loaded tractor-trailers were transporting cattle to and from the feed lots and had become more and more frequent. A steady stream of trucks approached from both directions and became a real safety concern. Although the truck drivers generally gave as much room as they could, the increasingly frequent occasions when two of them would pass nearby in each direction gave them no choice but to hug the white line that was to our immediate left. Under those conditions, with little or no shoulder to work with, it was necessary on more than one occasion to yell our code word, "Bail!" and head into the grass to avoid catastrophe. The close calls from the nearby passing trucks, along with the brisk crosswinds, created many cases of severe wind buffeting where we nearly lost control of the bikes. This portion of the day's ride had become the most difficult and dangerous part of the trip.

At about twenty-one miles into the day, Merj's parents followed us into a rest area in the support vehicle. They had been part of the trip since Garden Valley, Idaho and had stopped to offer their last assistance and encouragement before heading back to Ohio. John and Aili had done a great job over the previous four weeks in diligently providing food, water, and encouragement whenever the need arose. It was also enjoyable sharing each day's experiences over the evening dinner. As the panniers were loaded on the bikes we bid them goodbye and wished them a safe trip home.

With the panniers back on the bike, the effects of the trucks and wind were magnified. Fortunately the shoulders widened in a few miles and riding a safer distance off the road became possible. Before long a sign appeared that announced a scenic overlook a half mile ahead. Having spent weeks cycling through the western mountains where breathtaking scenery was a regular occurrence, a scenic overlook in Kansas was unexpected. As one would expect on the flat plains, the overlook was located, by necessity, at the top of what appeared to be a manmade hill.

The anticipation of a breathtaking Kansas Kodak moment was almost unbearable; the bikes were parked in the pull off area and the camera was hastily located. Gazing out from the Kansas version of Hoosier Pass, we saw what had to be the world's largest feed lot. In the shadows of feed silos, hundreds of cattle were enclosed in pens that extended nearly a mile along the road. The unmistakable odor was especially strong as the wind blew across the feed lot and directly toward us. It was impressive in its own way, but a little strange that a feed lot had warranted a scenic overlook. Maybe there was something else of a scenic nature that had been overlooked? It was hard to say because the feed lot was such an overwhelming part of the view.

Entering the small town of Cimarron, the early morning clouds had darkened considerably and were becoming quite threatening. Worried about nature's call to Merj and the air pressure in my rear tire, we stopped at a gas station/mini-market to take care of both issues. Being a product of the 50's and 60's, it was still possible to remember filling up tires for free at the neighborhood filling station. I also recalled driving over the hose by the gas pumps that rang a bell announcing a customer's presence. Upon hearing the bell, a friendly attendant would spring to life and fill the tank, check the oil, and wash the windshield. Such days were long gone and so was the free air.

Paying for air was a real source of personal irritation, but having no other options, I dropped two quarters in the greedy machine and proceeded to get no response. After dutifully "tapping" the balky device, it still failed to dispense the air that had already been paid for. In retrospect the effort to get the pump started was probably more than a casual tap. It was more a golden opportunity to not only "nudge" the machine back to life, but to take out frustrations at having to pay for something that God had granted to the people of the Earth for free. I went inside to get a refund of the fifty cents I had lost in the machine. After eloquently presenting a case in a fashion resembling a Johnny Cochran closing argument, the large woman behind the counter shook her head. "Too bad buddy," she said shrugging her shoulders.

Walking back to the bike an unintelligible stream of words not learned in Sunday school crossed my lips. Unfortunately the problem with the rear tire had become acute. While trying to fill it from the worthless piece of machinery that masqueraded as an air pump, it had lost more air. It was impossible to continue on with the low pressure. The town of Cimarron seemed to offer few options to solve the problem until a glance across the street a few short yards away revealed a fellow and his dog setting in front of an old-style gas station. Although the gas pumps had been removed and the building was clearly not being used for its original purpose, it was obviously being used for something so a request for help was in order.

Pushing the bike toward the middle age bearded man and his

dog, it was hard to avoid noticing a collection of old farm implements around the former filling station. Not sure if he had nodded off, I asked softly if he had an air compressor. "Sure," he said
and instructed me to follow him into one of the old service bays.
His name was Tom and he called his furry little companion Bud.
Hearing the dog's name caused a quick memory of the desk clerk
back in Syracuse who called anything that moved Bud. As he
turned on the compressor and hooked up the air hose, I noticed
an immaculate Harley Davidson motorcycle at the garage
entrance. As we filled the bike tire, he said, "She's only a year old,
but I ordered a new Hundredth Anniversary Edition that oughta
be here in a couple o' weeks." Much like a pet owner saying goodbye to old Spot for the last time, he looked fondly at the motorcycle, "I really hate to part with her."

We finished filling the tire and Merj, joining us from her
extended restroom visit, expressed concern about the increasingly threatening sky. Tom looked skyward and proclaimed, "I'm a
meteorologist, follow me." He motioned toward the "office"
where we assumed he would be able to determine if the weather
might be taking a turn for the worse. While walking the short distance, we turned to each other and exchanged one of those "Yeah,
sure" looks. Not wanting to seem ungrateful, however, we followed Tom inside.

Tom sat down behind a computer screen and called up a local
radar site. After looking at the assortment of green and yellow
images on the screen, "There's a couple of strong storm cells
about fifteen miles south, but they won't be a problem," he confidently stated. Although relieved to hear the forecast, finding out
about Tom's meteorological background became a necessity. He
seemed to expect the question, and producing a certificate from
the National Weather Service, he delivered an oral history of thirty-two years of forecasting the weather. "I spent a few years near
you guys with the weather service at the airport in Cleveland,"
Tom explained, adding, "The Cimarron area is the documented

windiest part of the country." Having a certified meteorologist confirm that our wind based fears had a basis in fact was somehow comforting. I wondered though if Tom had any training in snakes or hills; two other fears that regularly found their way into the consciousness of at least one member of our team.

Walking back outside to the bikes, comforted by the weather forecast and by Tom's unquestioned credentials in offering it, the conversation with the friendly fellow continued unabated. Tom asked many questions about the bike trip and shared his dream of riding around the perimeter of the country on his motorcycle. He told us, "I want to write a book about it, and I've got a lady friend English teacher in town who said she'd review and edit it for me." Of course his companion Bud would tour with him. To show the dog's good training, Tom touched the motorcycle and Bud dutifully jumped up onto it and found his usual riding position on the back of the saddle. It was obvious that the small dog had spent considerable time there. Tom explained, "Me and Bud have ridden more than 80,000 miles together. He's a great conversation starter."

After sharing our experiences with the narrow shoulders and speeding cattle trucks, Tom lowered his voice and talked softly about a tragedy involving a young married couple three years earlier. Apparently the young folks had recently married and were riding across the country on bicycles for their honeymoon. Unfortunately, on the same stretch of road that had caused such concern earlier in the day, a cattle truck struck them and both were killed. It was a sobering and troubling revelation.

The conversation turned to all of the antique farm machinery that occupied much of the area around the gas station. "I restore 'em and then sell 'em to collectors and other people," Tom explained. He talked of restoring classic cars, mostly Corvettes, and showing no hurry in getting on with his day, he handed us a business card, which read, "Honest Tom Kelsay, Proprietor, Cimarron Tractor Company."

Although Tom's meteorological skills were not in question,

the dark clouds gave reason to feel a certain urgency to get back on the road. With reluctance, we bid him goodbye and headed toward Dodge City. This chance encounter in Cimarron, Kansas had left us shaking our heads. What were the odds of running into a retired meteorologist in the vast plains of Kansas when there was a need for reassurance about a threatening storm? Tom was the type of quiet, unassuming, helpful person that others had told us to expect in Kansas. His moniker, "Honest Tom," was probably not necessary.

The remainder of the day's ride toward Dodge City was a continuation of the wind blown cattle truck dodging experiences of the morning. Tom's forecast had been right on target. Although rain always seemed imminent, the skies never opened. A stop at a Comfort Inn just after entering Dodge City was met with rejection, as the young lady behind the reception desk informed us that there was no room at the inn. She suggested alternative lodging at the Boot Hill Bed and Breakfast. A quick call verified that a room was available, and after thanking her, it was on to downtown Dodge City.

The Boot Hill Bed and Breakfast was, as expected, located at the top of Boot Hill. The actual Boot Hill was only a few hundred yards long, but it was a very steep and challenging climb on a fully loaded bicycle. Although we had called just a few minutes before arriving, the B and B owner acted surprised to see us. After explaining that it was us who had called from the Comfort Inn, he laughed and explained that the young lady at the reception desk had called and told him to, "watch out for two old people on bikes." Although thankful for her concern, we were a little troubled by her description.

THE WRONG SIDE OF THE TRACKS

Dodge City, Kansas is a town of 21,000 people with a history that is as colorful as any in the West. Dodge City was founded in 1872

and was located not far from Fort Dodge, which had been established a few years earlier. Its location along the Santa Fe Trail
made it a busy center for travelers and buffalo hunters. After the
buffalo were decimated, cattle took over as the major business of
the area, and Dodge City became a stopping point for cowboys
driving herds from Texas. It was those cowboys that established
Dodge City's reputation as a place famous for gambling, drinking,
and prostitution. It was during this period that Dodge City developed a number of descriptive nicknames such as Cowboy Capital,
Queen of the Cowtowns, Wickedest Little City in America,
Beautiful Bibulous Babylon of the Frontier, and Buffalo Capital of
the World.

Dodge City had two distinct sides separated by railroad tracks
that ran through the middle of town. No guns could be carried or
brought into the north side. On the south side, however, guns and
just about anything else were allowed. We wondered if the expression describing someone as being "from the wrong side of the
tracks" might have originated here. Many differences of opinion
on the south side were settled in the streets, and the Boot Hill
Cemetery became the final resting point for the losers. The law-
less nature of Dodge City allowed famous lawmen such as Wyatt
Earp and Bat Masterson to build their reputations there by trying
to tame the unruly citizenry.

In 1876 Wyatt Earp became deputy marshal in Dodge City
and soon hired several other deputies. Among them was his friend
Bat Masterson. He quickly established a few rules for the town's
rowdies, one of which was to keep their misdeeds on the south
side of the tracks. If they stayed there, they would be left alone but
if they crossed the tracks they would be arrested. Just to be sure,
he kept loaded guns at strategic points around town so that he
could always be ready to deal with any eventuality. Earp left
Dodge late in 1876, but returned a year later. Having established
the reputation of a tough lawman, he was able to settle some of
the town's disputes with talk, but other conflicts still required his

considerable gun fighting skills. Within a year or two, Dodge City settled down and Earp became bored and moved on to Tombstone, Arizona. Surprisingly, he lived to the ripe old age of eighty before his death in Los Angeles in 1929. Among his legacies is a post office near one of his old mining claims along the Colorado River on Route 62, bearing his name, "Earp, California 92242."

Today Dodge City is a popular tourist attraction. An authentic replica of Front Street has been constructed with an assortment of businesses from the late 1800's. Those familiar with *Gunsmoke*, the popular western of the 60's, would recognize the restored Long Branch Saloon. It wouldn't have been surprising to see Marshall Dillon stroll in looking for a beer and Miss Kitty. The historically accurate buildings were open to the public, and visitors were able to wander in and out of them at their pleasure. Every so often there was a re-enactment of a shootout on the main street that could be watched from the safety of nearby picnic tables. A short climb up Boot Hill brought us to the famous but very small cemetery. A sign informed visitors that the deceased who had taken up permanent residence there, had been buried with their boots on. Hence the cemetery's name. Over the cemetery fence and across the street awaited the Boot Hill Bed and Breakfast.

A very short walk from the B and B stood the Kansas Teacher's Hall of Fame. This structure had to be the mother lode of teacher's stories and the evening's pastime for Merj, but unfortunately it was closed. The staff must have left at 3:00 and was now home grading papers and doing lesson plans. The same building housed the Gunfighters Wax Museum. Gunfighters and teachers together in the same building was an interesting combination. Maybe Merj's years of complaining about classroom discipline had some basis after all?

Downtown Dodge City was home to a park, with a restored steam locomotive and visitor's center. Nearby was another of the so-called Kansas cathedrals. As an engineer it was easy to wax poetic about the grain elevators and bore anyone unfortunate enough to be within ear shot. Even Merj, though, had to admit that the structures in Dodge City were impressive. Having way too much time available allowed an opportunity to sit on a park bench and count eighty of the cylindrical shaped cells, each probably fifty feet or so high. The concrete complex, operated by the Dodge City Co-Op, was located adjacent to the railroad and was painted a bright white. It dominated the Dodge City skyline. Maybe the grain elevators really were the inspiration behind the castle in the *Wizard of Oz*.

Day 46 - 2213 Miles Down, 1574 To Go

SOME KINDA NUT

After a breakfast of pancakes and juice prepared by Clare and Craig, the B and B owners, it was time to "get outa Dodge." I had waited a week to utter such a humorous comment, so Merj's chuckle was appreciated by her witty husband. Another morning of battling winds began the day as did more fields of corn and wheat and the ever-present feed lots. A large processing plant about five miles out of town may have been the destination for many of the cattle trucks that had contributed to the difficult riding of the last couple of days.

The windy, warm day had begun to raise a concern about a diminishing water supply so a sign welcoming travelers to the town of Mullinville was met with a certain relief. Just outside of town a long line of wind blown "artwork" attached to posts offered a "greeting" to passers by. Craig, at the previous night's bed and breakfast, had spoken of these "whirligigs," as he called the tin signs decorated with pictures and words. The devices were four or five feet high, and spaced every six or seven feet, extending for about a quarter mile. They were attached to their supports in a way that allowed them to spin in the wind. Today's wind had caused them to spin rapidly which exposed a litany of sometimes profane points of view. The creator of this creative expression of free speech had an obvious dislike of certain politicians and showed no reluctance in venting his feelings.

The search for water ended a short time later when an elderly lady, watering the flowers in her front yard, quickly volunteered to fill our water bottles. While chatting in the shade of the front porch, her young great granddaughter played happily at our feet. When asked about the neighbor with the whirligigs, she said he was "some kinda nut." He was apparently intending to run for State Representative, and according to our affable water supplier, had little chance of winning. She had heard that he had been in the Army and surmised the experience may have contributed in some way to his current outlook on life. She was proud of the quality of her water, which was agreed by all to be much better than that found back in Dodge City.

The remainder of the day's ride into Greensburg, Kansas was a continuation of the heat and headwinds of the early morning. Not even the barbed wire had been able to slow down the strong winds of the day. At least it was comforting to know that with the winds a blowin' a storm wasn't a brewin'. Arrival in Greensburg showed a temperature of 96 degrees on the sign in front of the motel.

Conversation in the air conditioned lobby with the husband of the motel owner, an 84 year old World War II veteran, yielded numerous stories of the war and the fact that the largest hand-dug well in the country was located just outside of town. He went on to explain that the well was dug "back in the 1800's" to supply water for the steam locomotives that moved freight and passengers along the nearby railroad. Our usual complaint about the winds was met with, "These ain't nothin', they get a lot worse than this." It was tempting to ask the old fellow when the last time he rode a bike into those nothin' winds was, but a respect for elders rightfully kept the question unasked.

Day 47 - 2261 Miles Down, 1526 To Go

OKAY, THAT'S ENOUGH BUTTERING UP, LARRY

An early start out of Greensburg was met with a relative calm but fear that there may in fact be a storm a brewin'. A stop about eleven miles into the day, in the small town of Haviland at an old fashioned still functioning gas station, was an opportune time to take a break. Larry, a middle age fellow working at the gas station, had just cleaned the restroom and invited a needy Merj to make use of it. Larry was a friendly gentleman, and since there was no one else at the gas station, or for miles around for that matter, he had time to chat. It didn't take long to learn that Larry had been a mechanic for years at the local Chevy garage, and the conversation quickly moved to fond recollection of the Chevys of our youth. He pointed to a sporty well-preserved red '64 Corvair coupe parked along side the garage. I recalled Merj's Corvair for Larry's benefit, and took a photo of the two of them in front of his vehicle.

Next to the gas pumps was an old fashioned washing machine complete with attached wringer. When asked about its function, Larry responded, "We use it for washing rags and chamois." Why it happened to be located between the gas pumps rather than inside the station was a question that went unasked. An old boarded up hotel across the street gave a feeling that Haviland's best days might have been behind it. Larry explained with a certain sadness, "Unless the farmers around here get some rain pretty soon we're in trouble."

He explained that not long ago there had been two schools in Haviland, one public and one private, and that students were split about evenly between both schools. Because of the loss of population, enrollment at the public school had dropped to a level that endangered its funding from the state. To solve the enrollment problem and maintain funding, the town was forced to close the private school and eliminate it as an option. It was an unfortunate story that could have been repeated in many of the small towns in western Kansas.

Larry showed a lot of curiosity about the bike trip and talked of being an avid cyclist himself before a successful battle against prostate cancer slowed him down a few years ago. He expressed a concern about safety and his concern prompted stories of the cattle trucks of the last few days. "Jeez I hate to be nosey," he asked, "but have you had any flat tires?" When told there had been two flats, both of them on my bike, he winked at Merj and said, "That's because he's much heavier than you." With another wink he admitted, "I'm just trying to get some brownie points."

Not wanting to lose the decent riding conditions, it was time to bid Larry a fond farewell and head out. New companions joined the trip about twenty miles into the day in the form of hundreds of grasshoppers. When alerted by the passing bicycles, the insects would jump a foot or two into the air. Their jumping height was just high enough to bounce off our bare legs and make a pinging sound as they made contact with the spokes. One of them jumped high enough to make a noticeable sound bouncing off Merj's plastic helmet. Merj's snake-in-the-spokes fear apparently didn't translate to grasshoppers. The grasshoppers soon diminished and a modern home with a nearby garage appeared a short distance later. Normally these things would have been unremarkable, but the garage not only had a car parked inside of it, but an airplane with its wings fully extended as well.

The small community of Pratt, home to 3,600 people, provided a chance for a mid-morning break. A sign announced that the town was the home of the Miss Kansas Pageant and that three Miss USA candidates had come from Pratt. The residential area of town was composed of neatly maintained homes and the business district showed some relative prosperity. A large, red brick Methodist Church with a white steeple on top completed an all-American feeling in Pratt. The fact that the Miss Kansas pageant was held there wasn't surprising.

Pratt didn't qualify as a big time city though; it didn't have a Wal Mart. Passing through one small town after another had caused a pattern to emerge. Although Wal Marts may have been a sign of a city's commercial status, they also seemed to be a contributor to the demise of many of the small downtown areas. The pricing and large variety of goods available under one very large roof made the family-run businesses that traditionally occupied Main Street uncompetitive. Maybe it was purely coincidental, but no visible Wal Mart in Pratt along with a functioning downtown area seemed to give validity to the theory.

Although jumping grasshoppers and increasing temperatures continued to be annoying diversions, that were more than offset by the general friendliness of the motorists of Kansas. More so than previous states, the people of Kansas expressed their encouragement by a short blast of their vehicle horns, a smile, and wave. Sometimes the horn was a wake up call from of a cycling daze and sometimes the wave was no more than the raising of an index finger off the steering wheel. Regardless, their friendly gestures were always appreciated. On today's ride a convoy of school busses passed going the opposite direction, and, almost without exception, acknowledged our presence with a Kansas one finger wave.

A stop for rest about eight miles out of town at 90th Avenue gave more reasons for questions that would likely never be answered. The street numbers had been steadily increasing since leaving Pratt, but there had been very few signs of human habitation anywhere for the last seven miles. The streets, much like those back in Jeffrey City, went nowhere, but unlike Jeffrey City, these *never* went anywhere. At 90th Avenue there were no signs of development of any kind. Evidently the city planners in Pratt had anticipated significant future urban sprawl. Urbanization of 90th Avenue was likely a few millennia away.

The road east of Pratt included some ups and downs over the sand hills of the Great Plains. Merj summarized her disappointment, mumbling, "This wasn't on the agenda for today." After one fairly good climb by Kansas standards, a stop at the top gave an opportunity to unofficially designate it as Pratt Pass. The day's ride also gave evidence to an animal native to the area which we had not yet seen; we came across our first armadillo road kill. Having a good basis of comparison from previous road kill, it could be said that the armadillo represented the ugliest of the hundreds of dead critters that had decorated the roadway shoulders. Alive, armadillos are far from attractive; suffice it to say, being dead did nothing to enhance their already much diminished natural beauty.

HEY MR. CARNEGIE, CAN YOU SPARE A DIME?

The day had turned clear and very warm, and the small town of Cunningham provided an opportunity for a break. While waiting for Merj outside a mini-mart, an older fellow approached with his wife and, clearly not wanting to be intrusive, politely asked about the bikes and the trip. The couple was from Arkansas and a trailer behind their truck had obviously been serving as their lodging as they toured the West. They were fascinated by the trip. "Never met anybody doing something so crazy," they said. When asked why the people of this part of the country insisted on calling the nearby river the "Ark-Kansas," he laughed. "They don't want anything to do with Arkansaw." Our list of Arkansas acquaintances continued to grow by leaps and bounds. The friendly gentleman had been a truck driver for 32 years and asked about our experiences with truckers. When assured that most of them had been very accommodating, he said, "Well, there still are some very good people out there." It was hard to disagree.

Outside Cunningham, the surrounding landscape began to turn greener and was occasionally interrupted by clumps of welcomed shade trees. The rustling of the leaves on the trees and the presence of a small lake every once in a while gave the area a feeling much like that of home. A small group of horses grazing near the road represented the first animals for miles that had not been restricted by the fences of a feed lot. After a day that included sixty-five miles of hot, windy cycling, the corporate limit of Kingman, Kansas was a welcomed sight.

Kingman, much like Pratt, was a community with a well-maintained downtown area. The functioning, comparatively prosperous small Kansas towns that had been part of the last half of the day's ride were a pleasant change from the near ghost towns that had become all too common. The Kingman library offered a chance to research the road ahead and catch up on e-mails.

A very helpful librarian by the name of Linda assisted setting me up on the computer for e-mailing. Linda also spent a considerable amount of time working at the copy machine trying to get useable copies of maps for the days ahead. Through no fault of her own, it took a number of copies to get the areas mapped that were needed. When it came time to pay the ten cents per copy for our work, she was careful not to charge for the trial copies that had been wasted. When given a dollar, she even refused to keep the dime left over from the nine copies. No amount of arguing was going to get her to change her mind, as she kept repeating, "No, no, no that just isn't right and I'm not going to do it." Linda represented an old-fashioned honesty and sense of fairness that was becoming more common than not with the folks of the West and Midwest. It would not have been a surprise if she, like Tom Kelsay, had produced a business card that stated, "Honest Linda, Librarian." Again, the adjective would not have been necessary.

Linda explained that the library in Kingman was a Carnegie Library and got its designation as a result of money donated by industrialist Andrew Carnegie for its construction in the early

1900's. Andrew Carnegie, a highly successful businessman of the late 1800's, built a fortune in the steel industry. In 1901 he sold his Carnegie Steel Company for 250 million dollars, then and now, a huge sum of money. Carnegie then retired and devoted the remainder of his life to philanthropic activities. Prior to his retirement he had written an essay entitled "The Gospel of Wealth," in which he stated that wealthy men should live without extravagance, provide moderately for their dependents, and distribute the rest of their riches to benefit the welfare and happiness of the common man — with the stipulation to help only those who would help themselves. One of the areas specified for donation was public libraries. Carnegie believed education was the means to improve people's lives and libraries provided one of the main tools to help Americans build a better future. Before his death in 1919, at the age of 84, Andrew Carnegie had allegedly given away ninety percent of his wealth to charitable causes.

The library in Kingman was one of 1,679 new library buildings in communities large and small throughout the country that received a portion of the forty million dollars that Carnegie donated to libraries. To receive funding for a library, a community simply had to supply the land for the new building and funds for operating costs. Fifty-five Carnegie Libraries were eventually built in Kansas. Some have been razed, but many, like Kingman's, still serve as libraries. Many more serve as community centers, museums, office buildings, or restaurants.

Day 48 - 2331 Miles Down, 1456 To Go

A BIT OF KANSAS LUXURY

The road out of Kingman toward Wichita was one that had been a worry because of expected congestion in the metropolitan area.

To avoid the heaviest traffic, we planned a route using Linda's maps that would avoid most of the busiest areas. The route swung eastward along very lightly traveled roads bordered by alfalfa and occasional farmhouses. The bright red sunrise and the pleasant smells of the freshly cut alfalfa made the early morning ride one of the more enjoyable of the trip. The rural images that I had formed in my mind some time ago, were finally being played out on this warm morning in central Kansas.

The countdown to Wichita began at 375th Street, and much like Pratt, there was nothing around of note. The smooth, easy cycling continued along recently plowed rich farmland with occasional small rural roads crossing at right angles. About fifteen miles after crossing 375th Street a sign welcomed travelers to Wichita and the immediate beginning of commercial development. After thirteen more miles of cycling, some of which put us onto city streets with heavy traffic, the night's lodging at the Castle at Riverside came into view.

Wichita, Kansas was named for the Wichita Indians, the first inhabitants of the area. The town was first plotted in 1865 and "busted-wide-open" when the Santa Fe Railroad arrived in 1872. Originally a cow-town, Wichita in the 1890's became a trading and milling center. In the early 1900's the population of Wichita nearly doubled when a large reservoir of oil was discovered nearby. In 1925 Walter "Hamburger King" Anderson, one of the founders of White Castle Restaurants bought his first one in Wichita with a loan of $60. Anyone familiar with a White Castle "Slider" had to be forever grateful to Walter for bringing such pleasures to the American dining public. Anyone familiar with a Slider also remembers that it took at least six or eight of the microscopic burgers to properly satisfy an appetite.

In the 1920's a group of Wichita businessmen put much effort into attracting the aircraft industry to town. Their efforts were amply rewarded; over the years, such major manufacturers as Learjet, Cessna, and Beechcraft built major facilities in the

Wichita area. Maybe it was more than the efforts of the business-men though. The organization, Wings Over Kansas, gives a por-tion of the credit to the Kansas described in an anonymous quote. "Kansas sometimes seems to have more sky than ground. So much sky that people walk outside and naturally look up. So much sky that it seems at times to overtake the ground. So much sky that it almost seems to invite dreamers and explorers to test the limits."

Today Wichita is home to more than 330,000 people, and is the largest city in the state. With a total metropolitan population of 550,000, about one in five Kansans live in the Greater Wichita area. Downtown Wichita has the state's highest buildings and the largest industries in Kansas.

The evening's lodging, The Castle at Riverside, was located within a residential section of the city along the Little Arkansas River. The Castle represented a luxurious departure from the many ho-hum motels that had been the norm. Col. Burton Harvey Campbell, one of Wichita's wealthiest residents, built the castle from 1886 to 1888 for $80,000. The structure was pur-chased for $300,000 in 1994 by native Wichitans, Dr. and Mrs. Perry Lowery, who then spent two million dollars restoring it to its original splendor. The interior of the castle included a 250-year-old staircase imported from England, a 650-year-old Grecian fireplace and a parquet parlor floor consisting of four dif-ferent types of wood. Many of the twenty-eight rooms, including ours, were equipped with large luxurious bathrooms, in room Jacuzzis and fireplaces, and all the latest electronic niceties. A bal-cony off the room looked out on the nearby Little Arkansas River.

The Castle hostess suggested a nearby tearoom named the Riverside Cup of Tea for a late lunch. A short walk in 100 degree heat had us in front of a very amiable elderly hostess who sug-gested a seat on a comfortable sofa while the table was being read-ied. Sitting in the nicely appointed parlor in wrinkled shorts and tee shirts made us feel very much out of place. The other people in the parlor and the dining room were nicely attired; many of them adorned in hats that looked as though the Easter parade had just finished outside. Of the thirty or so people in the restaurant, many engrossed in serious discussions of the state of society in Wichita, there was not a single man.

A trip back to the hostess desk to question whether our attire was appropriate, and whether men were in fact welcome, produced a laughing response. "Of course you are!" My suggestion that a flashing neon Bud Light sign might increase the male customer base was met with the same good-natured laugh. The table was finally prepared and the young lady who owned the tearoom escorted the only male in sight and his wife to a table near the kitchen. The walk to the table past the ladies in their expensive headwear had a feeling somewhat akin to being seated in the restaurant back in Syracuse. Inquiring eyes lifted from their food and wondered about this interloper with the disheveled look, invading their lair. In spite of the paranoia, as the only rooster in the hen house, I was treated very well. Our lunch of a turkey sandwich with bread pudding for desert was reasonably priced and quite tasty.

An afternoon of sitting in the comfortably air-conditioned parlor at the Castle eating pistachios and listening to classical music was a bit disorienting. The radical change from the previous night's stay in Kingman with a gang of construction workers blasting country music was a little difficult to adjust to. As the hostess spread out a late afternoon table of wine and cheese, it became clear that adjusting to the differences in atmosphere over twenty-four hours would be made much easier.

Not wanting to miss any of the ambiance of Wichita, the accommodating hostess arranged for a cab trip to downtown. The cabby showed up in a beat up Oldsmobile and after a meandering ride that seemed much longer than it should have, he deposited his wide-eyed patrons in a restored entertainment district called Old Town. During the ride the cabby talked about his hobby of rock climbing and repelling. Although a cordial fellow, his driving and general conversation showed that an unfortunate fall on his head might have been part of a past climb.

The Old Town section of Wichita was a nicely restored area of brick buildings and wide walkways that had a comfortable, safe feeling. Unfortunately arriving after 6:00 PM meant that most of the restaurants in Old Town were already closed. The Old Town Brewery, a brewpub with their own home brewed beer selection, was open. While enjoying an especially good raspberry wheat beer and looking around the pub, it appeared the presence of a couple of cross-country cyclists significantly raised the average age of the patrons. On the positive side, wrinkled shorts and tee shirts fit in much better there than in the tearoom, and the ratio was about 50/50 male and female.

The ride back to the Castle was courtesy of the same cabby. It was quite possible that on a typical weekday evening in Wichita, there was only one cab on duty in the entire city. The return trip was along a different and even longer route than the earlier one. This guy obviously had time on his hands and needed the fare. The amenities of the Castle were waiting, including a long spell in the swirling, warm water of the Jacuzzi. It was difficult to imagine that the next day would include a ride back to the reality of basic lodging in rural Kansas!

Day 49 - 2382 Miles Down, 1405 To Go

NOT HAPPY UNLESS THERE'S SOMETHING TO COMPLAIN ABOUT

Based on the descriptions from locals of areas to avoid and traffic congestion, the ride out of Wichita was expected to be troublesome. Combining the information on local maps, along with the input of the Castle's hostess, resulted in a route that avoided those areas, but required riding through the center of downtown. The ride was also somewhat complicated as we began later than normal in order to enjoy the hearty breakfast of blueberry pancakes and fresh fruit that was part of a stay at the Castle.

The temperature was already in the high seventies and there wasn't a cloud in the sky as the day began. Today's high temperature was predicted to be a worrisome 105 degrees. It became apparent that it was going to be stifling, as the cycling through the modern buildings of downtown blocked any breeze. Bicycling in Kansas is perfect for anyone who enjoys complaining about things they can't control. If the wind was too strong, the cycling was too tough. If the wind died, the weather was too hot. Fodder for complaining was never hard for us to find.

The ride through the downtown business district soon transitioned into a more residential and commercial suburban area. About thirteen miles into the day, after crossing a railroad track, the city ended and the rural countryside of yesterday morning picked up again. It was as if the railroad had produced some sort of invisible barrier separating the city folk from the country folk. Unfortunately a delayed restroom break for Merj now meant there was no "cover" and a bit of tension began to build within our small eastward bound bicycle caravan.

Stopping a few very warm miles later in the small town of Benton offered an opportunity to relive those tensions and to chat with a curious older local by the name of George. George, clad in a sweat stained baseball cap and standing next to a well used pickup, had time on his hands and wanted to talk. He was truly a local. "Me and my four brothers were born here and we've lived within five miles of Benton ever since," George said. Although now retired, he had previously worked on local farms and for an area fertilizer company. When asked, George explained that the crops along the road west of Wichita were not maize, but were in fact milo. Milo, much like maize, was a plant that resembled corn but grew to a lesser height and was used as livestock feed. He laughed when I told him that a few days ago we thought that it might be sugar cane. In his mind he was likely thinking, who are these people? They wouldn't know the difference between a potato and a pineapple! He was probably right.

George went on to explain that the area around Benton used to look much like the classic farm image of Kansas. In the not too distant past, a local farm occupied a quarter section, an area of 160 acres, and consisted of a farmhouse, a barn, and acres of cropland. That image, according to George, was long gone. To be profitable now, "A farmer needs 3,000 acres or more and a lot of money to buy equipment," said George. "A lot of the farmers around here grow sunflowers for their seeds and oil. A lot of 'em are startin' to grow cotton now too."

The uncomfortable warmth of the morning was making it necessary to think about getting back on the bikes. I had to ask George about the Kansas winds. "This has been one of the least windiest summers in recent times," he told us. Our complaining about the weather of Kansas was obviously falling on deaf ears. In the minds of locals, this was an absolutely glorious summer for which anyone experiencing it should be eternally grateful. It was probably time to abandon the search for someone with a more sympathetic ear.

As temperatures in the evening's stopping point of El Dorado reached 104 degrees, buying a newspaper and an afternoon of relaxation were in order. The local paper, *The El Dorado Times*, offered an interesting snapshot of life in eastern Kansas. The newspaper told of a local event, The Prairie Port Festival, that would be the main entertainment in town over the coming weekend. As part of the festival, a queen had been crowned, and she and two of her attendants happily appeared on the front page of the paper. It was the type of photograph they would likely share proudly with their children and grandchildren in years to come.

The paper told of a medallion that had been hidden somewhere in town as part of the festival. Each day another clue about its location was published. The lady who had found this year's medallion was also prominently displayed on the front page of the paper. Her happiness was enhanced by a $150 prize. Between the images and articles in the local newspaper, and the friendly offer by the owner of a local bakery to make fresh cinnamon rolls for our early morning departure, the comfortable feeling of Midwestern America had found its way to El Dorado, Kansas.

Day 50 - 2417 Miles Down, 1370 To Go

ARE Y'ALL FROM MISSISSIPPI?

Leaving El Dorado required a three-mile ride through well-kept residential and commercial development. Downtown El Dorado was a well-done mixture of old and new, complete with brick sidewalks and old style street lamps. Beautiful large brick churches were frequent sights in this city of 12,000. A race was being organized in front of the local hospital, and runners with numbers pinned on their shirts lined the street stretching in preparation to begin the race. A small carnival, including a Ferris wheel and merry-go-round, was being set up in the parking lot of a shopping center.

On the eastern side of town, the Kansas Oil Museum, complete with a couple of old oil derricks, was getting ready to welcome visitors for the day. The people of El Dorado seemed to have a pride in their community and, as a result, were taking good care of it. The comfortable feeling of last night continued to grow. Had a backyard baseball game broken out, or had the aroma of fresh apple pie filled the air, the Norman Rockwell image of Americana would have been complete. Later learning that *Beetle Bailey* cartoonist, Mort Walker, grew up in El Dorado didn't come as a surprise.

Back in Benton, George had talked of the Flint Hills east of El Dorado, and at about fifteen miles out of town they began. The landscape consisted of clumps of trees that abruptly ended at a barbed wire fence to be replaced by fields of blue stem grass as far as the eye could see. The fields resembled a stretched bed spread with that occasional wrinkle, usually present on those occasions when the male half of the bicycling team made the bed. A passing lane appeared and thoughts of long climbs in Colorado flashed through our minds. We quickly remembered that this was Kansas and *not* Colorado, and our dread quickly disappeared. It was the first time since leaving Pueblo that we reached speeds of over thirty miles per hour. Ah, the simple pleasures of riding down from a "Kansas summit."

The evening was spent in Eureka at a motel in front of Eureka Downs, a large horse race track. Unfortunately a visit to the track was not possible as its season only ran from May until July. Norm, the co-owner of the motel, showed Merj a couple of rooms, and after long and painful contemplation, she picked one. Probably because there didn't appear to be any other prospective paying customers in sight, Norm was remarkably patient with us. To the untrained eye, the selected room looked remarkably like the two rejected ones. Apparently there is something to motel room selection that females know and males do not.

Norm went on to explain that most of the people around Eureka worked in the farming or oil industries. The Kansas Oil Museum back in El Dorado was testament to the importance of oil to the area, although no evidence of oil pumping activities were seen during the day's ride. He went on to say that the young people of Eureka, "Get their education and leave town because there's nothin' for them to do here." When asked about local restaurants, he suggested a small downtown restaurant called The Paddock for lunch. It seemed that the horse racing theme was very much alive in Eureka.

The Paddock was a typical Main Street, small-town restaurant that had become commonplace during the trip. While talking to the waitress about the location of a library, a friendly lady at the neighboring table indicated that she was the town's librarian. She patiently gave instructions on how to find the nearby library and headed back to work. Not long after, tired but well-fed, we followed her.

Upon entering the small, brick library, it became obvious that it was another of the Carnegie libraries that were becoming common in Kansas. The librarian and a friend were waiting behind the check-out desk and immediately began a guessing contest as to where we were from based on our "accents." When they asked for a few more words to give them a clue, I was tempted to doctor my "accent" and maybe get an answer like Mississippi, but ultimately rejected the notion. After our dutiful recitation of the Gettysburg Address or some such thing, and intense pondering, the librarian confidently ventured, "It's Wisconsin." When told that Wisconsin was not the correct answer, her friend, after serious contemplation, said, "Then it's Michigan." "Still not right but getting warmer," I said. Finally, in unison, they both guessed Ohio. The friend had grown up in Columbus, Ohio and felt that had given him the edge in guessing the origin of our so-called accents. It was tempting to tell him the people of Columbus don't even talk the same as the people from Cleveland, and, regardless, who said Ohioans had accents anyhow?

While the librarian helpfully connected us to the Internet, a young woman walked into the building with a pleased look on her face. The librarian recognized her as a regular and asked, "How's everything going?" The young lady seemed especially happy responding, "Things are goin' great." She revealed the source of her pleasure, exposing a two-day-old tattoo on her ankle. She was somewhat large to begin with and the swollen, tattooed ankle made her leg look a bit like the trunk of an elm tree. While the four of us profusely complimented her over the beauty of the ankle artwork, she casually unbuttoned the top couple buttons on her shirt and displayed a tattoo from an earlier time. After showing her body art, the newly tattooed library patron headed out the door with nary a book in tow

Back at the hotel, Norm offered assistance in planning the next day's ride while we continued to complain about the now 97 degree heat. Norm was a pretty good-sized fellow and sympathized, "A brisk north wind would be what it takes to cool off fat people like me on a day like this." When asked about the increasingly frequent number of dead armadillos on the shoulders, Norm told us, "They migrated north from Texas and Oklahoma over the last ten years." Armadillos seemed to be a creature in search of a useful niche in the overall scheme of things. Their migration north could not have been welcomed. Where was the Kansas Immigration and Nationalization Service when it was most needed?

Day 51 - 2454 Miles Down, 1333 To Go

ARE WE THERE YET?

Because of another predicted warm day, the ride out of Eureka had a clandestine feel as it began at 5:45 under the cover of darkness. The riding was comfortable with mostly gentle ups and downs along expansive grassy plains. Occasionally a small herd of cattle, startled by our presence, stampeded away from the highway. The eastward progress was evident by a steady increase in the humidity of the air. It seemed to become ever more apparent on this warm morning as perspiration began to flow freely.

About twenty miles into the morning, an "oasis" on the Kansas plains appeared in the form of the Lizard Lips Grille and Deli. While leisurely enjoying a mid morning break outside the deli, a family of cyclists rolled in and parked their bikes along the side of the deli. The family consisted of a husband, wife, and two teenage daughters, none of whom looked very happy. Their chosen transportation was one tandem and two single bicycles. "We started in Washington D. C. and we're hoping to get as far as Montana," the father volunteered.

The mother walked with a noticeable limp and complained of a very painful knee. Although the original plan was to cross the whole country, the knee problem, plus the girls' need to get back home for school would make it impossible to complete the entire trip. There was real concern by the mother as to how far she would even be able to go during this day, so she asked many questions about the road ahead.

The father was a fit looking individual probably in his early forties. The girls were obviously disinterested, and appeared to be searching for a telephone to call their friends back home to find out who had broken up with whom. Anyone who has raised two daughters through their teen years, could easily translate the looks on their faces. I could see the predictable question forming, "Are we there yet?" The poor father had placed himself in a difficult situation. He was faced with two daughters who looked as though they would like to take the next train home, and a wife with a knee that was killing her. To make matters worse, the bike trip was probably his idea.

It was tough not to sympathize with the father. It was very possible that he too had a long held desire to complete a cross-country bike trip. He likely convinced his wife and kids that the idea of bicycle touring would be a good way to see the country and enjoy quality time together. The trip started with great expectations, but as time went on it became clear that reaching the West Coast would not be possible, so Montana would have to do. Now as his family looked at him as though they were on the *Bounty* and he was Captain Blye, there was a feeling of mutiny in the air. This poor fellow was going to need his best negotiating skills to keep the group heading west. It felt good to know that Merj not only volunteered for our trip, but was also an infrequent complainer and almost always maintained a happy outlook. The things that she found to gripe about were usually the same things that I found worthy of a complaint. The look of frustration on the father's face made me feel bad for him, but lucky for our own good fortunes.

The small town of Yates Center was the location of a restaurant that pretrip research had suggested was worth a special visit. The restaurant was called Frannie's and was owned and operated by an elderly lady who served good, old-fashioned food at equally old-fashioned prices. Maybe it was because of the magazine description of the restaurant, but Yates Center had become another of those small rural towns that had formed a mental image. Preconceived notions were quickly dashed, as a string of junkyards became the first impressions of the town. To make matters worse, it was soon discovered that the restaurant wasn't open. A faux Egg McMuffin at a mini-mart would have to do.

The legendary winds of Kansas awaited us on the ride due south out of Yates Center. The winds, steady at twenty to twenty-five miles per hour and gusting to thirty-five miles per hour, came directly at us and can only be described as absolutely brutal. No type of drafting technique worked. Gutting it out became the only option. I began to feel like the poor fellow with his disgruntled family back at the Lizard Lips Grille and Deli. After thirty-two years of marriage, it was not necessary to exchange a lot of verbiage to understand the true feelings of one's spouse. The body language of the fairer member of our cycling duo expressed a certain degree of dismay at being where she was and doing what she was doing. It was hard to disagree though; these winds were difficult to negotiate. Fortunately, after fifteen miles or so, the route turned east toward the evening's destination of Chanute and the brisk head winds, thankfully, turned into more easily negotiated cross winds.

Day 52 - 2516 Miles Down, 1271 To Go

FASTER, MERJ, FASTER!

The ride out of Chanute began under uncharacteristically cloudy skies and cooler temperatures. It had rained during the night and the fresh smells of the morning were a delightful change from those that had become customary. A short time after beginning the day, more of the small farm images of Kansas began appearing. It was about time. This was our last full day in Kansas. The small amount of traffic allowed for comfortable side by side riding and a much-improved attitude when compared to yesterday's wind blown afternoon. A small clump of trees afforded an opportunity for the morning's restroom break. Unfortunately the noises created by a short trip into the trees was just enough to wake every dog in the area. A barking Jack Russell Terrier with his eyes trained firmly on two sets of bare legs caused a quicker than planned exit from the seclusion of the grove of trees.

The Jack Russell was the first of a few dogs that decided to give chase on this otherwise easy cycling morning. The usual tactic in dealing with dogs was to ready the dog spray in one hand and pedal like crazy to try to outrun the barking pursuer. If the dog was able to catch us, a last defense before resorting to the spray was a sharp yell to "go home!" Usually one or the other worked well. A short distance after encountering the yipping Jack Russell, the out-run-them method was severely tested as a long-legged whippet charged out of his yard directly at us. The whippet is a close relative of the greyhound, and it is a virtual impossibility to outrun them. This one, however, with his tail wagging vigorously, looked at the two of us as objects of playful entertainment. After a quarter mile or so, he realized that the people on the bikes weren't giving him much of a workout, so he turned and ambled back home. It was clear, though, that dogs were becoming a more frequent problem.

At mid-morning a kindly older fellow pulled up along side in a Chevy El Camino and asked, "Are you guys lost?" After convincing him, and also ourselves to a certain extent, that this road was part of the planned route, he chuckled and said, "Well take 'er easy," and rattled away in his old vehicle. The El Camino should have been designated the Kansas state vehicle. It's a combination of car and truck that ceased production in the 70's, but had found resurrection in Kansas. There were way more of them than there should have been.

The stereotypical images of Kansas continued toward Pittsburg through gently rolling countryside with wide expanses of corn, milo, and beans that were occasionally interrupted by white farmhouses. A noisy flock of chickens in front of one of the houses added to the images of the day. A stop in the small town of Walnut provided an opportunity for a mid-morning break at another gas station. This one also advertised boots and saddles for sale. Main Street in Walnut consisted of a number of pickup trucks parked in front of a mixture of abandoned and occupied storefronts. It was a scene that had been repeated in many earlier small towns.

Pittsburg, without the *h*, Kansas would be the evening's destination and the last night spent in the state. Pittsburg was the largest town since Wichita and came with all the amenities necessary to satisfy most any weary cyclist, save one. After rejection of the offerings of two national hotel chains, Merj finally found one to her liking. Going from hotel to hotel is problematic enough in a car, but doing it on a bicycle along a busy four-lane commercial street is a bit more of a challenge. But patience and meeting challenges were what had gotten us this far, so a seemingly endless quest for the perfect hotel was a challenge we could meet. The lack of lodging options in the tiny rural towns along the way had resulted in more than a few sub-par accommodations. Merj's opportunity to actually choose between multiple hotels, any of which would have been acceptable, was probably her way of exorcising some of those lodging memories.

Kansas had been a state that in many ways lived up to its advance billing, although it took a while. Western Kansas had been one cattle truck adventure after another, along with the unmistakable odors announcing each upcoming feed lot. The central part of the state represented a little more of the traditional image of Kansas, but not quite. The area east of Wichita began to present itself as the "real" Kansas we had envisioned.

Throughout the state, the people were invariably friendly and helpful. Some like Honest Tom and Linda the Librarian were confirmation of solid Midwestern values. Gestures from the horn honking index finger waving motorists seemed genuine and were appreciated. The winds, although allegedly less than normal, were at times a challenge. That was to be expected, and in retrospect, they could have been a lot worse.

Day 53 - 2575 Miles Down, 1212 To Go

missouri

"I just want to get to heaven."

SHOW ME THE FOG

After all the one-stoplight towns, Pittsburg was a veritable metropolis. Riding through downtown required negotiating at least a *dozen* stoplights. A low fog created an eerie halo around street lights and added a different dimension to the early morning ride. The fog thickened east of Pittsburg and created visibility problems for passing motorists, but also some interesting photographic opportunities. A snapshot of Merj on a bicycle disappearing into pea-soup fog had a certain surrealistic look. It was quite possible that disappearing was something that had crossed her mind during the climbs back in the Rockies.

Not far out of town, in a fog that was now very thick, a large sign presented itself and proclaimed: WELCOME TO MISSOURI

THE SHOW ME STATE. Missouri was state number six and a real feeling of progress toward the Atlantic took hold of us. After all, the Mississippi River was only a state away, and everyone knew the East started there.

Another measure of our progress was the daily edition of *USA TODAY*. The recent series of larger towns had meant that the paper was available on a regular basis. On the last page of the first section of the paper a large colorful weather map showed the day's weather forecast throughout the country. Not only did the map offer an unfortunately repetitious red coloration indicating high temperatures for the next day's ride, but also a visual measurement of our progress. Looking at the map each day allowed a comparison of how much had been covered and how much lay ahead. The *USA TODAY* map had begun to show us that there was clearly less in front of the bikes than behind them.

Through the thick fog and across the road from the welcome sign, the faint glow of a large illuminated gas station sign appeared. Inside the gas station a group of mailmen sat under a cloud of cigarette smoke drinking their morning coffee. The mail delivery would have to wait until this morning ritual had run its course. The talkative, animated fellows immediately recognized that we did not live on their postal routes, and the questioning began. It was always enjoyable to talk about our experiences, and most people seemed genuinely interested. These postmen were no different, in fact, they were especially inquisitive. After answering their questions, it was time to ask our new acquaintances a question of our own: What was the story behind Missouri's Show Me State motto?

Unfortunately they had no idea, but some help from the State of Missouri produced two versions. The most widely accepted involved a Missouri U. S. Congressman named William Duncan Vandiver who served in the House from 1897 to 1903. While giving a speech at a naval banquet in 1899 he stated, "I come from a state that raises corn and cotton and cockleburs and Democrats, and frothy eloquence neither convinces nor satisfies me. I am from Missouri. You have got to show me."

The other version had the motto originating in the mining town of Leadville, Colorado. During a miner's strike in the mid 1890's, a number of lead miners from southwest Missouri were imported to replace the strikers. The new miners were unfamiliar with the mining techniques in Colorado and required frequent instruction. Their bosses began saying, "That man is from Missouri. You'll have to show him."

Not phased by their lack of Missouri history, the postmen poured another cup of coffee and appeared to be settling in for the morning. In our case, though, the fog outside beckoned, and it was time to get back on the road. Before getting on the bikes, however, tire inflation concerns caused a search for an air pump and a couple of quarters. After a quick search, an air hose appeared hanging on a hook just around the corner of the garage. Further examination showed that the quarters wouldn't be needed; the air was FREE. The State of Missouri was already turning into a pleasant experience.

The Welcome to Missouri sign was still shrouded in fog, but that didn't prevent our ritualistic state line photographs. The deed done, it was time to ride on toward the Mississippi River. The surrealistic feeling created by the foggy conditions, along with the free air that had fully inflated my bike tires and spirits, made for an enjoyable ride.

Fields of corn, milo, and soybeans, barely visible through the fog, gave Missouri more of a Kansas look than Kansas. Had it not been for a friendly fellow who worked for the Missouri Department of Animal Services, the soybeans probably would have been identified as lima beans or baked beans or some other erroneous bean. The ever-thickening fog had made everything wet and water dripped in a steady stream off the front of our helmets. On this first morning in Missouri, rolling terrain with an increasing number of ups and downs greeted us through the fog.

Merj had developed a technique of dealing with the rolling roadway that consisted of pedaling furiously on the last portion of the downhill and using the momentum to help carry her uphill. She called the technique "blasting," and generally it worked quite well. The morning fog prevented us from seeing what lie ahead, so much of the blasting was guesswork.

Many of the rural roads in Missouri had been given letter rather than numerical designations. Much of the day's ride was on a road identified as "A" with intersecting roads designated as "M," "J," "O," and "JJ." Apparently when the number of roads exceeded the twenty-six letters of the alphabet, it was necessary to name additional ones with doubled letters. Since there were likely a great many roads waiting, was there a JJJ Road or maybe even a JJJJ Road ahead? We occasionally used to call our daughter Jennifer JJ, so we stopped to take a picture of the sign as the fog began to lift.

"ONCE YOU'VE MADE IT THROUGH KANSAS YOU'VE GOT IT LICKED."

At about thirty miles into Missouri, a sign welcomed travelers to Golden City, Population 804. Golden City was a small, two-stoplight town with the usual collection of downtown businesses. A Main Street favorite of the locals called Cooky's Café offered an opportunity for a mid-morning break. Cooky's was a classic small town restaurant that consisted of a long counter, a variety of tables and booths, and a glass enclosure holding the day's assortment of fresh pies. There was a certain tension among the staff at Cooky's on this particular day as a health inspector had chosen the restaurant for an inspection.

A local fellow, seeing that we were cyclists, stopped by our table to chat. He was a former cyclist himself, and had set up a hostel near town to assist cyclists or other travelers passing through the area. He proceeded to inform us, "I had a young couple on bikes stop at the hostel two days ago. When they got here, the woman was suffering from heat exhaustion and had to be flown home." The look on Merj's face showed considerable dismay as she listened to the woes of a fallen female comrade. He went on to offer encouragement, though, by assuring her, "Once you've made it through Kansas, you've got it licked." If that was true we asked, why did other touring cyclists refer to Missouri as Misery?

Another local cyclist joined the conversation and explained it to us. "The rest of your day will be through the Ozark Plateau, and you've got a few ups and downs before you get to Ash Grove. But," he further explained, "the Ozark Mountains will give you some challenges." The happy, relieved look resulting from "Once you've made it through Kansas you've got it licked," to the much different look Merj gave upon hearing, "The Ozark Mountains will give you some challenges," made for yet another noticeable emotional contrast.

Heading out of Golden City, the fog lifted and the sun and humidity were beginning to make the morning's ride a bit more uncomfortable. An aromatic vegetable like smell greeted us about eight miles out of Golden City. A short time later a field of cucumbers came into view. A woman had stopped her car along the road and was scavenging the few vegetables that were left in the recently harvested field. A strange looking machine, presumably the one used for picking the cucumbers, sat parked behind a tractor next to the road. A John Deere farm implement store a short time later provided a lot full of interesting, but unrecognizable, farm machinery.

It was always interesting to see the odd looking machinery that had been invented over the years to perform specific farming tasks. As strange as it may sound to a "normal" traveler, the impressive string of farm machinery displayed along the side of the road at the John Deere store gave reason for a panoramic photograph. Other than the "scenic" feedlot back in Kansas, it was the first time we had used the panoramic camera setting since the mountains of Colorado. Who would have guessed that a photo of strange looking machinery would have been the reason for a panoramic memory?

The picturesque farm machinery was soon replaced by more rolling hills and the approach of two westbound cyclists. Upon seeing us, they stopped their heavily loaded bikes and waited for our approach. After the exchange of a few brief words of introduction, it became obvious from their accents that this duo consisting of an older gentleman and his middle age son were not from "these here parts." They soon explained that they were in fact from the Netherlands and were cycling from Washington, DC to Denver.

A few years ago the two of them had biked from the West Coast to Denver before the son had to return to Europe. This trip was to be a cross-country completion of that one. They talked of doing other long trips together in the USA including one in Alaska. Of all the bicycle trips that they had done, New Zealand was the country that had most impressed them. They were friendly and enthusiastic and obviously enjoyed each other's company. The father, a 66-year-old, looked fit and not a day over 65.

This cordial father and son team talked of upcoming steep climbs in the Ozarks and of the very friendly people they had met while getting this far. In one small town a few days earlier, a bank had invited them in for coffee and toast. The teller then called a local newspaper that came out to the bank to interview them for a story. The fact that neither one of them was wearing a helmet prompted a question. "Helmets aren't used in the Netherlands," they laughed. We light heartedly responded, "Yeah, but you're not in the Netherlands." They shrugged, as if to say, "So what?" The friendly twosome asked the standard questions about hills ahead and we told them the hills were gentle rollers. The look of relief in their eyes should have been an indicator of what awaited us.

FIRST BATH IN THIRTY YEARS

The morning was becoming increasingly warm and all four of us realized it was time to get going again. In parting, the subject came up of an earlier Dutch cross-country cycling couple that had been encountered back in Wyoming. They responded that the Dutch are a bicycling people. We responded that, with all of the Dutch in the United States this summer, there couldn't be that many left back in the Netherlands. They politely laughed at our awkward attempt at international humor and we parted ways.

The missed hint of hills ahead became reality a short time later. The hills became steeper and more frequent as exercise induced perspiration began appearing rather profusely. Wooded areas began to replace the pastures and croplands that had become the norm for the past couple of weeks. Two buzzards circled overhead as if to tell us, "Keep moving or you're ours!"

The letter identified roads of Missouri continued and in a very short distance we had turned from "A" to "Z" and were now on "K." Frequent stops for rest and water under shade trees were necessary as the heat, humidity, and hills were beginning to take their toll. While grinding up another long incline and worrying about the diminishing supply of water in our bottles, a surprising offer of aid came from a young woman standing in front of her house.

The woman, probably in her thirties, was attired in a housecoat and invited us to join her and her daughter, Katie, on the porch of her weather-worn house. We chatted with the very energetic and bright Katie, a young lady of maybe three years of age, while her mother, Susan, went inside to fill the bottles with ice and water. Upon her return we talked for some time amid a few old appliances and other assorted household items stored on her front porch. Susan, sensing our fatigue said, "You guys really look tired, why don't you spend the night here?"

Susan was obviously not the wealthiest person in Missouri, but it would have been difficult to imagine a friendlier or kinder person. The thought of spending the evening with her and Katie crossed our minds. But a reservation already made for the evening in Ash Grove awaited, and it was time to head back into the hills and heat. Before leaving their humble dwelling, however, Susan and Katie happily posed for a picture in front of their home.

The steep ups and downs continued and the fatigue of a hot sixty mile day must have been very obvious because another yell from a friendly Missourian offered a room in their home for the night. Merj's blasting strategy wasn't working quite as well as she had hoped. The climbs were too long and momentum from the downhill blasts only lasted for maybe a third of the climb. The rest was a low gear, sweat inducing, "Man it's hot," questioning, "Why are we doing this?" kind of experience. A large cluster of shade trees off the edge of the road offered an opportunity to spread eagle on the grass and enjoy some of Susan's refreshing cold water.

The Missouri countryside soon began sprouting political signs like tulips in the spring. It appeared that an upcoming primary election had brought out numerous candidates for the County Recorder job. Why the Recorder's job would be so attractive was a mystery. County office holders in Missouri must be compensated very well. To add to the political feel of the hot afternoon, a sign welcomed us to Dade County. Unlike its Florida counterpart, it was doubtful that hanging and dimpled chads would play a part in the hotly contested Recorder's election.

A day that began in Kansas in a thick fog ended over seventy sweat-stained miles later at a small bed and breakfast in Ash Grove, Missouri. Joan, the owner of the Maple Tree Inn, met us downtown and asked that we follow her to the night's lodging. After arriving, she requested that the bikes be left in a building behind the house for the night. The small structure was outfitted with various woodworking tools and served as her husband Fred's workshop. Joan showed us to an upstairs room that consisted of a large bed, a partitioned toilet stall in the corner, and an old fashioned four legged porcelain bathtub near the door. The evening's lodging justifiably received quick approval from the very selective half of our twosome.

There was no shower in the room so the bathtub became the only option available to cleanse us of an odor that resembled a Kansas feed lot. Not having taken a bath in thirty years or so, the experience was one accompanied by a certain amount of clumsiness. The normally simple task of hair washing became a source of entertainment for Merj. Her sarcasm was poorly disguised as she watched me pour pitchers of water over my lathered head with a fair share of it ending up on the nicely finished wood floor. The consolation was that her obvious enjoyment of my tribulations was a good antidote for a tough day on the road.

After finally mastering the art of taking a bath, a bench under a tree in front of the house afforded an opportunity to relax and chat with Fred and his precocious granddaughter, Jade. As if he had known us for years, Fred talked of growing up on a farm in Iowa and of restoring the Maple Tree Inn himself. The original house was built in 1872, and Fred's handiwork was displayed in a photo album that documented the progress of the restoration. Fred was rightfully proud of his work. As the conversation of life in a small western Missouri town and cross country bicycle trips flowed freely in the shade of a large, perfectly shaped maple tree, Joan appeared and asked, "Why don't you guys join us for dinner?" Dinner had not been part of the evening lodging, but Joan's generosity was much appreciated, and her offer was quickly accepted.

The dinner table was set in a fashion that was reminiscent of the Sunday dinners that were a traditional part of growing up in rural Ohio. After blessing the meal, Fred passed around helpings of chicken, green salad, potato salad, cabbage, with chocolate cake and ice cream for dessert. The day on the bikes had made us hungry, and eating Joan's home cooking without looking like our last meal had been back in Colorado took more than a little restraint. As we enjoyed dinner, Fred talked of his interest in restoring old vehicles and of a collection of his work out back. The mention of old cars allowed me to launch into descriptions of vintage cars I had owned over the years. In spite of Merj's gentle attempts to change the subject, Fred and I clearly bonded over a discussion of old Chevy trucks.

After the last bite of chocolate cake disappeared, we carried our dishes to the kitchen and Fred and I headed out back to take a look at his collection of vehicles. We started with a very good restoration of a 1934 International tractor, and moved on to a half-dozen or so International Harvester, and Chevy trucks in various stages of restoration. Fred proudly opened the doors of three or four of the trucks to show interiors that were in remarkably good original shape. He started the engines of a couple of them to prove that they were more than just open-air museum pieces.

After walking around the yard, Fred said, "Follow me, I got something I want to show you." In a short time he guided me to a garage that held three of his most prized vehicles; two late 40's vintage Studebakers and a similar generation Dodge pick-up truck. His justifiable pride showed as he described the features of each vehicle in detail. Having done the same thing with my own modest collection, I knew the pleasures of talking to others about an old car that had been the source of hours of enjoyable labor.

Dusk descended on western Missouri, and as coyotes howled in the background, we headed inside to rejoin the ladies. Jade had dug out Fred's high school yearbook and everyone had a little fun around the kitchen table at Fred's expense. One change since those days in Iowa in 1959 was the increased likelihood of a sunburn on the top of his head, should he decide to spend an afternoon in the summer sun without his baseball cap. Fortunately, Fred took the good-natured teasing well and deftly changed the subject by telling us of Joan's sixty-fourth birthday the following day. She planned on celebrating her birthday by getting up early and preparing a breakfast of pancakes and eggs for us. After much discussion, we convinced Joan that her birthday would better be celebrated by sleeping in.

Day 54 - 2649 Miles Down, 1138 To Go

"THERE'S A BETTER WAY TO GET ACROSS THE STATE."

Leaving the Maple Tree Inn before sunrise accomplished two equally important objectives. The first was the daily need to avoid as much of the heat as possible. The second was to sneak out before Joan awoke and felt an obligation to fix our breakfast. After all it was her sixty-fourth birthday. The house was pitch dark as we left our room, and we were careful not to turn on lights or make any noise that would awake the hospitable birthday girl. Feeling our way down the darkened stairway, every third or fourth step let out a potentially wakening groan. We fumbled out the back door and into the dark workshop, located the bikes, and, after the normal morning preparation, stood ready to take on another hilly, hot Missouri day.

Not far outside Ash Grove the challenging rises and falls of yesterday began anew. From the look on Merj's face, it was becoming obvious that, if things continued as they had started, completing this day's ride would take some words of encouragement from her riding companion. Individually the hills were not a particular problem, but the fact that they kept repeating over and over again like a large geologic wave-machine made them both energy and psychologically draining. Facial expression soon turned to verbal expressions. The day had all the makings of a very long and difficult one.

An early morning break in the small town of Walnut Grove, population 690, offered an opportunity for another Egg McMuffin wannabe at a gas station. Maybe waking Joan and partaking in her blueberry pancakes might not have been such a bad idea after all. It was no use wondering what might have been, though, more hills were in the offing and the morning was getting hot and muggy. Soon after the break, one of the higher crests in the road offered an aerial view of a green valley shrouded in a low-lying fog. The picturesque image temporarily diverted attention from the roller coaster cycling. Fields of tall corn and an occasional farmhouse sporadically interrupted the undulating terrain. Intermittent trees offered cooler respites, but water and Gatorade were being consumed at a rate faster than any day yet. Luckily the evening's destination of Marshfield appeared before dehydration became a problem.

A long shower and nap in the selected motel left us revitalized and ready for a walk back outside into the stifling air. Fortunately a strip-mall near the motel housed a number of businesses, but most fortunately, a Hallmark Card shop. A stop in the store provided an opportunity to talk with the elderly couple who managed the shop. Luckily, save our presence, the establishment was otherwise empty. As he listened to our planned route, the kindly gentleman next to the cash register spoke in disbelief. "You guys are crazy if you go that way. That's a real tough ride, there's better ways to get across the state," he said.

This was music to Merj's sweaty, sunburned ears. She quickly agreed with the Hallmark man and added the phrase that is not music to every husband's sweaty, sunburned ears, "I told you so." Not wanting to sound offended by this clear challenge to my trip-planning expertise, I responded to the elderly gentleman in a gracious, yet firm fashion, "So you've got a better idea?"

"Sure do," he said confidently. He spread out our sweat-stained collection of Missouri maps on his glass counter top. Before long the native Missourian, with the aid of a felt tip pen, had drawn a line on the map designating a new route across the "Show Me State."

Day 55 - 2697 Miles Down, 1090 To Go

"GET OUTTA THERE, THERE'S CHIGGERS IN THERE!"

The alternative route suggested by Merj's newfound hero would take us south out of Marshfield and east toward Mountain Grove. Ten or so miles out of town, sights familiar to those travelling the rural roads of our native northeastern Ohio began appearing. The white farmhouses with no electricity, the horse drawn farm implements, the hoof prints, and "road apples" along the shoulder were obvious indications that Amish people lived in the area.

The Amish are direct descendents of the Mennonites of Germany and Switzerland. They arose in the 1600's as a distinct community of believers who strictly adhered to biblical law. The first Amish came to America in the 1720's seeking good farmland and religious tolerance. It is estimated that there are 150,000 Amish living in seventeen American states including about 5,000 in Missouri.

The Amish live in modest homes on rural farms, and travel by horse drawn vehicles. Their lifestyle evolves around a close-knit family, a strict adherence to their faith, and the productive use of their land. The Amish do not believe in technology, and as a result, electricity is not permitted and only horses and horse drawn implements are used for farm work. The young and old work side by side to ensure that skills are passed from generation to generation. The Amish make little distinction between work and play and find leisure a foreign concept. Many, but not all, find tourists somewhat silly or at best merely annoying. Most Amish want nothing more than to be left alone.

The benefit of riding a bicycle through an Amish area is that road shoulders are many times wider to provide for the safe passage of their buggies. What works well for buggies usually works well for cyclists. Such was the case south of Marshfield as the comfortable ride through Amish country was only interrupted by an occasional abrupt change of direction to avoid souvenirs left by the horses. Tall functioning windmills made the Amish farms visible from some distance away. At one of the farms, an Amish family stood around a well under the windmill drinking water on the already warm summer morning. A short time later, a large coop of noisy chickens on a well-kept Amish farm serenaded us. The Amish farms were easy to identify, since, just like in Ohio, the curtains in the windows of the farmhouses were pulled to one side. Also like home, occasional vans passed, full of Amish men headed for construction sites.

The revised route soon put us on a divided four-lane highway with wide shoulders, constructed for the Amish buggies. Hundreds of wheel tracks on the dark asphalt gave evidence of the Amish's frequent use of the shoulder. Not far off the road shoulder a Santa Fe Railroad train thundered by in the opposite direction. The engineer acknowledged our presence with a friendly wave and an ear piercing blast of the locomotive's air horn.

Santa Fe locomotives had long been special to me. In my early teen years, like many other boys of that era, I set up and operated a model railroad in the basement of my parent's house. The pride of the model fleet was a Lionel Santa Fe diesel electric locomotive. The red and silver Santa Fe paint scheme, complete with the large stylized arrow on its sides, represented something both powerful and beautiful at the same time. Hour after hour the Lionel engine made its way around the intricate three-railed arrangement of tracks and switches that had been carefully laid out over two sheets of plywood.

It is quite possible that the Lionel O scale work of art may have traveled as many miles as the real one that passed this morning. We had seen a number of other Santa Fe locomotives over the last couple of weeks, but this one was a dead ringer for the one that had provided so much enjoyment forty years earlier. It was as if the horn blasts and friendly wave were meant to acknowledge a middle age man's musings of his youth.

After leaving the Amish area, the comfortable shoulders disappeared and the heat of the day arrived with its usual vengeance. In the small town of Seymour, a McDonald's supplied an air-conditioned rest and a chance for brief conversation with a seventy-year old fellow from Arkansas. After patiently answering his questions about the trip, he responded, "Well, it really is great to be fulfilling a lifelong dream, but I'd rather be traveling across the state in my Lincoln." Since, among other niceties, the Lincoln's air conditioning was likely first rate, it was hard to argue with our newfound acquaintance from Arkansas. It was also noticeable that these unanticipated and frequent encounters with Arkansans had us beginning to talk like them.

The new route did not do away with the need to get over the Ozarks; it just made the grades more gradual. Gradual grades meant longer climbs to achieve the same elevations. In some ways they were similar to the ones a thousand miles back. The armadillos that had migrated north to Missouri also apparently had difficulty with the grades, or more likely, the vehicles that negotiated the grades. With their hard shells largely intact, the deceased armadillos were like cobblestones on an old city street. Some of the locals had told us that the nocturnal animals jumped into the air as the lights of an approaching car came upon them only to meet their demise on the grille of the oncoming vehicle.

Our intended stopping point of Mansfield arrived much sooner than anticipated. The early arrival caused a dilemma for Merj; do we stop here, or do we continue on another eighteen miles or so to the next town of Mountain Grove? Even though the day was warm, continuing on would make the next day's ride eighteen miles shorter. In the comfort of a cool truck stop, the decision was made to proceed. While leaving Mansfield, a sign proclaimed the town as the home of Laura Ingalls Wilder, author of *Little House on the Prairie*. Knowing that Merj had been fond of the 80's television show of the same name, inquiring whether she wanted to take the two-mile trip off route to visit the home seemed appropriate. Her terse response of "absolutely not," showed that the question was in fact very much inappropriate.

Near Mountain Grove, the evening's new destination, a broken down truck on the shoulder gave an opportunity to help its two disheveled occupants. Like many others, the two of them sort of "gee whizzed" our trip and expressed "admiration" but no desire to duplicate it themselves. Helping the fellows required our standing in the high grass off the shoulder. They immediately admonished us, "Get outta there, there's chiggers in there!" they shouted. A young man mowing the grass at the McDonald's earlier in the day had given the same warning. Now, Merj had more to worry about than snakes. In fact, as she remounted her bike, the scratching had already begun.

Upon reaching the evening's lodging in Mountain Grove, concern over rumored construction to the east necessitated a call to the Missouri Department of Transportation (MDOT) to get the real facts. The call was taken by an accommodating fellow named Bob Edwards. Bob was a former cyclist and understood the importance of knowing about road conditions. After a phone explanation of what lay ahead, he said, "I live in Mountain Grove, so I'll stop by your hotel on my way home to give you guys more details."

After work, Bob showed up with a stack of information. He spread Missouri maps and computer print-outs around the small table in the room, and began a detailed summary of the road ahead. By the time he finished, there was no excuse for us not knowing every chuckhole from Mountain Grove to the Mississippi River.

After finishing the planning, Bob explained the subtle differences in speech between the southwestern and southeastern portions of Missouri. "Around here," he said, "we say 'you-uns'. A little farther down the road, they'll say 'you-all'. When you hear them change to 'you-all' you'll truly be in the South," Bob explained with the confidence of a linguistic expert. Having spent much of our recent life in the South, we could have told him the correct pronunciation was "y'all," but decided it wasn't worth alienating a very nice fellow. Bob's cooperation went way above the call of duty and was greatly appreciated. The enthusiasm and assistance offered by the people in the small rural towns of America continued to amaze us. In fact, it was so commonplace that it had almost become an expectation.

Day 56 - 2748 Miles Down, 1039 To Go

"WHEREVER THE BUICK TAKES US."

The ride out of Mountain Grove began with a flat tire before even leaving the motel parking lot. For those keeping score, and Merj was, it was three for me and none for her. Maybe Fred with the Corvair back in Kansas wasn't just buttering Merj up. Maybe my few extra pounds were the difference. Regardless, once on the road, the ride became like those of the last few days including dodging an ever-increasing number of dead armadillos. The day also brought a return of the high jumping grasshoppers from Kansas, and occasional clusters of pine trees reminiscent of the ones in the Rockies.

The pines evidently represented a cash crop, as logging trucks became more and more frequent co-occupants of the roadway. The discarded chunks of bark falling from their beds, became obstacles to avoid. The destinations of the logging trucks soon became evident as an occasional lumber mill announced its presence in the hot sultry air with the pleasant smell of sawed timber. The hot day had also produced blisters in the asphalt that made audible popping sounds as the bicycle tires rolled over them.

The day's ride offered a subtle reminder of the description of "red necks" that had been used by western Missourians to describe the folks of southern Missouri. The term was familiar, and, had been used by Merj on occasion to describe me as I cheered for any Chevy driver in a NASCAR race, or loaded up a bowl of grits for a breakfast dose of roughage. A good family friend, who grew up in Kentucky, occasionally corrected Merj by explaining that I had a ways to go before qualifying as a red neck. According to her, my affliction might better be described as being "pink around the collar." Whatever the case, today's ride produced a small town called "Hillbilly Junction" and a mailbox for the Herrod family that was nicely lettered except that both of the r's in the name were backwards. To add to the red neck feeling of the day, some pretty mangy looking dogs decided to give chase, and in a couple of cases, provided a pretty good challenge. There was no question about it. These were my kind of people.

After a typical day of about fifty miles on the bikes, a sign announced our arrival at the small town of Birch Tree, Missouri, population 634. While checking into a nice, locally owned motel, the lady behind the counter showed a certain amount of unexpected contempt. When she asked for advance payment by credit card *and* a form of identification, I pleasantly asked, "What exactly is the problem?" The answer was to the point, "We had a bunch of bikers in here a couple days ago and they did a lot of damage to the place." I tried to explain that our bikes did not have engines and that the chosen transportation of the "bikers" she referred to probably did. It made no difference. We and our "biker" brethren were one and the same. "Show me the ID or move on," she said. We acquiesced; testament to the fact that the only other lodging option in town had not passed the Merj test.

As it would turn out, Birch Tree would become home for two nights. Efforts to reserve a room in the busy summer resort town of Van Buren for the next evening were impossible. The spare time would be put to good use, however, by planning the route ahead. To do that a good Kentucky map was needed, so a trip to a gas station across the street was in order. After working my way past a parking lot full of jacked up, muddy pickups, their equally muddy owners, and the blue smoky haze of the gas station interior, the friendly young lady behind the counter politely informed me that no Kentucky maps were available. Since half of Missouri remained to be conquered, not having access to a Kentucky map at this stage of the game was not yet cause for alarm.

Dinner choices were limited, so a decision to eat at the fast food establishment next to the hotel was not a difficult one. Two young women behind the counter took our hamburger order and warned, "It may be a while before your burgers are ready." While killing time, I noticed that one of the young ladies was attired in an Ohio State Buckeyes tee shirt. When asked if she had attended Ohio State, she told me, "No, I bought this here in town yesterday." Since the hamburgers were nowhere near ready and there was more time to kill, I asked her if she had heard of Ohio State. She indicated that she hadn't, and although having heard of the State of Ohio, had no idea where it was located. She had never heard of Cleveland, Columbus, or Cincinnati and neither had the coworker who was working behind the counter with her. Both young ladies had recently graduated from the local high school and were considering their future educational options. Frankly, we were at a loss for suggestions. A while later the food arrived, and after trading orders with some of the other eight or ten people that had also been waiting in line, everyone ended up with something close to what they had asked for.

While eating our gourmet meal, a trio of elderly ladies sat down at an adjacent table and dove into their own appetizing selections. The ladies were obviously enjoying each other's company, and before long they invited us into their discussion. "We're all widows," one of them divulged, "and all of our husbands died within the last ten years."

Since the death of their husbands, this threesome from Kansas had made many trips together. Though they weren't sure exactly where this one would take them, their discussion led us to believe it might be Williamsburg, Virginia. They giggled like a bunch of teenagers and joked that the trip toward Virginia, "May take us through Nashville, but then again it might not!" We asked them where they would be going the following day. "Wherever the Buick takes us," they said gleefully.

Day 56 - 2800 Miles Down, 987 To Go

KILLDOZER

The small town of Birch Tree was a short walk over a rise from the motel. Unfortunately, like so many of the others, this community had seen more prosperous days. An abandoned lumber mill that had evidently employed many Birch Tree residents making hardwood flooring was a sign of hard times, as were remnants of a long abandoned railroad. An old train station and a Frisco Line caboose were permanently parked on a short section of track in the town square. The Mercantile Exchange was the dominant building in town, but, like most of the other buildings around the square, was abandoned and boarded up.

The only remaining operating businesses in downtown Birch Tree appeared to be an AmVets hall, a U. S. Post Office, and a small quilt shop. After a visit to the post office to mail audiotapes home and a discussion with two friendly and inquisitive postal employees, it was time to dutifully follow Merj into The Hideaway Quilt Shop. Once inside the store, it didn't take long to engage in conversation with Marlana, a very pleasant middle-age lady who, along with her sister, operated the shop.

In a short time, we discovered that the husband of Marlana's sister had purchased the building housing the store, and the two sisters started their quilting business even though neither knew how to quilt. Soon after setting up shop, some of the ladies from the area taught them quilting, and they had since gotten pretty good at it, as far as we could see from their handiwork in the store.

It didn't take long for Marlana to find out that she and Merj were both retired teachers, and that they shared similar reasons for their decisions to leave the elementary classroom. Once again it was fascinating to stand off to the side and watch two former teachers engaged in an increasingly animated discussion about their common experiences in education. In some ways it almost appeared that they were validating each other's decision to retire early. There were more than a few "yeah, me to's" sprinkled into the conversation. Marlana, now widowed, had been married to the principal of her school.

At a break in their discussion, I jokingly suggested to Marlana that a comfortable chair for husbands in her store might increase sales. Just for good measure, she could nicely arrange a couple of six-month-old *Sports Illustrated* or *Popular Mechanics* magazines to provide quiet entertainment for the captive males. After advancing the theory that comfortable husbands would allow more unfettered time for wives to shop, and in turn buy more, she politely said, "I'll take it under advisement." Marlana was much too nice a person to flat out suggest that the idea bordered on moronic.

The building that housed the quilt shop had an interesting history that Marlana fortunately had the time to share. The relatively small one story building once served as a blueberry and then a pickle canning operation. "When a load of blueberries arrived, a loud whistle would blow letting everybody around here know that there were jobs at the plant." Marlana further explained that after the canning operation folded, the building housed freezer lockers. Freezer lockers were rented by people in Birch Tree to store their frozen foods in the times before individual household freezers became common. We laughed imagining Merj walking down to the freezer locker to get a bag of Bird's Eye frozen beans before preparing an evening's dinner.

Marlana continued, "The lockers were eventually removed and the building was used for some kind of tire molding operation." She wasn't sure what that meant, but we guessed that it might have been a recapping business. After the tire molders closed down, the building was used to grow mushrooms. When Marlana and her sister took over the store, a great amount of time and effort went into cleaning out the dirt that had been used to grow the mushrooms.

While Merj ambled about the store, for some unknown reason Marlana and I began a discussion of old cars. Marlana owned a '69 Dodge GTS and wanted to find a buyer for it. Previously, the car had meaning for her, but that was no longer the case. At some time in the past, the car got away from her. It rolled down a hill straight toward family members at the bottom. As a result of the near disaster, Marlana's brother named the car Killdozer from a movie that was popular at the time. She regularly referred to the car as "him" and asked for help in finding what he was worth. I gave her some ideas from my own experience and a couple of old car web sites that could help her price it correctly.

Marlana was a very thoughtful person and asked in an embarrassed sort of way, "How are you two getting along after spending so much time together?" It was a question that had been asked by a few of our friends back home who had been sending messages and encouragement via e-mails. E-mails from men had especially expressed doubt of their own ability to survive the constant companionship that a trip like this one necessitated. Fortunately, we were able to answer that our relationship was, in fact, proceeding quite well. Merj and I shared a mutual desire to complete the trip, and to do it in a way that allowed for considerable time off the bikes. Maybe equally important was my philosophy of beginning each day with the simple statement, "I'm sorry." Something was going to go wrong at some time during the day, and it was sometimes best to get the apology covered in advance. It was a method that usually worked at home and was especially effective on the road. Marlana seemed to accept the explanation as reasonable. "It might be a good idea to continue that same approach for another month or so," she suggested.

Marlana was a lifetime resident of the area and shared stories of the more prosperous times in the town's past. Her smooth Southern accent was gentle and soothing. The melodic hint of the South in her speech stood in sharp contrast to the heavier twangs of others in the area. She had an infectious energy and enthusiasm that was obvious to anyone in her company. Her sense of humor and tolerance were especially noticeable. She showed interest in my stories of the road even as Merj rolled her eyes in the background. Marlana, feeling her life was now in the proper perspective, told us, "I just want to get to heaven." This charming, kindly woman deserved a spot there.

Leaving the store, it was necessary to negotiate a hydraulic lift machine parked on the sidewalk by the front door. Marlana's sister's husband, the building owner, occupied a raised platform about ten feet off the ground. He was repairing joints in the concrete block front of the building, and was in no particular hurry on the hot summer morning. It didn't take long to learn his name was Jim and that he was a retired state employee. In an accent much thicker than Marlana's, but nonetheless appealing, he talked of his new "off the clock" attitude about life. In a nutshell he summarized, "I do things when I want to, and if I don't want to do 'em I don't do 'em." He went on to explain, "I fell off a ladder a few times and that's why I bought the lift."

Jim was in the process of remodeling the other half of the building for an expansion of the quilting business. He lowered the lift, stepped onto the sidewalk and insisted on showing us his progress to date. Jim was rightfully proud of his handiwork, and equally proud of the fact that he worked on it only when the mood hit. His reasons for living in this small, nearly abandoned town were much like those we had heard from others. "Birch Tree's not crowded, except every once in a while it gets crowded." Heading through the park back to the motel, a crowded Birch Tree was just about impossible to imagine.

As the day turned to evening, Alice, the lady who had been on duty at yesterday's check in, was still working behind the desk. Alice had warmed up to us "bikers" to the extent that she seemed to now actually enjoy our company. We had to admit that our feelings about the lady who had made checking in a little more complicated than usual had also noticeably improved.

Alice had also lived her entire life in the area and told of the town's former times. She talked of growing up when, "Most of the people around here worked at the hardwood flooring company or on farms outside town." She went on to explain that, "A movie theater and a lot o' downtown stores made Saturday nights so crowded that it was hard to get through town." She laid the cause of the town's decline on the fact that, "A lot of the old people died and the younger ones moved away because they didn't see any opportunities around here." Sitting outside the motel office in a rocking chair listening to the crickets and talking to Alice on the warm night, it was clear that Saturday nights in Birch Tree were not what they used to be.

Alice talked about growing up in a town where nobody locked their doors at night. She explained that a number of families in the area formerly lived on welfare. When welfare eligibility was tightened a few years ago, most of the welfare recipients were forced to seek other employment. According to Alice, "A lot of 'em headed for the hills around town to set up meth labs." These modern day moonshiners had made Missouri number two to California in production of the illegal drug. She went on to say, "The law's catching up to 'em, and so a lot of 'em are moving south into Arkansas." Before long she hoped Missouri would lose it's number two ranking.

After asking Alice if she wanted an ice cream cone, I walked next door to provide satisfaction of my own sugar fix. The evening clientele had arrived and the town barber's perfection of the mullet was apparent. It was also clear that the local tattoo artist had been doing a brisk business. Regardless of hair styles or body art, the folks around the restaurant were friendly, accommodating and offered valuable advice for the next few day's rides. The lessons learned about not judging books by their covers were again brought home in the small southern Missouri town of Birch Tree.

Days 58 - 2800 Miles Down, 987 To Go

"THAT WAS SOME LITTLE DISPLAY YOU PUT ON BACK THERE."

Leaving the motel in Birch Tree in the early morning, Alice came out of the office and made sure to wish us luck in the rest of our journey. This initially somewhat antagonistic lady had undergone a metamorphosis, and over the period of a day had come to realize that all bikers aren't built alike. Apparently not judging a book by its cover applied to others too.

The day's ride was a planned short one of only thirty miles with a destination of Van Buren. The cycling began in a fog and continued with some fairly good grades through forests of pine and deciduous trees. The smell of the fog-concealed pines was a pleasant addition to the morning's ride. The crests of hills presented panoramic views of fog covered valleys with mist covered mountains in the distance.

The short ride put us at the evening's hotel by mid-morning and offered a whole day to partake in the recreational activities available in Van Buren. It was obvious that recreation in the small town centered around the Current River. After renting two truck inner tubes, a fellow by the name of Grubb carted us along with a van full of people up river to be dropped off. The float from the starting point down the Current River was a slow leisurely one only occasionally interrupted by small very manageable rapids. The slow trip of about three hours was enjoyable and relaxing until about a quarter mile from the end. A large tree had fallen into the river along the bank and the river currents were such that an unwary floater could be swept into its branches. Merj, aware of the situation, gently floated past the tree without a problem. Me, however, not paying attention and thinking about who knows what, got caught in the current and pushed directly into the entanglement of the tree branches. After finally getting myself extricated from the tree in the rapidly moving water, a pain in my right shoulder became very noticeable. The movements associated with pushing and pulling my way through the tree branches had caused a problem with the shoulder that made the last short portion of the inner tube ride somewhat painful.

A grinning Merj, having seen the adventure in the tree, greeted me as I walked onto the shore. "That was some little display you put on back there," she said. My original thought was to let the shoulder pain go without comment, but Merj's mocking of my dilemma required a change in thinking. A try for sympathy was now called for so the right shoulder suddenly became a source of pain and agony unequalled in the annals of man. It appeared to be successful. Merj quickly cried, "Oh my goodness, you've ridden almost three thousand miles on a bike without any problems and now an inner tube and a tree are going to get you!" I wondered now if maybe the attempt at sympathy had gone too far, so a quick assurance that everything would be fine was offered. Privately, though, the shoulder really was quite painful and the same thought that Merj expressed had crossed my mind too. After all those miles, would floating in an inner tube down a lazy river be my undoing?

Day 59 - 2830 Miles Down, 957 To Go

"THERE ARE PEOPLE AROUND HERE THAT'LL MESS WITH YA IF YOU'RE NOT CAREFUL."

The planned predawn departure from Van Buren was frustratingly delayed by an inability to get to the bicycles. Responding to our request, the folks at the lodge had secured them the night before in a locked room. Unfortunately at the early departure hour, there was no one around to unlock the room. After a two-hour wait in increasingly warm and humid air, a young employee showed up with a key for the storage room and unlocked it. The only benefit of the long morning wait was an opportunity to stretch and test yesterday's raft ravaged shoulder. Since it only seemed to hurt when my arm was raised to shoulder height, the biking would be fine. Throwing a ninety-mile an hour fastball, alas, would not be possible, but then again, in over fifty years it hadn't been possible anyhow.

After a foggy start, the construction that Bob from MDOT had promised three days earlier became reality. The combination of fog, road construction, and the absence of shoulders caused us to shout the warning word, "bail," on more than one occasion, along with the accompanying detour into the grass. Approaching the crossroads town of Ellsinore, it was obvious that a significant meteorological event had occurred recently. Sections of forests had been blown down while others nearby stood strangely, undisturbed. The pattern of destruction made it obvious that a tornado had recently visited Ellsinore. A short distance from the first signs of the tornado, a stop at a makeshift service station showed further evidence of the storm. The original facility had apparently been blown down by the tornado and a small group of construction workers were in the process of rebuilding it.

After using a restroom housed in a wooden shack, and while

taking a rest next to a temporary trailer that served as a mini-mart, two of the workers interrupted their break and approached. Noticing the loaded bikes, they became interested in finding out what was going on. While answering their far-reaching questions, one of the workers strongly suggested, "You call the paper in Poplar Bluff so they can do an article about your trip." Evidently having some prior experience with the newspaper, he proceeded to write the paper's phone number from memory on a scrap piece of paper. Telling him that we usually try to avoid attention and even sneak out of most towns under the cover of darkness made no difference to this friendly, but persistent, construction worker. While handing over the scrap piece of paper with the phone number, he made us promise that we would contact the *Poplar Bluff Daily American Republic* as soon as we got to town. There was nothing to be gained by arguing with him, so we agreed.

Climbing back on the bikes, the same worker inched closer and warned us to be careful. His warning seemed more serious than the casual, "Now you be careful out there." The troubled look on his face caused some concern, so further questioning as to what he meant was needed. He drew closer, looked around and softly said, "There are people around here that'll mess with ya if you're not careful." Merj glared at me with one of those "What have you gotten me into?" looks. After assuring both of them that two full canisters of pepper spray were at the ready for any emergency, the morning's ride began anew. While riding away, my hope was that Merj had bought the pepper spray defense argument. It was clear, though, that if people really wanted to "mess" with us, the pepper spray would probably have been like shooting an elephant with a BB gun.

Thoughts of people wanting to do us harm were quickly put out of mind, and it was back to the heat and hills of southeastern Missouri. About half way to Poplar Bluff, a well used white Ford pickup truck pulled up behind us, and a blast from the truck's horn was obviously intended to get our attention. Horn blasts from passing motorists were frequent occurrences, as some drivers seemed determined to make sure we knew they were there. Mumbling the usual, "Yeah, yeah, we hear ya," under our breaths the Ford driver pulled up next to us. My first thought was, "We're gonna get messed with!" It didn't take long to realize that the pickup driver was the construction worker from Ellsinore. Was he trying to mess with us? As it turned out, he was still worried about our safety. He, along with his colleagues in the truck bed, had ridden out to make sure everything was okay.

FINDING GOD

Poplar Bluff, a community of 17,000 people, had been long awaited. According to the old gentleman who managed the Hallmark store back in Marshfield, Poplar Bluff marked the end of the Ozark Mountains and the beginning of the flat Mississippi bottomland. The flat cycling was something that Merj had been looking forward to since entering Missouri. The gentle hills of the last few miles into Poplar Bluff, however, had her doubting the old fellow's information. It soon became evident though, that when it came to hills, the fat lady was beginning to sing.

The lodging in Poplar Bluff was new and comfortable and had a computer available for patron's use in the lobby. The affable young lady behind the reception desk greeted us with a cheerful, "How y'all doin'?" It was now official. After over 2,800 miles of cycling, we were in the South.

Finally reaching the South caused a robust appetite and need for an equally robust supper. Inquiring where one could obtain such a meal, the helpful desk clerk suggested a nearby steakhouse. The walk to the restaurant was a short one, and once seated inside, our twenty-something waitress, Amanda, asked about our day. After offering the standard response of okay, the same question of her brought an enthusiastic response of "great!" "I spent the day with my friends who helped me find the meaning of God." It sounded as

though her search might have been ongoing for some time. Its successful completion seemed to have put her at ease.

As Amanda brought the salads, she talked of being an only
child and growing up in a stable family atmosphere. She explained
that her home was the usual hangout for high school friends, and
that many of them regarded her parents as their friends. When
delivering the steaks, Amanda talked of attending a local community college and of her plans to become a social worker or foster
parent. Her upbringing had caused her to want to try to offer sta-
bility to youngsters who may not have been as fortunate as she had
been. While she explained her goals and aspirations, we offered
encouragement and unsolicited advice. Finally, after bringing the
desert, Amanda surprisingly informed us, "It's on me." When
asked why, she responded, "You guys have helped make my day."
The feeling was mutual.

Day 60 - 2874 Miles Down, 913 To Go

FINALLY, A FLAT TIRE FOR THE FAIRER HALF

The selected road out of Poplar Bluff was a four lane highway with
considerable truck traffic. The wide smooth shoulders, however,
made the riding feel safe. As the morning progressed into a head
wind and past fields of soybeans and corn, the skies darkened and a
thundershower threatened. Worried that cover, should the thunderstorm become reality, was limited, a decision was made to
reroute to a local road that paralleled the highway. Before heading
off route, however, another flat tire caused a fifteen-minute delay.
The score was now, Phil four, Merj nada. Maybe it *was* the weight.

The well-paved bypass took us along more fields of corn and
soybeans and our first encounters with cotton. Before long the
rain began to fall. It began as a light sprinkle and steadily

increased in intensity. A stop under the covered entrance of a church was quickly interrupted by the onrushing charge of two large, barking dogs bent on no good. We quickly remounted the bikes and the rain continued to increase, but on this hot humid Missouri day, it actually felt good.

Not long after leaving the church, the rain stopped and it was back to the original four-lane highway. Soon after rejoining the busy roadway, Merj began complaining about her bike's handling. After miles and miles of cycling and four of my own, it finally happened to her; flat tire number one. Fortunately her tire-changing hero quickly came to her aid, and she was back on the road in a few minutes. After the day's tire problems, we had no spare tubes left in the equipment pack. A flat now would require a last resort: the patch kit. Fortunately, about ten miles later a Wal Mart stop in the "big time" town of Sikeston afforded an opportunity to replenish the tube supply.

Traffic in the twin towns of Sikeston and neighboring Miner was heavy due to an annual rodeo that was underway. Not having seen evidence for hundreds of miles of the ranch like atmosphere that had spawned rodeos out West, such a big event in southeastern Missouri seemed strange. For all we knew it could have been a biker's rodeo, or a skateboarder's rodeo, or a quilter's rodeo. Whatever type it was, a lot of people had come to be part of the experience. Not far from Miner, the traffic dwindled and the free and easy cycling made for an enjoyable afternoon's ride. More fields of corn and soybeans spread for acres and acres over the flat fertile Mississippi River valley as the evening's destination of Charleston drew near.

Day 61 - 2944 Miles Down, 843 To Go

———

illinois

"How am I going to get over that thing?"

WHOLE LOT O' SHAKIN' GOIN' ON

While leaving Charleston in the early morning, more than the usual number of people took an opportunity to honk their horns and wave. The thought crossed my mind that Merj might have somehow slapped a sign on my back that said something like, "HONK IF YOU LIKE BIKERS." Finding no such sign, it was obvious that the encouragement was genuine and it was appreciated.

The flat ride from Charleston toward the Mississippi River included a stretch along a levee, constructed to protect the lowlands from a rising river. On this peaceful summer morning, it was hard to imagine the upheaval that occurred in this same area nearly two hundred years before. According to *Goodspeed's History of Southeast Missouri*, early in the morning of December 16, 1811,

the people of this area "were visited by a violent shock of an earthquake, accompanied by a very awful noise, resembling loud but
distant thunder, but more hoarse and vibrating, which was followed in a few minutes by the complete saturation of the atmosphere, with sulphurious vapor, causing total darkness." The first
person account continues, "The screams of the affrighted inhabitants running to and fro, not knowing where to go or what to do,
the cries of the fowls and beasts of every species, the cracking of
trees falling, and the roaring of the Mississippi, the current of
which was retrograde for a few minutes, owing, as is supposed, to
an eruption in its bed, formed a scene truly terrible."

The scene described by the eyewitness is what later became
known as the New Madrid earthquake. Unfortunately, the same
terrifying scene would be repeated a month later. The second quake
was larger than the first and still is the largest recorded earthquake
to have ever occurred on the North American continent. Between
December of 1811 and March of 1812, 1,874 separate smaller
quakes occurred with their epicenters in the general area of New
Madrid, Missouri. The quakes and aftershocks were felt over the
entire country except for the Pacific coast. Large areas sank into the
earth, new lakes were formed, and forests were destroyed over an
area of 150,000 acres. By March of 1812 most of the houses in New
Madrid had fallen into the Mississippi River. The earthquake was
said to have rung church bells as far away as Boston.

The morning's ride was only about fifty miles south of New
Madrid. Although it was difficult to imagine what it might have
been like during the earthquake, the flat bottomland looked vul-
nerable to any significant change in the normal patterns of the
nearby Mississippi River. Surprisingly, the events of 1811 and
1812 caused the reported death of only one person, mostly due to
the very sparse settlements that existed then. Such an earthquake
today would cause considerable death and destruction. There are
a number of scientists that predict that such an event is possible
and even likely.

No earthquakes seemed in the offing, so today's crossing of the Mississippi River was a much-anticipated event. It would mark the unofficial entrance into the "Eastern" United States. Since a South Carolina town in the eastern U. S. was the trip's ultimate destination, feelings of accomplishment began to form. Perceived images of the final ride onto Hilton Head Island occasionally visited our minds. At the risk of creating some sort of curse that would prevent successful completion of our journey, we tried to put them aside

Crossing the Mississippi however, would undoubtedly involve negotiating a bridge of some sort. Bridges, especially high arching ones, were a source of worry for Merj. More specifically, looking over the edges of high places caused her a near paralyzing anxiety. An earlier car trip through Montana's Glacier National Park had caused her to relocate to the back seat with her head between her knees to avoid any knowledge of the steep drops outside the car window. The fear was real, and whenever it cropped up, calm discussion and encouragement were required. Knowing of Merj's building fear was cause for my own sympathetic anxieties.

About a dozen miles into the day and still with no Mississippi River in sight, a stop at a mini-mart for a break allowed for a question as to what had happened to the river. Had there been a recent earthquake that had moved the river's course farther east? The lady behind the counter was quick to assure us that the river was where it had been for the last two hundred years or so, and that it wasn't far away. Merj's questions about the inevitable bridge were answered, but not in a way that provided her the comfort she seeked.

A short distance from the mini-mart, around a bend in the road, an arching steel structure spanning the Mississippi River appeared. The look on Merj's face as the bridge came into view clearly wondered, "How am I going to get over that thing?" The half-mile approach to the bridge allowed just enough time for her anxieties to build. The fears were at full strength a short time later, and I made a suggestion that we walk the bikes across.

The narrowness of the structure and the fairly heavy truck traffic made the option one worthy of consideration. The only other viable method was to ride over the bridge but avoid the edges as much of possible. That required Merj riding down the middle of the eastbound lane with me riding behind her, to hold up the truck traffic and keep her from getting run down. After weighing the two options, Merj chose to ride rather than walk across the bridge. From my point of view a few irate teamsters didn't compare to the prospects of marital discord for another thousand miles. The truckers would likely express their displeasure, but we would never see them again. I couldn't (and didn't want to) say the same for Merj.

The Mississippi River crossing was intended to be savored and enjoyed as one of the signature events of the entire trip. A stop at the top of the bridge to take a photograph of the early morning traffic on the wide river and to memorialize the experience was anticipated. As so often happened, events didn't always work out as expected. At a pause in truck traffic, we began a mad dash down the middle of the eastbound lane over the Mississippi River. The photographs of the river became quick on the fly snapshots from the high point of the arching structure. Within a few minutes the bridge grade turned downhill toward Illinois and the occasional blasts from truck horns increased in frequency. Landing on terra firma in Illinois was met with great relief and a sense of accomplishment on Merj's part. We avoided eye contact with the truck drivers who were backed up behind us and now passed in aggravation. The acknowledgement of our accomplishment would likely have involved a different finger than the one finger waves of encouragement back in Kansas. Sometimes it was best to just look the other way.

After making sure all of the trucks and other vehicles had passed, we continued on a few hundred yards to a parking lot in Confluence Park. The park was appropriately named as it was located at the confluence of the Ohio and Mississippi Rivers just outside the city of

Cairo, Illinois, a small town of about 4,200 people.

Cairo was named for the city of the same name on the Nile River in Egypt. The southernmost city in Illinois is part of what was called the "Little Egypt" area. The reference to Egypt came from the area being able to supply northern and central Illinois farmers enough grain to survive the harsh winter of 1830-31. The farmers were said to be like Jacob's son in the Bible, "Going down to Egypt to obtain some grain." During the Civil War, it served as a strategic location against a possible Confederate invasion of the North from Kentucky. When one of us would mistakenly pronounce the town's name in the same way as the one in Egypt, a correction was always forthcoming. In that part of the country it was to be pronounced as Care-row.

The stay in Illinois was brief by any measure. A jogger who had just finished his morning run along the bank of the river offered to take our picture in front of a sign that came as close as could be found to welcoming visitors to Illinois. Once the photo commemorating the entrance into state number seven had been completed, and since there was nothing else of importance to accomplish in Illinois, we mounted the bikes and headed for Kentucky. The entire crossing of the state was accomplished over a distance of about a half-mile and in about fifteen minutes.

kentucky

"You guys do know, don't you, that the grass in Kentucky isn't really blue?"

A WAL MART IS NOT THE ONLY SAVING PLACE

The problem with Kentucky was that to get there from Illinois a person had to cross the Ohio River. Unfortunately crossing the Ohio River would involve negotiating another bridge much like the one over the Mississippi River. Since the earlier crossing was judged to have been a success, a mad dash down the middle of the eastbound lane over the bridge was again chosen as the preferred method. Fortunately the trailing group of truckers was different from the Mississippi River bridge, but their reaction to being delayed was much the same. There's a certain feeling of insignificance when a cyclist looks in his rearview mirror and sees the entire field of vision filled with the grille of a Peterbilt. If that first truck driver in line had been a little less patient, it's possible there could have been chalk outlines drawn in the road in the shapes of two middle age people with poor judgement.

Fortunately the first trucker was cooperative, and shortly after reaching the safety of the other side, we located the small sign hidden in a dense growth of trees that welcomed visitors to Kentucky, WHERE EDUCATION COUNTS. Riding a bicycle in three states in a single morning gave us a certain feeling of giddiness and sense of accomplishment. It didn't matter that we had had our feet on the ground in all three in the span of about twenty minutes. It was still three states of the lower forty-eight, and there were only four more to go.

Having previously traveled the eastern part of Kentucky in an automobile, we were familiar with the hills of the Appalachians, but western Kentucky was an unknown. Always the pessimists, there was an expectation that the whole state resembled the mountainous east.

The western area, paralleling the Mississippi River, however, was much like the Missouri side: flat with easy cycling. The wide, slow moving Mississippi plied its way south, distanced from the road by a railroad and overgrowth. Barges laden with unknown cargoes made their way up and down the busy river that bisected Middle America. There was an instinct to look for a fence, some whitewash, and Tom Sawyer and Huck Finn.

The euphoria of crossing the river was soon replaced by a realization that Paducah, the evening's destination, was still over thirty miles away. Leaving the river and heading toward the small town of Wickliffe, the road became more rolling and passed through areas of dense woodlands. A short stop in Wickliffe provided an opportunity to question a small group of locals about alternative routes to Paducah. As sometimes happened, a conversation with a knowledgeable resident caused us to consider a change in plans.

The original route to Paducah, although shorter, was judged to be too hilly and a longer, but flatter, route was suggested. This revelation required a huddle with Merj and a serious discussion of the merits of hills versus shorter distance. The last time the longer, flatter route had been chosen, the result was a muddy construction site and eventually a ride in a pickup truck. Knowing the effect of the recent Missouri hills on the female member of our little team, the resulting choice of the longer, flatter route was not surprising. For a split second I considered posing the question, "If hills are to be avoided at all cost, why do the bikes have twenty seven speeds?" Over three decades of matrimonial bliss, however, had not come to pass by asking such questions.

The flatter route toward Paducah produced rolling terrain and fields of milo, corn, and soybeans. The otherwise enjoyable ride was complicated somewhat by narrow shoulders and a fair amount of traffic. A Baptist church in the tiny town of Barlow, declared on a sign out front, "WAL MART IS NOT THE ONLY SAVING PLACE." Was this reference to Wal Mart enough to consider Barlow "big time?" What exactly were the rules when it came to designating towns as big time? Regardless of the nagging Wal Mart question, Baptist churches were becoming more and more plentiful along the rural roads of Kentucky.

A stop for brunch in the small town of La Center at the Bluegrass Restaurant allowed an opportunity to enjoy a tasty fried egg and ham sandwich. By now it was probable that the blood flowing through our veins had developed the consistency of mayonnaise. While munching on the sandwich, it was hard to miss the John Deere paraphernalia and an autographed picture of Miss Kentucky that hung proudly on the restaurant wall. Miss Kentucky, as would be expected, appeared quite fit and healthy. It was likely that her visit to the Bluegrass had not included a fried egg and ham sandwich. The congenial waitress, upon our inquiry, explained, "You guys know, don't you, that the grass in Kentucky isn't really blue?" Although we attempted to convince her that we in fact knew that, the look on her face questioned the intelligence of the two northern interlopers in her nearly empty restaurant.

A large fellow in coveralls weighing in at at least four hundred pounds watched the interaction with passing interest from a nearby table. As he slowly ate his morning fare and glanced at the local paper, there was every indication that his place at the table had been occupied for some time and was likely to be occupied for most of the rest of the morning. An occasional grin as he overheard our lively discussion with the waitress revealed a mouth noticeably lacking a significant number of front teeth. Regardless of his lack of recent dental care, he, like so many of the others that had been encountered, seemed to be a genuinely nice person just going about the day's agenda. On this particular day, that agenda appeared to be uncluttered.

The remainder of the day's ride to Paducah was accompanied by an increasing amount of traffic and my fifth flat tire. The morning had turned sunny and pleasantly warm with low humidity. Changing a tire in such comfortable conditions was almost pleasurable. The gentle ribbing about the disparity in the number of flat tires made by the other team member rolled off my happy tire changing back like water off a duck. Nothing was going to affect the good feelings of this beautiful first day in Kentucky. The same question was once again repeated, though. Why had one bike had five flats and the other only one? The phenomenon would remain an unanswered cycling mystery.

The last few miles into Paducah were along a four-lane highway with wide shoulders and gentle grades. Paducah, a city of 40,000 situated at the confluence of the Tennessee and Ohio Rivers, was much larger than anticipated and provided a comfortable evening's stay. William Clark, of Lewis and Clark fame, founded Paducah in 1827. The name of the town came from a large tribe of Indians that inhabited the area called the Padoucas. Before Clark's arrival, enemies armed by Europeans reduced the once proud tribe to slavery. William Clark, wanting to preserve the tribe's memory by making sure people could pronounce their name, used the current English spelling.

Day 62 - 2993 Miles Down, 794 To Go

WHAT'S A HUNDRED BUCKS AMONG FRIENDS?

The ride out of Paducah included navigating five or six miles of busy commercial development and a section of four lane divided highway. A brilliant red sunrise helped make the troublesome road conditions a little more tolerable. A stop in Calvert City at a gas station that had been converted into a used car lot supplied a much-needed opportunity to use the facilities. When asked for permission to use the restroom, the fellow working in the service bay casually lifted his head from under the raised hood of a '69 Mustang Mach I and nodded toward a well-used but clean one-holer at the back of the station.

Merj's trips to the restrooms of America always provided a chance to kill time and talk to locals. The fellow under the hood of the Mustang was the latest source of companionship during such lengthy visits. The old Mustang was in pretty good shape, and he was justifiably proud of the improvements being made on the engine.

While growing up in the sixties, the automotive preferences of the high school male population was generally divided into two camps, Ford lovers and GM or more likely, Chevy lovers. There were always a few that argued the merits of Chrysler products, but the avid and much more numerous Ford and Chevy guys usually drowned them out. A person was one or the other, and in many cases, the preference reflected the vehicle that their parents drove. I had grown up in a decidedly Chevy family, and tolerance for the opinions of the Ford guys was only politely tolerated.

For we Chevy fans, the Mustang had been a problem. When it first appeared in 1964, there was no comparable model from GM. The timing of the Mustang introduction couldn't have been worse for a high school senior, Chevy fan. When the arguments between the two camps were the fiercest, we only had five bullets in our six shooter. In fact, it wasn't until the fall of 1966, when the Camaro made the scene, that those of us in the Chevy camp had something comparable to challenge the gloating Ford lovers with. The wait was worth it. A few years later, I happily plopped down $2,741 in cash to buy my first new car: a '68 Camaro Rally Sport.

Over the years the rivalry between Chevy and Ford has pretty much disappeared. After all, the passions aroused by a Taurus or the modern version of an Impala are hardly comparable to those of the offerings during sixties. The one exception is the rivalry between the Mustang and the Camaro. In spite of the end of Camaro production in 2002, the competition remained pretty much in place. Most current owners of restored, early models, however, have mellowed over the years. Acknowledging a well restored car from the opposite camp was not as difficult as it had been a few decades earlier.

The Mach I Mustang in Calvert City was a decent restoration and deserved accolades from a fellow car collector. Seeing another sixties era muscle car always offered an opportunity to expound with detailed descriptions of the three cars I had back home. Merj's eyes usually rolled back in her head as such discussions began, and a look that clearly conveyed "there he goes again" almost always came over her face. Such a look was obvious as she emerged from the restroom. After an especially impassioned description of the '69 Camaro Indianapolis 500 Pace Car that formed a third of my small collection, the fellow under the hood of the Mustang raised his head and declared, "You got a fine ride there." Who could argue with the observation of such an astute student of classic cars?

The ride out of Calvert City toward Princeton continued along a busy roadway with easily negotiated ups and downs. The heat of the morning caused reason to stop at a fast food hamburger restaurant for an air-conditioned break and a large Coke. The restaurant was empty, and as we sat at a table drinking the

Cokes, a neatly uniformed, middle age lady busied herself ready-ing the dining room for the expected noon hour rush. Our cycling attire usually drew attention to the fact that we were "different" and the lady in the restaurant, along with some of her fellow employees, took the opportunity to ask the customary questions.

Where did you start? Astoria, Oregon. How long have you been on the road? About two months. Where are you headed? Hilton Head Island, South Carolina. Have you had problems with anybody? Nope, nobody's messed with us yet. Any flat tires? Yep, about six. Where do you stay at night? Motels. Why are you doing this? Boyhood dream. What's been the best part so far? The people along the way and the mountains of the West. How was Merj talked into this? Not sure, you gotta ask her. Where do you go to the bathroom? There's not enough time to tell you. Are you guys crazy? Maybe.

Although we never tired of responding to people's questions, the melodic Southern accent of the lady in the restaurant made the usual question and answer session even more pleasant than usual. The smooth "y'alls" flowed freely. If there were any doubts before about being in the South, they were clearly dispelled by the classy lady in western Kentucky.

The morning ride continued through the small town of Eddyville on an absolutely gorgeous summer morning. A short dis-tance later, we met our friends Bob and Barbara from back in Ohio. They had come down to meet us and provide support to Nashville.

Before our leaving for the West Coast, Bob had wagered a hun-dred dollars that I would not make it across the country. His confi-dence was based on thinking that Merj would, at some point in time, insist that we deposit our bikes in the closest dumpster and take the next bus home. He knew that like most husbands who had invested a number of years into a harmonious marital relationship, I would not be able to say no if the demand were ever presented.

Now, with the trip about three-quarters complete, the look on Bob's face, although showing a happiness in seeing us, also reflected the distinct possibility of losing a hundred bucks. His well-known frugality over the many years of our friendship had given extra meaning to the wager. A number of our mutual friends had offered encouragement through e-mails, and many had mentioned the delight they would share in seeing Bob part with the hundred dollar bill. A hundred dollars to Bob was five hundred dollars to anyone else. It would be a special reward and had been a topic of discussion along the many roads of America we had already covered.

In the back of my mind, the thought of losing the bet on a technicality created by the two mile *downhill* ride in the pickup through the construction site in Wyoming occasionally reared its ugly head. Bob was frugal, but certainly he wouldn't use that forced truck ride to back out of the bet? On second thought, what kind of a buddy bets *against* his friend?

Bob and Barbara left us and drove on to Princeton, about ten miles down the road, to check into the hotel and ready a home cooked lunch. The remainder of the day's ride continued along rolling terrain with small fields of various crops and widely spaced homes. The beautiful morning and scenic rural landscape made for an enjoyable experience. Merj seemed to have jets in her biking shorts as she set a blistering pace to Princeton. The thought of a home cooked lunch and good conversation with our friends seemed to motivate her.

The accompaniment of our friends also meant the removal of the panniers and their temporary, at least for a couple of days, transport in the trunk of the car. The panniers on my bike had grown to a fairly robust fifty-five pounds, much of which consisted of "souvenirs" that had been collected along the way. A prominent contributor to the added weight was the zip lock bags full of dirt from each state. Merj's plan was to assemble the samples into a layered display in a large glass vase, with each uniquely colored layer representing one of the states on the trip. Surprisingly, judicious searching provided for a variety of soil samples that varied enough so that I had come to believe that such a project had some merit. Besides, at this late stage it was not wise to question the artistic genius of one's daily bicycling companion, and long term wife. There were times though, when the thought crossed my mind that a wiser choice might have been to collect air samples from each state. Although certainly not as striking, the weight would have been considerably easier to deal with.

Day 63 - 3044 Miles Down, 743 To Go

LAST TRAIN TO CLARKSVILLE

The early morning ride out of Princeton was unusual in that it was cool enough to warrant jackets to combat the early morning temperatures. It had been some time since any type of long sleeved outerwear had been required, even during predawn starts. The tingle in our fingertips on this chilly morning was a pleasant change from the warm beginnings to most of the days over the last few weeks. The pleasant ride through downtown Princeton at dawn, showed a community that was nicely maintained and one that had tried to preserve its heritage through a fair amount of historical renovation.

The road out of Princeton took us through rolling terrain, past a busy and dusty stone quarry, and into a picturesque countryside. The fields bordering the well-paved and lightly traveled road consisted of corn, soybeans, and our first glimpse of tobacco. Having never seen tobacco in its crop stage, a stop for an early morning break and picture was in order. The natives that passed as the pictures were being taken had to chuckle to themselves about the two Yankee travelers photographing such an ordinary tobacco field. In reality, the closest to a tobacco field we had ever gotten was a pack of Winstons behind the counter at the local mini-mart. The local Kentuckians probably shared the same thoughts as the hundreds of other natives that had passed us during the trip: "Those people are a bit strange."

Tobacco has historically been a very important part of the Kentucky agricultural economy and culture. The tobacco grown in western Kentucky is generally of the dark fire-cured and dark air-cured variety and is used primarily in smokeless tobacco products such as snuff, chewing, and pipe tobacco. Kentucky is the most tobacco-dependent state in the United States. Although North Carolina grows more tobacco than Kentucky, tobacco represents a larger percentage of Kentucky's agricultural income. Tobacco currently accounts for about fifty percent of Kentucky's crop receipts and twenty five per cent of the state's total agricultural cash receipts.

More fields of tobacco appeared and the beautiful cool morning continued, as the ups and downs became a little more severe, but not worthy of complaint. The effects of the many mountains we had previously negotiated gave a certain perspective to these western Kentucky rollers. Had they occurred in the first week of the trip, complaining would have been the order of the morning. At this stage, however, they had become just a mild annoyance. Before long the rolling terrain produced small herds of cattle and an occasional old barn. The weathered barns soon became a much-photographed part of the landscape. At times the word "obsession" may have again quietly crossed Merj's lips as a call for a pause and photograph of yet another old barn broke the calm of the late summer morning. Maybe she was right. The barn thing was a bit unusual.

The notorious Kentucky dogs made their presence known, as on more than one occasion quick acceleration was required to outrun a canine bent upon our destruction. One hard charging dog who exhibited a certain interest in our undertaking interrupted a particularly interesting old barn photo session. A short time later, while outrunning an unusually persistent white terrier, a truck passed with an odd, almost sweet smelling odor. As so often happened, our minds wandered trying to determine what inside the truck had created the smell. In the case of odorous truck, we guessed that its contents could very well have been from one of the distilleries in the area. A reasonable hypothesis, but like many of our other guesses, there was a chance that it was incorrect.

The ride through downtown Hopkinsville produced a busy commercial area and a number of restored brick buildings. Unlike many of the small towns west of the Mississippi, the villages of Kentucky generally appeared to be more prosperous, and many had functioning downtown business districts. Just south of Hopkinsville, a large, older fellow in a lumbering well-used dump truck passed us from the opposite direction; he rolled down his window and gave us a big grin and a vigorous thumbs up. Such simple, friendly acknowledgements continued to provide a good feeling and a certain amount of encouragement. We made a vow to never again pass a bicyclist loaded with gear without acknowledging him or her in some fashion. It really did make a difference.

The road from Hopkinsville to Clarksville, the evening's destination, became much busier, and watching the rear view mirror for approaching traffic became a bigger part of the cycling experience. The scenery, however, remained pleasantly rural as we passed fields of soybeans and well-maintained farmhouses. The unmistakable chirping of bobwhites provided a welcomed change from the din of passing vehicles. Roadside flea markets became more and more numerous and the traffic increased as Fort Campbell and the Tennessee line approached. The flea markets seemed a natural fit amid the hilly landscape and weathered buildings, with their own "antiques" scattered around adjoining yards.

All semblances of rural Kentucky peace and tranquility ended at the Tennessee state line, which was also near one of the main entrances to Fort Campbell. Our traditional picture taking session at this state crossing was distinctly non-traditional as a steady stream of traffic roared past us on the busy multilane highway.

There was a certain nostalgia for the charging herd of cattle at the Colorado crossing. Our chances of survival seemed better with a live bovine than confrontation with the inanimate bulldog on the hood of a Mack truck. With eleven miles to go to Clarksville, we grew anxious contemplating what lie ahead. The ride into the city was not going to be a pleasant experience.

For once, anticipated dread turned into reality. The last eleven miles of the day were some of the most difficult of the trip. The grades were easily negotiated, but the traffic on what was now a six-lane highway through a heavy commercial area required more time checking the mirrors than looking ahead. On more than one occasion we shared the feeling that, after all of the miles and all of the obstacles that had been dealt with, our demise would surely be found on this congested stretch of Tennessee highway.

Bob and Barbara shared that same opinion as they came out to check our status, give directions to the night's hotel, and question our sanity. Bob had to be thinking, "There's no way both of them are going to make it to Clarksville, that hundred dollars is mine!" It would have been hard to find someone to bet against his thinking, but the remaining miles were safely negotiated and two physically strong, but psychologically scarred, cyclists checked into the Riverview Hotel in downtown Clarksville.

Clarksville, straddling the Cumberland River, is the fifth largest town in Tennessee. The city was established in 1784 and was named for Indian fighter and Revolutionary War leader General George Rogers Clark. The town grew and prospered during the early 1800's, and in 1861 made the momentous decision to join with the South in the Civil War. A short time thereafter, the city fell to Union forces. After the Civil War the Cumberland River helped the community prosper and it became well-known for the production of dark fired tobacco, it's primary money crop.

In the Twentieth Century the area has profited from communication and mechanical technology, and is no longer dependent upon an agricultural base. With nearly 4,000 employees, the area's largest employer is nearby Fort Campbell. The fort is home to over 23,000 soldiers and 40,000 family members and the headquarters of the famed 101st Airborne Division. Clarksville is also the home to Austin Peay University, and such luminaries as track star Wilma Rudolph and famed University of Tennessee women's basketball coach Pat Head Summitt.

When not concerned about impending death on the ride into town, the old Monkees song from the sixties, "Last Train to Clarksville," kept rattling through our minds. Questioning why they would have sung about this particular Tennessee town when other more famous cities such as Memphis, Nashville, Knoxville, and Chattanooga were available as subjects was yet another mystery of Twentieth Century life.

Clarksville proved to be a fitting destination after the excitement of the latter portion of the day's ride. A pleasant stroll with our friends along a riverside park bordering the Cumberland River and an enjoyable dinner was a good tension-relieving antidote. The friendly restaurant staff used their innate Southern hospitality to make the dining experience a rewarding one. A slow after-dark stroll along the river walk back to the hotel, with the lights along the trail reflected in the slowly moving waters of the Cumberland River, provided a fitting end to a day of great differences. A ride that had begun with bucolic rural scenery and had been truly enjoyable, had ended with the hope of surviving the day in one piece.

Day 64 - 3102 Miles Down, 685 To Go

tennessee

"Sometimes I just draw the words out s'long that I just gotta chop 'em off to get to the next one."

"THINGS JUST AIN'T WHAT THEY USED TO BE."

The early morning departure from Clarksville followed a portion of the Cumberland River through the usual commercial development that would be expected in a good-sized established community. Barges being pushed by tugs slowly moved their cargoes upstream as the traffic on land began to increase. A short distance from downtown, the day's planned route turned south toward Nashville onto a quiet, two-lane road known as the Pat Head Summitt Parkway.

While negotiating the rolling highway, certain thoughts of inadequacy crept into my vacuous mind. Coach Summitt was probably no older than me, and while still very much alive, she had had a road named after her. What had I done in the same amount of time to warrant any such accolades? Not much, at least in the eye of the public. The only comfort lie in the fact that it was doubtful that the coach ever rode a bicycle across the country. She was probably a lot smarter than that.

After the previous day's nerve-wracking ride into Clarksville, the planned route to the much larger destination of Nashville was carefully designed to avoid a reoccurrence. Most of the information for the less traveled route was gleaned from discussions with hotel and restaurant personnel in Clarksville. The trip that had begun the previous winter with meticulous planning of every day's ride had now degenerated into a general idea of a route whose daily details were not usually firmed up until the night before.

This approach had started in eastern Colorado with some divergence from the original plan. It reached a full day-by-day philosophy in the Hallmark store in western Missouri where the original route was abandoned for good. The daily planning had unexpected rewards, as there was always a certain feeling of freedom knowing that there was flexibility to meet changing weather, terrain, or other physical conditions. The route planning almost always required input from knowledgeable locals, so conversations with people along the way became a necessity and often led to other interesting discussions. There was a certain "foot lose and fancy free" feeling that we both found satisfying. It felt like the way one should cross the country on a bicycle.

A stop at a restaurant about nine miles into the day supplied what had become a customary breakfast of scrambled eggs, sausage, and toast. A native of the area sat nearby and studied the crossword puzzle in the local morning paper. Much like the fellow back at the Bluegrass Restaurant, he too weighed in at four hundred or so pounds, and was in no hurry to get along with his day. In a thick Southern drawl, he asked, "How's your trip goin'?" We answered his question with as much detail as he seemed willing to accept.

With a certain amount of dismay in his voice, the long time

native explained, "This area has growed from about 30,000 to a little over a 100,000 people in just the last thirty years or so. Things just ain't what they used to be." He went on to say, "A lot of the newcomers work over at Ft. Campbell or at the Trane air conditionin' plant." The rural farming nature of the area, much like other parts of the country, was undergoing a fundamental change, and a lot of the old timers were having a tough time accepting it.

Our rather large breakfast companion had a heavy Tennessee accent that required careful listening attention so as not to continually ask him to repeat what he had just said. In some ways it was like listening to an individual who had immigrated to the United States and learned English as a second language. I tried to understand enough words in order to string together some meaning from the conversation and be able to answer in a reasonably intelligent fashion. Regardless of the difficulties, the smooth, Southern drawl was a comfortable and pleasant rendering of the English language, and the fellow speaking it was equally pleasant.

The morning warmed and the cycling proceeded through wooded rural areas of long drops downhill to small rivers, and equally long climbs back up only to be repeated again. Merj, now an eagle-eyed-dead-snake-spotter, pointed out number fifty twelve miles into the day. This one, like most of those that proceeded it, was in a rather bad state. A similar count of dead armadillos had started back in Kansas but had been abandoned in Missouri. There were so many of them, that to keep count had become an exercise in futility. The folks back there had often referred to the ugly critters as "possum on the half shell."

Snakes, however, were still worthy of counting. After all, there was still the possibility that one of them could magically come back to life, become entangled in Merj's spokes, and bite her each time the wheel came around. Attempts at gentle ribbing about this phobia continued to be met with stern facial expressions, clearly indicating such comments were not welcomed.

The slow pace of life in rural central Tennessee was again noticeable when a stop at a gas station produced a rather indifferent woman behind the counter. Upon dutifully presenting ourselves in front of her to pay for the usual mid-morning snacks, she barely looked up from an intense telephone conversation. Without any unusual effort to listen on our part, it was clear that she was in a heated discussion about the purchase of a horse. Being totally unaware of the criteria that one uses in the purchase of a used horse, and realizing that mileage on the odometer and remaining life on the tires are unlikely considerations, her conversation became one of interest. At least two criteria became clear when she asked the person on the other end of the phone, "Does that horse rear or buck?" It seemed to be a pretty good question, even to a couple of Yankees whose closest encounter with a horse had been the kind that takes a quarter to ride in front of Wal Mart.

The comfortable rolling morning ride proceeded through scenic rural countryside, past the town of Cheap Hill and the Sycamore River. In Ashland City a large banner was prominently displayed that announced CHEATHAM COUNTY MULE PULL - AUGUST 19-24. A mule pull may not have the roar and excitement of a big-time, arena filling tractor pull, but it was an appropriate form of entertainment in this part of the country. It felt right, and more than that, it felt good.

A REAL OLDIE MOLDY

Soon after leaving Ashland City, the shoulder widened and a sign pronounced the designation of the roadway as a bike path. The broad shoulders and the gentle grades of the recently reconstructed road made for a pleasant ride through the scenic mountains north of Nashville. After exiting an especially suitable stand of roadside trees that had served as a makeshift restroom, we had a surprise visit from Bob and Barbara. Barbara had brought tasty cookies that helped restore some of the energy expended after thirty-five miles of hilly cycling. While we chatted about the upcoming evening at a Day's Inn in Nashville, Bob said, "We went on ahead and made reservations at a better place than that Day's Inn." He further explained, "The rates are better too." He then proceeded to give detailed directions on how to find our new home for the evening.

A nagging unease came over both of us as our two friends headed down the road to run errands and await our arrival in Nashville. Over the years we had traveled extensively with our friends, and on those occasions where Bob was left in charge of the lodging, we had stayed in some "interesting" accommodations. Regardless of the lodgings, we always had a good time, so that comforting thought temporarily dispelled any concern over Bob's judgement.

After a little over forty-five miles of cycling, the crest of a hill after a long climb provided a panoramic view of the distant Nashville skyline. The view was a picturesque one; the downtown buildings were lightly shrouded in late morning fog and haze. The last few miles of the day's ride were through increasingly busy areas along roads that were undergoing areas of significant construction. Also noticeable was a change in the surrounding areas. The pleasant well-maintained, rural countryside of the earlier part of the day had given way to run-down housing and debris filled yards. Concerns about Bob's lodging choice began to reappear.

Unfortunately it didn't take long for the fears to be fully validated. Home for the evening was located off an exit ramp from Interstate 24 and was probably originally built as a chain motel in the sixties. Apparently little maintenance had been done since, so it retained most of its "charm." Part of the ambience included a swimming pool filled with water of questionable quality, dirty and worn carpeting, a badly rusted front door and an area of about five square feet of impressive black mold on the ceiling. The other clientele at the establishment, however, seemed to be quite comfortable with the surroundings. It was possible that some of them may have only occupied their rooms for relatively brief interludes.

Having completed their errands, Bob and Barbara joined us a few minutes later and the four of us examined our motel rooms. As usual, Bob had gotten the better of the draw. His room only had a couple of square feet of mold on the ceiling. The ladies offered the opinion that we would be spending the night in a "dump" and got no dissention from the gentlemen. No other options existed. The town, at least this portion of it, was booked for the evening. The good news was that we were saving a few bucks by staying here rather than the Days Inn. The bad news was that the savings weren't nearly enough.

Getting out of the motel and going someplace, anyplace, was an agreed upon necessity. The car offered an opportunity to escape our surroundings and spend most of the afternoon at a Nashville landmark called Opryland. The facility consisted of a very nice hotel, acres of enclosed gardens, and an abundance of shops and restaurants. The Grand Old Opry was located in an adjacent structure.

Opryland was very nicely done, and one of the "must see" attractions for visitors to Nashville. An especially interesting feature was a large, open, rotating restaurant and bar. The slowly rotating bar allowed a chance to relax, share stories of the road and contemplate what lie ahead for the evening back at the Bates Motel. Time was of no concern as the four of us viewed and reviewed the passing Opryland scenery with each turn the bar made.

Facing the inevitable, our quartet eventually ventured back to the humble lodgings, changed clothes, "freshened up," and prepared for a visit to downtown Nashville for dinner. It was decided that the secret to success in the hotel room was to never remove our socks or to not touch anything in the room with our bare hands. Turning on faucets with one's elbows or showering with one's socks on was considered a necessity in our low-budget temporary home in north Nashville. It was difficult to freshen up in an environment that seemed to encourage just the opposite.

The car ride downtown was complicated by traffic congestion caused by a pre-season Tennessee Titans football game. Such minor inconveniences were easily tolerated since the evening's return "home" was to be delayed as long as possible. Eventually a leisurely and tasty meal was enjoyed at a small restaurant in the entertainment district of Nashville. Conversation with the restaurant staff was helpful in the development of a plan to survive the next day's early morning ride out of town. The look on their faces, however, conveyed a certain amount of skepticism as to whether any well-devised plan would be successful. The look on Bob's face displayed a renewed confidence that maybe the hundred dollars could be saved after all.

Day 65 - 3150 Miles Down, 637 To Go

"ARE YOU GUYS CRAZY?"

An early morning departure from the motel was always part of the plan but setting an alarm clock proved unnecessary. Merj did not sleep the entire night, and her travelling companion had been awake since 3:00 AM contemplating an escape. As is often the case with such early morning problem solving, getting out of Nashville appeared fraught with nothing but trouble. Lying in bed wasn't going to solve the problem, so at about 5:00 AM, four sock covered feet hit the floor and preparations for a predawn departure ensued.

Bob and Barbara's room was still dark as the bikes were quietly rolled out into the dark, muggy air. They would be heading back home today, and waking them was not necessary as we had said our good-byes the prior evening. It was great having our good friends along the past three days and their presence and support would be missed. Their leaving marked the unofficial beginning of the final leg of the journey. All that was on the immediate agenda, however, was traversing the ten or fifteen miles necessary to get through Nashville.

The early departure and the fact that it was a Sunday morning allowed a relatively uneventful trip through portions of the city that had seen better days. In short order our route took us on an arching bridge over the Cumberland River into the heart of downtown Nashville. The generally unoccupied bridge gave an opportunity to snap an unobstructed picture of Merj heading toward the haze covered, tall downtown buildings. We cycled past One Nashville Place and then the Country Music Hall of Fame where a local shouted words of encouragement from a nearby curb. Although his comment was appreciated, this fellow was clearly not in full control of his faculties and may still have been feeling the celebratory effects of a Titans preseason victory the night before.

Another three miles through the "adult" section of town and past a somewhat deteriorated commercial section, including the Hubcap Heaven, delivered us to an office area and an increasing level of comfort. Hubcap Heaven may have had a ready source of inventory from some of the rolling stock that had been seen in the area. The road continued through a tunnel under runways of the Nashville Airport, and at about twelve miles into the day, a modern industrial park appeared. A relaxed feeling finally settled in and two miles later a stop at a McDonalds for breakfast allowed a chance to collect our thoughts.

While relaxing in the restaurant, a Nashville policeman sat down at the table next to ours and began to chat. The young officer confessed that he had followed us in his police cruiser for the last few miles. We would have felt a whole lot better knowing that he was there, but his trailing skills were pretty good apparently, as we had not been aware of being followed. "Are you guys crazy?" he wanted to know. Why was it that this question seemed to be the one most frequently asked when people were informed of our little adventure? That said, his reaction directly reflected the area we had just ridden through. He went on to say, "Do you guys know that, on average, we get about a shooting a night in that part of town?" We had no choice but to respond, "No sir, we didn't."

Our police officer friend continued, "The only people crazier than you two are a couple of Irish girls I ran into in Ethiopia." Wait a second, Ethiopia? After obvious questioning on our part, he responded, "I ran into 'em while I was over there as part of a UN sponsored refugee relocation program. When I asked 'em what they were doing, they said they were walking across Africa. I told 'em they're crazy and asked 'em if their parents knew what they were doing. You guys are almost as crazy." It was encouraging to learn that we failed to occupy the top spot on his list of those with questionable mental health.

The remainder of the day's ride continued along gradual up and down grades through the commercial areas of LaVergne and Smyrna. A local transmission shop advertised, SHIFT HAPPENS HERE, and a short time later Honest John's Used Cars proclaimed THE WALKING MAN'S FRIEND. A herd of cattle brought forth a familiar fragrance, in sharp contrast to the odors of the early portion of the morning. Soon after leaving the cows, Bob and Barbara called on the cell phone to make sure that Nashville had been successfully navigated. Their concern was justified and much appreciated.

Murfreesboro would be the destination for the evening and a newly constructed inn was chosen for the night's lodging. Outside the hotel a stretch limo waited for a large wedding party that had assembled in the lobby. The limo was unusual in that the vehicle that had been used to create it was a Hummer. It wasn't the smaller H2 model, but the military's climb-over-anything original version. A stretch Hummer was certainly a first. The twenty-eight year old driver was a smooth talker who regaled us with stories of athletes and country western stars that had graced the inside of the limo. He had a Bachelor's Degree in Business and had all the makings of a guy who would someday own the company.

Inside the motel at the registration desk an equally impressive young lady awaited our arrival. After some spirited but friendly negotiation, the price of a night's stay was lowered from $89.95 to $64.95. Contrasts with the previous nights lodging in Nashville were unmistakable. The ceilings of this almost brand new building were a bright white and devoid of any traces of the ubiquitous black mold that had greeted us just a day before. The swimming pool actually looked fit for human habitation, and in fact, the lobby displayed a gurgling water fountain. Yes, it was back to the good old times of just two nights ago.

Getting into the shower to wash off the day's hot ride was, as usual, a priority. Equally important was to remove the remaining vestiges of our last motel, including the unseen but surely present bacteriological growth that must have taken up residence on our skin. The comfortable feel of new carpet under sockless feet was a pleasant experience that one usually takes for granted. Murfreesboro, Tennessee was our kind of place.

The City of Murfreesboro is located off Interstate 24 in central Tennessee and is populated by 69,000 people. The town was named after Colonel Hardy Murfree, a friend of the original owner of the land that the city currently occupies. Murfreesboro was briefly the capital of Tennessee from 1818 to 1826. Nearby Cannonsburgh Village, the original name of the city, has been restored to portray a vintage southern community. The restored village is the home of the "World's Largest Red Cedar Bucket" which was made in Murfreesboro in 1887.

The bucket brought to light an inherent problem with bicycle travel. Many of the local attractions were off the beaten path and required a commitment of time and energy to get back on the bikes and head off to "The World's Biggest Ball of Tin Foil," or whatever the local point of interest may have been. Unfortunately the "World's Largest Red Cedar Bucket" in Murfreesboro, all 1,000 gallons of it, would have to meet the same fate as the

"World's Deepest Hand Dug Well" in Greensburg, Kansas. It was just too much to ask a couple of middle age cyclists to remount their two wheeled transportation and head out to the oversized bucket on a hot, muggy day. The question did persist though as to what had possessed the good folks of Murfreesboro to construct a 1,000 gallon red cedar bucket in the first place.

A PRIVY AS SECURE AS FORT KNOX

After leaving the commercial area of Murfreesboro, the morning's ride passed through an attractive residential area consisting of large homes set back from the road behind well-manicured front yards. An exceptionally large brick home with a sparkling white fence gave the feeling of a modern day Southern plantation. Soon the housing changed back to the more traditional, modest dwellings that had become more typical of central Tennessee. The rolling terrain was generally easily navigated, but ahead more substantial mountains could be seen through the morning fog and haze. An occasional small herd of cattle and a large collection of goats provided four-legged companionship through a landscape consisting of wooded areas and meadows.

Another newfound four-legged "friend" in the form of a Tennessee dog roared out from a rundown farmhouse and gave chase until finally giving up. The house's yard was home to a dozen chickens that were tethered to individual vertically mounted steel tanks with holes cut in the bottom. Presumably the tanks were the chicken's homes. It was too bad that the dog wasn't tied to the tanks and the chickens were left to roam the yard unfettered. Our canine friend would have had to think twice before dragging one of the good sized steel tanks behind him as he chased us down the road.

The chickens were more examples of our naïveté. We later discovered that the leashed fowl were likely being raised for cock fighting. Allegedly their ultimate destination was South America, since cock fighting was illegal in Tennessee. It was also suggested that only the *most* naïve believe that all of the animals are really shipped out of the country.

Not long after, an early morning stop at a general store and "fillin' station" provided a chance to take a restroom and nutrition break. The lady behind the counter of the modest establishment was not having a good day, but nonetheless, politely handed over a restroom key attached to a wooden stick the size of a small two by four.

The restroom consisted of a padlocked privy adjacent to the fillin' station. The outhouse was like most and didn't lend itself to the urge to partake of a leisurely review of the morning newspaper while being occupied. The heavy padlock on the door was another mystery. Why would the storeowner think that anyone would want to occupy the place unless there was a *real* need to make use of it let alone steal something from its posh interior? And why the giant sequoia attached to the key? It was hard to imagine a conversation that might have began something like, "Oh boy Martha, let's take this key, it'll go real good with the towels we stole from the Holiday Inn last night."

The ride continued from the fillin' station through rolling terrain and the small town of Bell Springs where an old fellow in front of a bright white Methodist Church waved a friendly acknowledgement. The hills became more significant as the road headed south and an occasional sign announcing "Passing Lane Ahead" brought back fears last felt in the western mountains. Stopping at a Texaco gas station for a Coke provided an opportunity to consult with Katy, the young woman behind the counter, about the road ahead.

Katy, a sweet Southern lady, opined, "If you guys are goin' to Manchester tonight, the best place to spend the night is the Holiday Inn Express." She continued, "I've got a good friend named Eugene who manages the place and he'll take care of y'all." Katy then gave us a slip of paper with Eugene's name on it and a written request to "treat us good."

After thanking Katy and heading back to the bikes an odd sight greeted us near the gas pumps. Three large busses full of young members of a travelling drum and bugle corps had pulled into the gas station. One of the busses had unfortunately become hung up on the steep entrance. The rear bumper of the bus rested firmly on the road and prevented movement in any direction. The young drummers and buglers seemed amused by the situation. The adult driver did not.

The town of Manchester appeared about six miles later and a sign on the Coffee County Bank showed a late morning temperature of 92 degrees. The motel was located a few miles from downtown and required passing the county jail, a bail bondsman's office appropriately located across the street, and a local eating establishment known as the Red Neck Barbecue. While checking in at the Holiday Inn Express an inquiry was made as to whether Katy's friend Eugene was on duty. The lady behind the reception desk informed us that he was not, and that she was not aware of anyone with that name having ever worked at the hotel. So much for the VIP treatment.

The walk back from lunch passed a building identified as the Coffee County Arrowhead and Aerospace Museum. Upon opening the front door, it was quickly ascertained that the museum was empty save the husband and wife curators and the two of us. Judy, the wife, offered a personal tour and her offer was graciously accepted. The tour started with a room devoted to the biblical creation story and then to areas representing the time period when Native Americans occupied the area. Each successive room dealt with another significant historical period in central Tennessee. It was becoming clear with the proliferation of churches and the subject matter of the first portion of the museum that religion was a large part of the lives of folks in this part of the South.

The well-stocked museum contained a moonshine still and a restored drug store complete with bottles of old fashion elixirs. Judy talked of the area's well known Tennessee walking horses. Evidently Tennessee was known for its walking horses much like Kentucky was known for its thoroughbreds. She told of General Patton's stay near Manchester where he trained troops for World War II combat in Germany. Patton had chosen the area because of terrain similar to that found in Germany. A large Lionel Train display again brought back memories of that memorable Santa Fe diesel locomotive making its innumerable circles of the basement layout.

Behind the museum a larger, outdoor railroad layout was being assembled by a small group of men. The railroad was large enough to transport small children around the grounds. The men were working at a rather leisurely pace on the warm day and all were attired in striped suits. Judy explained, "These fellows are prisoners in the county jail and are part of a work release program. Each morning we pick them up at the jail and then return them at the end of the day." Their boldly striped outfits made an escape attempt problematic. Regardless of their attire, working on the railroad had to be a better way to spend the day than back at the county jail.

Day 67 - 3224 Miles Down, 563 To Go

HERMAN

It didn't take long to leave the town of Manchester behind and head into a gentle rolling countryside filled with fields and occasional homes. The cool morning made for a comfortable ride through the scenic landscape. Since leaving Nashville, a mountain by the name of Monteagle had been a subject of warning from many locals. As so often happened, the description of the mountain made it sound like an insurmountable obstacle.

As the mountain drew closer the descriptions became more

ominous. Merj, her antennae always tuned to rumors of steep climbs, was growing more anxious as the hill loomed a few miles down the road. Trying to console her by reminders that walking the bike up the hill was not a sin (although in my obsessive thinking it was, at least for me), or that if trucks could negotiate it we surely could, made little difference. No amount of psychological cheer-leading would help. In Merj's mind it was still a hill and it would certainly ruin the day's ride.

As Monteagle Mountain drew still closer we quickly passed through the tiny town of Hillsboro. School children waited along the roadside as the school year was just beginning in rural Tennessee. On occasion a parent would be waiting with their "young uns" as we rolled past. Each time we were greeted with a wide grin from the freshly groomed youngsters and a friendly acknowledgement from their proud parents. The opening of the school year and the browning fields of corn along the highway added to the feeling of late summer on this sunny mid-August morning.

The cycling continued free and easy over gentle rollers and through scenic fields of corn and soybeans as the tiny towns of Pelham and Mountain View were traversed in a quick order. An old barn proclaimed "IT'S FUN FOR THE FAMILY IN ROCK CITY" in large letters painted on its roof. The previous day's museum stop had provided information that Rock City was located near Chattanooga at the top of Lookout Mountain. Supposedly the view from the top of the mountain included six or seven states. That seemed a bit of a reach, but certainly two or three seemed plausible.

Lookout Mountain and Rock City sounded like interesting places. We had certainly been advised with each passing barn advertisement of the benefits of a stop at either of them, but the chances of making a visit there was very remote. The problem lay in the name itself or at least the part of the name that referred to a mountain. It, like the "World's Deepest Hand Dug Well," and "The World's Largest Red Cedar Bucket," would have to await another visit. Probably one done in a motorized vehicle.

At eighteen miles into the day we crossed the Dry Fork Creek and began the long anticipated ascent of Monteagle Mountain. Trees generally canopied the road and the dense forest and steep grade were reminiscent of the coastal climbs in Oregon. Even with the shade of the overhanging trees, the warmth of the morning caused a significant sweat to dampen our clothing.

At two miles into the climb, a cut swath through the forest allowed for a panoramic view of the area that we had traversed earlier that morning. The early portion of the day's ride stretched out for a long distance below, and the high vantage point showed that the climb had been significant. The patchwork of rectangular fields interspersed within the heavily wooded landscape made for a photographic opportunity. A summer haze hovered over the distant horizon. As pictures were being snapped, a rooster crowed loudly behind a house located on the opposite side of the road. It was the only house on the mountain so far, and the rooster didn't appear to appreciate the intrusion of humans in his domain. There was a hint of autumn in the air as the bikes were remounted for the remainder of the climb.

A mile or so later we reached the top of Monteagle Mountain. A break at a crossroads near the town of the same name gave us an opportunity to rest and reflect on the morning. The Monteagle climb had been a topic of discussion by well meaning natives for the last couple of days and, while not a walk in the park, the three mile, six percenter was not the ominous obstacle that it had been advertised as.

While pondering the remainder of the day's ride, a fellow rolled up in a white pickup truck with a Tennessee Department of Transportation logo on the door. He rolled down the window and in a smooth, friendly Tennessee drawl said, "I saw y'all comin' up the hill. Is everything okay?" The " feminine glow" caused by the layer of perspiration on Merj's face must have caused reason to question our status. After being assured that everything was just fine, he told us, "Y'all are at the highest point in this part of

Tennessee. It's all down hill to Chattanooga from here." Merj's glow quickly changed to giddy glee.

Before long we learned that our new friend was fifty-eight years old and that this long time resident of the area went by the name of Herman. Herman's slow drawl was more drawn out than most that had been encountered since crossing the Mississippi River. He was conscious of his own slow speech. "Sometimes I draw the words out s'long that I just gotta chop 'em off to get to the next one," he explained. Herman proceeded to give detailed descriptions of the road ahead and encouraged a continuation of the days ride to Jasper, about twenty-six miles or so down the road. The helpful, friendly attitude displayed by Herman was not unusual in this part of the country. Carefully listening to each of his words took a little more effort, but Herman's slow Southern accent was a real treat. It fit comfortably into the surroundings. Southern hospitality was alive and well in the form of a genial TDOT employee at the top of Monteagle Mountain.

The town of Monteagle, located just off I-24, appeared to be a small, thriving community with a functioning downtown and a very nice bed and breakfast. Just outside of town a sign claimed that the Hillbilly Restaurant served "The Best Food in Town." The restaurant appeared to be permanently closed, so "best food" was apparently a superlative not shared by many of the diners in Monteagle.

The ride continued along the Cumberland Plateau through more gentle ups and downs and past farms, wooded countryside, and through the small town of Tracy City. A stop for a break at the The Mountain Mart was followed by a fast, fun, three-mile, seven percent drop through scenic tree-covered mountains down to Jasper. The comfortably warm summer morning and low traffic volume made the ride an enjoyable one. Herman's suggestion to continue on to Jasper was good advice.

Day 68 - 3272 Miles Down, 515 To Go

TRAIL OF TEARS

The ride from Jasper to Chattanooga began with some fairly good climbs and about five miles into the day, the road dropped down to a large lake created by the Tennessee Valley Authority (TVA). The fog hanging over the lake and the surrounding green mountains made for appealing early morning photographs. A narrow steel bridge with low railings caused the usual angst on Merj's part, but riding down the middle of our lane and our "the heck with those eighteen-wheeled Peterbilts" attitude allowed us to navigate the structure. A sign near the lake indicated that the chosen route was following the Trail of Tears Corridor. Other earlier signs had also made reference to the Trail of Tears. When we discovered the origin of the roadway designation, we also uncovered an ugly part of American history.

During the formative years of the United States, the westward movement of settlers put them onto land inhabited by various tribes of American Indians. A general policy developed after the Louisiana Purchase in 1803 called for relocation of the Indians to lands west of the Mississippi River. One tribe in particular, the Cherokees, was greatly affected by the policy. The Cherokees inhabited a large portion of the southern Appalachian Mountains and had developed a lifestyle based on farming, hunting and fishing. The discovery of gold in 1829 on Cherokee land in northern Georgia intensified efforts to remove them from their native lands.

In 1835 the Treaty of New Echota was signed with the federal government which gave the Indians five million dollars for their land and two years to move beyond the Mississippi River to Indian Territory. The Senate ratified the treaty even though a majority of the affected Indian population was not in agreement with its provisions. President Martin Van Buren ordered enforcement of the treaty in 1838 and the U. S. Army, under the leadership of General Winfield Scott, began rounding up the Indians for relocation. Unfortunately, incidents of intimidation by the troops and theft of property by locals further inflamed the Indians' anger.

Although a few were moved by water, most of the Indians traveled over land along a route that crossed central Tennessee, southwestern Kentucky, and southern Illinois. The relocated Indians were then transported over the Mississippi and brought west through southern Missouri and the northwest part of Arkansas to the Indian Territories. They were moved in groups of 700 to 1,600, and a physician and clergyman usually accompanied each group. Food for the trips was gathered before hand, but was generally of poor quality and a severe drought reduced available supplies for the animals. For much of the trek wagons were used to haul possessions while the people walked along side. Travel conditions, illness, and the severity of the winter weather made death a frequent occurrence. It is estimated that about 4,000 Native Americans died as a direct result of the relocation. The Trail of Tears was a sad but appropriate name for this stretch of Tennessee where such suffering had occurred during an earlier time.

THE VINE THAT ATE THE SOUTH

Leaving the Tennessee River required a long climb through humid air along a tree-canopied road. Passing a fellow unloading beer from a truck begged the question, "Have you got any extra in there?" To which the response of, "You might fall off your bicycle," was offered. The beer would have been welcomed as the beginning to the climb had caused a condition that we referred to as "presweat." Presweat is that relatively short period of time when a dampness is felt but the oncoming deluge of perspiration is still yet to arrive. One knows, however, that it won't be long once a presweat condition is acknowledged. The morning's presweat was soon converted to full-blown sweat by the time the midpoint of the hill was reached. A big ugly dog sat on the front porch of a rundown house and casually watched two sweat-stained odorous cyclists pass by. It was a good thing he decided not to give chase. The uphill grade would have made it impossible to outrun him.

Despite numerous signs that suggested substantial fines for littering, the roadside of this portion of Tennessee was covered with a considerable amount of refuse. It is said that you can tell a lot about people by the garbage they discard. That being the case, it was safe to assume that beer was a popular beverage, and that the beer of choice in central Tennessee was either Budweiser or Natural Lite. The favorite soft drinks were Pepsi or Mellow Yellow. A smattering of just about every other brand was also present in the grassy area off the road shoulder.

Counting discarded beer and soft drink cans was but another example of the effects of many hours perched on top of a narrow bicycle seat. Sometimes we discussed whether our minds would return to some semblance of "normalcy" upon the return home. A bigger question was how normal they were in the first place.

The morning ride continued through fairly substantial ups and downs along the Tennessee River. The small town of Riverside, home of the Catfish House restaurant, passed quickly, as did Raccoon Mountain and the Raccoon Barbecue, which had been closed for some time. The first sightings of a Southern curse in the form of kudzu began appearing as Chattanooga neared.

Ah, yes, kudzu. The kudzu plant was introduced to the United States at the Centennial Exposition in Philadelphia in 1876. The Japanese displayed the plant in an ornamental garden constructed as part of their exhibit. American gardeners were captivated by the large leaves and sweet smelling blooms and used the plant for ornamental purposes. During the Great Depression, kudzu was promoted as a means to reduce soil erosion and thousands of acres were purposely planted with the vines. Unfortunately the climate of the Southeastern United States was very much to the plant's liking and the kudzu grew too well. The vines, which can grow as much as a foot a day in the summer and sixty feet a year, soon covered trees, power poles, and anything else that didn't move. Over the years the rapidly growing vine had taken over large parts of woodlands choking out the healthy foliage underneath. Kudzu now covered over seven million acres in the South.

The USDA declared kudzu a weed in 1972, and discovering this, I had many questions. Who exactly were these people who sat around a table and voted to declare a plant a weed? Was there someone who spoke in defense of the plant before it was forever sentenced to "weedom"? And, finally, what took them so long? A quote attributed to Channing Cope declares that "cotton isn't king in the South anymore. Kudzu is king!" A poem entitled "Kudzu" by James Dickey starts with, "In Georgia, the legend says, that you must close your windows at night to keep it out of the house." Common names for kudzu include: mile-a-minute vine, foot-a-night vine, and the vine that ate the South. Some creative Southerners have used kudzu for baskets, jelly, syrup, livestock food, and even quiche. We were reminded to keep moving lest the noxious plant engulf a couple of slow moving cyclists. The thought crossed my mind that worry of a kudzu attack made about as much sense as worry of a snake getting entwined in the spokes and biting the unsuspecting rider on each rotation.

As the kudzu lessened, the city limits of Chattanooga soon appeared along with new residential developments. Before long we came upon the long awaited Lookout Mountain with the equally long anticipated Rock City at its summit. As expected, the steep entrance road to the attraction was enough of a discouragement to cause us to sail on by. The road soon became a four-lane highway and traffic increased through the commercial areas closer to downtown. In the process we had entered the Eastern Time Zone. The fourth and final time zone was a watershed event as we were finally in the same time zone as our ultimate South Carolina destination.

CHATTANOOGA CHO CHO

The Holiday Inn Chattanooga Choo Choo supplied the night's lodging. The Choo Choo was a nicely restored train station complete with the locomotive of the same name and a number of railroad cars parked on parallel tracks that were used for sleeping and dining. Most of the lodging, however, was of the traditional brick and mortar variety. The complex included a few shops and restaurants, and a large model railroad display that recreated an earlier period in Chattanooga's history. The inn was one of the first phases of redevelopment of Chattanooga. Across the street, by contrast, stood a number of boarded up, run-down businesses.

Originally called Rossville Landing, Chattanooga was officially renamed in 1838 after the Creek Indian word for Lookout Mountain. As the area developed, cotton became a principle crop, and Chattanooga became an important port and then rail center for the shipment of cotton. During the mid 1800's the iron industry also became a significant part of the local economy and eventually led to a thriving steel industry. The city would later be referred to as "The Pittsburgh of the South."

During the Civil War, the Battle of Chattanooga was a turning point; the 1863 victory by Union forces has been described by many historians as the beginning of the end for the Confederacy. After the war, an influx of African-American workers helped build a strong industrial base, especially in the iron and steel businesses. By the late 1800's there were plow makers, stove works, boiler makers, machine shops, and pipe manufacturers within the growing city limits.

By the early 1900's the city had become known as a major rail and warehousing center for cotton and other agricultural products. During the first part of the century, however, the agricultural sector of the city's economy was significantly weakened by the destruction of much of the cotton crops by boll weevils. The growing popularity of automobile travel about the same time had a negative effect on the importance of Chattanooga as a rail center. Before the demise of the railroads, the famous bandleader Glenn Miller gave Chattanooga its calling card. Miller introduced the song "Chattanooga Choo Choo" in the 1941 movie, *Sun Valley Serenade*.

By the 1960's, Chattanooga, like many American urban centers, was having its problems. Decreasing population and increasing crime made the area a less desirable place to live and work. The Terminal Station was closed in 1970, but would later become the beginning of a turnaround. The boarded up station was bought by local businessmen and turned into the hotel where we were spending the evening. The Tennessee Aquarium was completed in the 1990's along with an IMAX Theater, the Creative Discovery Museum and the Southern Belle riverboat. Chattanooga had become a viable tourist attraction.

The stay in Chattanooga began with an electric shuttle bus ride from the Holiday Inn Chattanooga Choo Choo to the downtown business district. The shuttle busses offered pollution free transportation around town at no cost to the rider. The drivers were friendly and answered questions patiently. At the suggestion of one of the drivers, and some locals who were within earshot of the conversation, we headed for lunch at a popular local restaurant and then walked to the Tennessee Aquarium. The aquarium was a very well done exhibition of the aquatic inhabitants of the Tennessee and Mississippi Rivers. The displays were presented in an interesting fashion and the aquarium was a beehive of activity on the late summer day.

On the way to the aquarium, the shuttle bus passed the original Coca-Cola bottling plant. Although Chattanooga was the site of the first bottling plant, the popular soft drink was not originally concocted there. Coca-Cola syrup was invented in Atlanta in 1886 by a druggist named Dr. John Smith Pemberton. The syrup was originally advertised as a brain and nerve tonic. As legend had it, a man complaining of a headache walked into an Atlanta drug-store and asked the soda jerk to mix a Coca-Cola syrup. The soda jerk used carbonated water instead of the usual tap water. The aching man remarked that the drink tasted very good and Coca-Cola was born. Since many folks along the way had indirectly suggested that our consumption of a brain tonic might be a good idea, we had consumed a large amount of the tasty beverage since leaving Oregon ourselves.

Near the aquarium was an IMAX Theater that offered a cool respite from the warm summer evening. The theater was presenting a feature on the International Space Station. Like other IMAX Theaters, this one made the viewer feel as though they were part of the action.

The evening had turned misty as we waited outside to catch a shuttle bus back to the hotel after the movie. Nearby the Chattanooga Lookouts minor league baseball team played a home game in their small cozy ballpark. The misty rain illuminated by the overhead lights gave a strange feeling to the night.

The bus trip, although relatively short, gave an opportunity to glean more information from the driver and a friendly local about another product with a history in Chattanooga. This particular one was a cookie called Moon Pie. Moon Pies are best described as chocolate covered graham crackers separated by marshmallow. The four inch diameter cookies were invented in the early 1900's as a special treat for coal miners to brighten their long days underground. Rumor had it that the name originated when a miner said, "I'd like a cookie as big as the moon."

Moon Pies were a mostly Southern delicacy as Carolinians consumed more of them than the entire rest of the country. Although it had been a long time since either of us had eaten one, our collective memories of Moon Pies were that they were pretty good. Just talking about them on the bus had "set the hook." The exit from the bus at the hotel was followed by a beeline to a vending machine that luckily carried the tasty objects of our latest desires. Finding a Moon Pie in a vending machine in Chattanooga, though, should probably not have been considered a matter of luck. After all, that was where it all began.

Day 69 - 3301 Miles Down, 486 To Go

―――――――――

georgia

"Are y'all enjoyin' the Southern hospitality?"

THE MOTHER OF ALL YARD SALES

The ride out of Chattanooga began later than usual to avoid anticipated morning rush hour traffic. The planned day was a short one, so the prospects of yet another hot day were not a concern. The relative carefree feeling of the morning probably contributed to our getting lost, a mere few minutes after leaving the hotel. A helpful lady on a smoke break in front of an office building patiently redirected two misguided cross country cyclists back on track.

One advantage of the rural towns that had dominated most of our trip was the near impossibility of getting lost. Usually, there was one road in and one road out, so even for the most directionally challenged, the prospects of getting off course were slim. A

larger city like Chattanooga presented just enough options to create a navigational quandary. When presented with such choices,
we usually chose wrong.

The lady smoker gave good instructions, and the corrected
route bisected the commercial and industrial sections of southern
Chattanooga and headed toward the Georgia state line. Since it
was the last state we would cross, there was more than the usual
anticipation of our pending entrance into Georgia. The elusive
nature of the Georgia line, however, was cause for disappointment. Somehow we missed it. Circling back to its expected location failed to produce any evidence of our having entered The
Peach State.

Regardless, it was soon clear that the line had unwittingly
been crossed; the bikes now rolled over pavement in the City of
Rossville, and Rossville was undeniably in Georgia. A decision
was made to take the Georgia picture later looking back from the
friendly confines of South Carolina. Although technically a violation of the official state crossing ritual, we decided it wasn't our
fault that the people of Rossville had decided to hide the fact that
they inhabited a piece of Georgia real estate.

The road out of Rossville soon turned more rural and the up
and down riding meant a quick passing from presweat to full
sweat on the warm and sultry morning. Before long, signs directing travelers to flea markets and yard sales began appearing along
the roadside. Their frequency was cause for questioning locals as
to what was going on. It didn't take long to learn that the morning's route was taking us near the Highway 127 corridor. The corridor happened to be the location of an annual weeklong yard sale
that extended from Kentucky to Alabama.

The "Worlds Largest Outdoor Sale" was the brainchild of a
former County Executive by the name of Mike Walker. He con-
ceived the idea to prompt travelers to forgo the Interstate highways for the rural roads of Kentucky and Tennessee. The sale,
which began modestly in 1987 and had grown each year since, fol-

lowed U. S. Route 127 for most of its 450 mile length. The local buzz about the upcoming event was significant, and the folks along the sale route anticipated a busy week of peddling accumulated "collectibles and antiques."

It was a fortunate twist of fate that the timing of the trip had us in this part of the country before the sale would officially begin. Hauling plastic bags full of dirt from state to state was one thing, but the prospect of adding a "vintage" Singer sewing machine, a collection of National Geographics from the 40's, or an antique cherry dresser was a bit daunting. The expected increase in traffic was also something that was thankfully avoided.

Even though the morning's ride was off the main sale route, occasional collections of interesting items began appearing alongside the road. Merj's temptation to browse was apparent in her glances at the assembled heirlooms as we cycled past. The increasingly warming temperatures, however, made even Merj consider air conditioning and a shower in LaFayette a more desirable pastime. After over two months on the road, she was developing an ability to quickly sort through the available options and choose the correct one. Heat and humidity had a way of making such choices even easier.

The town of LaFayette provided lodging alternatives for the first night in Georgia, and lodging alternatives meant that choices had to be made. Merj made the usual well choreographed visitations to a couple of hotels having at least reasonable curb-appeal and pronounced one of them passable. She was really getting quite efficient in her secretive evaluation and selection process. Questioning the process was clearly something to be avoided in the interest of maintaining a cordial and pleasant team atmosphere. Based on significant "on the job training," it was possible that the feminine member of our cycling twosome would qualify as a certified hotel inspector by the time the front wheels found the Atlantic.

It didn't take long after arriving in town to realize that the local pronunciation of LaFayette was somewhat different than the one that most Northerners would offer. The very accommodating lady behind the hotel reception desk politely explained that the correct pronunciation wasn't La-fay-ETTE, but that the town was more properly known as La-FAY-ette. Although it appeared to be a "You say po-tah-o, I say po-tay-to" situation, the usual effort to acclimate to local conditions was judged the appropriate course of action. The admonition of Oregonians over three thousand miles ago had left a lasting impression.

The same young woman offered encouraging information about the road ahead. Her confident pronouncement that the mountains would soon be history was met with a noticeably uplifted attitude on Merj's part. The good news was cause to celebrate with a meal of three miniature hot dogs loaded with chili and cheese at a local fast food restaurant. The name on the menu identified the selection as "Three Dog Night" or some such thing. It was but another stop on our health conscious tour of America.

Day 70 - 3326 Miles Down, 461 To Go

DONKEYS AND OTHER THINGS

The early morning departure out of Lafayette was delayed somewhat due to the later sunrises that occur in the western part of a time zone. Although predawn departures using the bicycle headlights were acceptable in the rural areas of the West and Midwest, the busy commercial districts of the towns in the Eastern Time Zone made cycling in the dark a bit of a concern. A hint of mist and fog in the air was an added worry on this warm mid-August morning.

Cycling through the rolling Georgia countryside presented sections of busy roadway bordered by shoulders with deep rumble strips. The rumble strips were deep enough to awake even a comatose driver who may have veered from the straight and narrow. In our case they seriously tested Dr. Whitnah's dental work from back in Oregon. The day's selected route soon included a mile or so climb near the small town of Summerville and an opportunity to snap pictures of Merj riding ahead through the fog-shrouded low mountains. Although not sure it was the case, the summit was treated as if it were the last climb of any consequence that we would encounter on the trip. Suddenly, Hilton Head seemed within reach.

A respite at a Burger King in Summerville allowed an opportunity to sip on a couple of Cokes in air-conditioned comfort. Having witnessed up close the first Coca-Cola bottling plant just two days prior, there was a feeling to do our part to insure its continued profitable operation. A collection of old timers at a booth in the restaurant offered helpful information about the road ahead, warning, "Some of the drivers around here use their hood ornaments for aimin' sights when it comes to pedestrians and bicyclists." Looking around the neatly maintained town of Summerville, though, gave sufficient reason to believe that the people offering that opinion were probably pulling the increasingly muscular legs of a couple of gullible Yankees.

Outside Summerville, a mid-morning roadside stop for rest and water put us in front of a small building, identified as the Lily Patch. It seemed the nature of business at the Lily Patch was the sale of lilies. Next door stood a much larger structure that may have been home to the storeowners. Both buildings were somewhat weatherworn, but thought to be good representations of the rural Georgia countryside, so the camera was quickly readied for duty. The obsession with the weathered buildings of the South had not yet run its course. Fortunately, the weatherworn look of the buildings was not mirrored in the face of the experienced, yet youthful looking female cyclist who duly photographed them.

The day's ride was to end in Rome, a busy, good-sized com-

munity of 35,000. Rome's history, like many other communities in
the South, included important Civil War conflicts but also a visit
by General Sherman on his March to the Sea. The town's highly
developed transportation system made it an important cotton-
trading center in the late 1800's. A flood in 1886 destroyed railroads, bridges, and buildings and so inundated the city that a
steamboat traveled down the town's main street on the high
waters. Fortunately the boom following the flood included a
growing iron industry that helped the city withstand later down-
turns in the cotton business. Occasional floods would continue to
wreck havoc on Rome until a nearby flood control dam was completed in the 1940's. Like many other older communities, most of
the recent development in Rome has occurred in the areas surrounding downtown.

The ride through downtown Rome was a bit hair-raising
and left us confused as to the location of the night's chosen
lodging. Fortunately, frequent episodes of confusion were usually cleared up with conversations with locals or well-placed cell
phone calls. In this case, a call to the desk clerk at a Hampton
Inn provided directions. Unfortunately the direct route to the
hotel would place us on a divided highway. Divided highways
had given safe passage for more than a few miles of the trip, but
the good folks of Georgia had other ideas as to the appropri-
ateness of bicycles or pedestrians on their's. A sign at the
entrance ramp indicated that neither should consider using the
highway. Unfortunately the desk clerk's directions left little
choice but to make a mad dash down the ramp followed by a
half-mile sprint along the roadway shoulder to an intersection
near the hotel. Fortunately our very brief violation of Georgia
law went unseen by any of Rome's finest, and we found ourselves at the entrance road to the hotel. The quarter mile road
to the hotel's front door turned out to have a severe grade,
probably the steepest of the trip. Those people who believe in
such things as retribution would probably say that the short

heart thumper was just reward for our uncharacteristic earlier divided highway transgression.

An afternoon session with the desk clerk provided good advice on an alternate route for the next day's planned ride. While chatting with the helpful lady, an elderly man approached the desk with the clear intention of checking into a room for the evening. The gentleman, in a voice that clearly identified him as having spent most if not all of his life in the South, asked for a room on the first floor, "I'm too old to climb steps," he said. The charming fellow told me his name was Jerry and said he was from Monticello, Georgia, which was located somewhere between Atlanta and Macon.

The elderly gentleman went on to explain that he was a County Commissioner in Jasper County, and that the town of Monticello, Georgia served as the county seat. Jerry described Monticello as, "An old fashion town with a town square," and went on to say, "There's a decent sized town every twenty miles or so in Georgia." Apparently finding acceptable lodging and meals throughout the state would not be a problem. In Monticello he suggested a small local motel and a locally renowned restaurant. Jerry continued, "If y'all get there around noon I'll be there, 'cause I'm there every day."

As he continued, we learned that the County Commissioner's job in rural Georgia was one that would be of little interest to an aspiring millionaire. Jerry carefully enumerated his Jasper County Commissioner's pay and arrived at, "Forty one dollars a month for the first three months of the year after they take out for taxes." As the conversation continued, Jerry went on to say, "Don't come to Monticello in October 'cause my daughter's gettin' married and I got the whole town tied up." It was easy to insure him that a room in Monticello in October would not be needed. We may not have been setting world records in crossing the country, but Monticello would be ancient history by the time October rolled around.

Jerry was very proud of his hometown and strongly suggested that it be added to our trip itinerary. He offered a business card, "Look me up if you make it to Monticello." It would be easy to find him, he said, because, "I'll be in bib overalls and wearin' a straw hat. I'll show you some donkeys and other things." Donkeys and other things? As Jerry headed back outside to his waiting wife, we pondered what he meant. To us a donkey was just a four-legged relative of a horse. In the South, did the word "donkey" have some sort of double meaning? Fortunately, we only had to wait a few days for the answer.

Unfortunately lunch required walking back down the steep entrance road to a good local restaurant that had been recommended by the hotel desk clerk. A warm walk back up the hill and more conversation with the friendly desk clerk, Linda, followed a good spaghetti lunch. Linda had grown up in Rome and was quite familiar with the area. She too encouraged us to make Monticello part of our trip and to stop in a town near Monticello called Milledgeville as well. Milledgeville had served as Georgia's capital before the state government was relocated to Atlanta in the mid 1800's. She also explained that the nearby town of Madison was spared destruction during Sherman's March to the Sea because the general had fallen in love with a woman there. It was too bad the General did not have a bit of a wandering eye. Had that been the case, many other Georgia towns may have been spared a fiery fate.

Linda explained, "Most of the people around here work at one of the big hospitals, or the Suzuki plant where they make four wheelers, or at Keebler where they make Rice Crispy Treats." Memories of Rice Crispy Treats were that they, like Moon Pies, were pretty good. The idea of making a quick early morning detour past the plant to sample the first treats of the day was given serious consideration. After all, the basis of Rice Crispy Treats was a breakfast cereal.

Day 71 - 3373 Miles Down, 414 To Go

"AROUND HERE THEY DON'T DRIVE, THEY AIM."

The road leaving Rome included more of the gentle ups and downs that had become the norm for the last few days. After a short distance, we passed through the residential portion of the city and were soon back in the rural Georgia countryside. The small community of Cedartown greeted us at about eighteen miles into the day, and provided a refreshment and restroom break at another McDonald's.

This one, like most of the other daily stops, was outside normal mealtime. It seemed that the main occupants of restaurants at such times were older folks who tended to congregate in the booths and discuss the problems of the day. Many times it appeared that such congregations were frequent and regular in nature. The conversations were usually animated and most often appeared to be of a friendly nature. It was not unusual that these conversationalists would notice the unique nature of our transportation and begin to ask us questions. Their inquiries were welcomed because it allowed an opportunity to in turn ask our own questions. The local knowledge of older citizens who had gathered for mid-morning coffee klatches was usually very helpful and reliable. On this particular morning, we were again warned about the behavior of local drivers. As one older gentlemen stated, "Around here they don't drive, they aim." Having heard a similar reference to cars being used as weapons of bicycular homicide the previous day, there was cause for concern. Maybe there really was something to worry about.

Cedartown was a small community complete with tree-lined streets and a nice downtown area. Typical of many of the small towns, however, was the obvious presence of a few empty Main Street storefronts. Regardless, there was a fair amount of activity and the economy of Cedartown seemed to be doing quite well.

Outside of town, we passed a store that specialized in the sale of Confederate paraphernalia such as shirts and flags. More and more Confederate flags and Georgia flags with the Stars and Bars began appearing in homes and businesses. There was a move afoot to allow the citizens of the state to vote for a preferred state flag. One of the flags under consideration had the Stars and Bars occupying about half of the flag surface. Signs, many times displayed with a Confederate flag, asked passers-by to "LET US VOTE." The issue was obviously one of importance to a number of Georgians.

Near the evening destination of Bremen, the rear tire went flat on the bike that was carrying dirt samples from nine previous states. Maybe we were learning the basis for truck tires being much bigger than their automotive counterparts. Were there such things as heavy-duty, bicycle tires? If so, they may have been a wise investment. Regardless, a good sized nail was extracted from the tire, and flat tire number six was repaired in short, sweaty, greasy order.

Another question that went unanswered was why most of the flat tires seemed to occur on the rear wheel. One would think that the front wheel would pick up most of the road debris before it would find its way into the rear tube. The bicycling gods appeared to want to test my tire changing ability, puncturing the more difficult tire to change more frequently.

Day 72 - 3419 Miles Down, 368 To Go

DUMBER THAN FENCE POSTS

Biscuits and gravy, a recurring favorite Southern fare, supplied an early morning energy source as the ride out of Bremen began before dawn through already humid air. As good as the biscuits and gravy were, they unfortunately stayed lodged somewhere between the fifth rib and the belt buckle for most of the morning. Such was the case on the warm ride toward the good-sized community of Carrollton.

Carrollton was to be the location of a turn south on a four-lane highway toward the evening's destination of Newnan. As sometimes happened, our preferred route presented an insurmountable problem that would require a change of plans. The entrance to the intended roadway had a sign that announced, "Bicycles and Pedestrians Prohibited." Two days before when an identical sign appeared, we made a mad dash the short distance to the hotel road. Unfortunately, the distance we would need to travel on this four-lane highway was far lengthier, so mad dashes were out of the question.

The quiet Sunday morning offered few options for seeking advice other than a pair of young employees on a smoke break outside an empty fast food restaurant. The last inquiry of an employee on a smoke break had offered sound advice for exiting Chattanooga, so these two were approached with anticipation of positive results. Such optimism soon faded and was replaced by more accurate observations by the female half of the team such as "dumber than fence posts" and "clueless." Sometimes it was impossible to imagine how some folks actually got dressed in the morning and found their way to work. The two smokers would be of absolutely no help. We hoped that they had dropped breadcrumbs on their way to the restaurant so as to find their way home at the end of the shift.

A barely perceptible wave of worry made its way through a couple of fifty-something cyclists as the light morning traffic failed to present us with any other sources of information. While pondering our latest dilemma, a lone early morning visitor to the restaurant drive-through passed close enough to allow us to get his attention. As he rolled down the window of his well-used Chevy pickup, initial impressions were not favorable. The truck driver was a bearded, deeply wrinkled, old fellow who rightfully seemed more interested in getting into his breakfast than helping a couple of "damned fools" on bicycles. Fortunately, initial impressions of the man behind the wheel were off target.

After sensing the slight degree of panic on our faces, he placed his hand on his chin and slowly pondered a way out of our problem. Before long he proclaimed a solution in the form of a rural reroute that bypassed the prohibited highway and rejoined the original route at a point where bicycles, and presumably pedestrians, would again be welcomed. His very thick, but delightful, Southern accent required careful listening on the part of the pair of "damned fools" on bicycles, but before long the new route was carefully crafted in the form of a hand drawn map on the unused side of a napkin. Not wanting his food to get cold, we thanked our newfound friend profusely and watched him disappear into the thick muggy air behind a cloud of blue exhaust smoke.

The old fellow's detour proved to be a good alternative and before long we were back on the two-lane segment of the original route. The remainder of the day's ride traversed some fairly challenging terrain while passing through the small towns of Clem, Whitesburg, Sargent, and Arnco toward the evening destination of Newnan.

Near Newnan a couple of Georgia dogs decided to venture out into the warm morning air. Georgia dogs had learned well from their Kentucky and Tennessee brethren, as these two unusually inspired ones tested the mettle of a pair of road-hardened travelers. Fortunately, the road-hardened travelers prevailed. When it came to dogs, a sense of confidence bordering on cockiness was inching its way into our psyche. In the presence of a hundred-pound plus Doberman bent on doing no good, however, such arrogance could disappear in a moment.

Day 73 - 3457 Miles Down, 330 To Go

"I SERVED JUNIOR RIGHT HERE NOT TOO LONG AGO."

Newnan was a big enough community to generate a significant amount of early morning traffic, so even a 6:30 departure put us on a busy two-lane road complete with non-existent shoulders. Apparently the folks in this part of Georgia were anxious to get to work, as the morning rush hour was a little earlier than anticipated. In a break from the norm, a decision was made to take up temporary residence in a bank parking lot to wait out the traffic. We had a self-congratulatory attitude in the empty lot; at least on this occasion, we had exercised some degree of common sense. Common sense had not always been a particularly strong personality trait during the last couple of months, so there was a certain satisfaction when we realized we still had some.

Even common sense had its limits, though, so after a wait of a half-hour or so, the road beckoned a couple of impatient cyclists back to a rolling ride through the Georgia countryside. The rural landscape consisted of a series of scenic small farms with neighboring fields of hay and straw and small herds of cattle. A roadside rest offered the sweet summer smells of a nearby field of freshly cut and baled hay. The advantages of slowly experiencing the rural highways of America were never more evident than enjoying the late summer sights and smells of the small Southern farms.

There was something about the bucolic setting of the South that left a different feeling than other rural parts of the country had. The under-populated areas of the West had a certain appeal in their starkness and large vistas. The farming areas of the Midwest never quite lived up to the romantic images we had visualized prior to the trip. Maybe it was the fact that they were huge operations, charged with the mass-production of food. By comparison, the Southern farms tended to be nestled in the rolling green countryside, with well-kept houses surrounded by orderly fields of produce. Ironically, the farms of the South were more like the images we had had of Midwestern farms than those of the Midwest had been. It didn't matter where we found preconceived images of American farm life. The important thing was that we had found them.

Nearing the town of Griffin, the comfortable, rustic feeling quickly came to an end as the traffic again increased. The traffic concern was reason to quickly plan an alternate route to the hotel district and lodging for the evening. On the fly rerouting was usually easily accomplished by consulting one or more of the maps from a growing on-bike library. In fact, the weight of maps was beginning to challenge that of the bags of colorful dirt. The maps and dirt were becoming much like the ballast on a sea faring ship, except that ballast on a bicycle was not a usual requirement. At least the roads were beginning to flatten out, so the added weight didn't seem as noticeable as it had been. Such a realization was never shared with Merj. My gentle complaining about carrying the increasing number of "souvenirs" continued unabated.

Griffin was of sufficient size to offer a multitude of hotel accommodations, so the chief hotel inspector of our twosome again swung into action. Soon a short list of three prospective lodgings was made and each was revisited for a final more detailed inspection. A fear began developing that the length of the evaluation period may put us in a position of being shut out of any place to stay. Fortunately, after much deliberation, an acceptable hotel was selected and the bikes, maps, bags of dirt, and bike riders soon found themselves surrounded in air-conditioned comfort.

A fortunate byproduct of the selected lodging was its location in the midst of an area of shops and restaurants. A short walk to an Applebee's provided good food and good conversation with patrons and staff. Soon a six-way conversation ensued with a friendly Deputy Sheriff, an Air Force Captain, a local resident, and the waitress. Questions of the trip dominated the discussion, and as always, we enjoyed telling incredibly detailed tales of the road. At times the thought crossed our minds that a captive listener may not always share our exuberance, but nonetheless, we continued to babble on.

The Applebee's was located fifteen minutes or so from Atlanta Motor Speedway, so the restaurant occupants soon deftly diverted the bicycling conversation to NASCAR. The diversion was so well done that two long-winded cross-country cyclists didn't pick up on it until it was too late to redirect the discussion back to the trip. The waitress was quite proud of the fact that a number of the drivers had visited the Applebee's over the years. "I served Junior right here not too long ago," she beamed. Anyone familiar with NASCAR, and people in the South are definitely familiar with NASCAR, knows that Junior is Dale Earnhart, Jr. It just didn't get any better than that.

Day 74 - 3496 Miles Down, 291 To Go

MY COUSIN VINNIE

So as not to be confused with people who don't learn from their past experiences, we postponed the ride out of Griffin toward Monticello until after the morning rush hour. After four or five miles of fairly busy residential areas, the road headed into more of the gentle rolling farmland that could have been the subject of a Georgia picture post card. Traffic lessened, and in spite of the increasing heat, the scenery and easy riding made the morning very enjoyable.

Monticello had been a much-anticipated destination since the encounter with Jerry, the Jasper County Commissioner, back in Rome. Jerry's description of the small community and his reference to donkeys gave us good reason to see the town and find out more. Ironically, the donkey question was resolved well before crossing the Monticello City Limits. Outside the small town of Jackson, the sight of a donkey among a herd of cattle caused a quick halt to our progress and a photograph. While Merj and I discussed the possible reasons for a donkey amid the cattle, a local resident happened by and provided us with the answer. Much like the llamas out West, the donkeys were added to the herd to protect the cattle from coyotes. A guard donkey was a concept that would take some getting used to. It wouldn't be something to lose sleep over, though; after all, the idea of guard *llamas* had been accepted as fact just two months prior in Sisters, Oregon.

Jackson was a nicely preserved community complete with a downtown square that was home to a Western Auto store. It had been quite a while since either of us had seen one of those stores. Western Auto was founded for the purpose of supplying parts for Ford automobiles by George Pepperdine in Kansas City about 1910. Over the years the offerings of the stores had included a variety of goods extending well beyond auto parts. Western Auto had been a staple of small towns throughout the country for years. I had spent many happy, youthful hours in my hometown Western Auto leafing through Lionel electric train catalogs and admiring the sporting goods. Another wave of fond memories made their way into the mind of a middle age, two-wheeled tourist.

There was a comfortable feeling in the quiet southern town of Jackson, Georgia. A sign at a local bakery advertised FRECH BREAD. Without going inside, it was not possible to determine whether the sign maker was promoting French bread or fresh bread. Two friendly ladies on the town square talked about the recent battle by towns folks to keep a proposed Wal Mart from moving into the area. They were successful; it was clear that Jackson had no desire to go "big time."

The ride out of Jackson continued through the beautiful rolling Georgia countryside toward Monticello. About eight miles from town, a long bridge carried the road and a couple of bicycles over the shallow rock bottomed Ochmulgee River and out of Butts County into the much-anticipated Jasper County. The morning had grown very warm, so a rest stop at a small country store on the Jasper County side of the river became a necessity. While parking the bikes in front of the Sac-O-Suds a voice from across the highway summoned us to a roadside produce market.

The voice came from behind a long table that displayed a variety of Georgia produce. A collection of peaches prominently exhibited on one of the tables seemed like a refreshing way to beat the oppressive heat, so the bikes were left at the store and the riders departed for the produce stand. Peaches in Georgia were certainly to be expected, but we wondered whether it was possible to buy just two. "You bet," said one of the four individuals manning the stand. For fifty cents apiece we were soon partaking in two juicy symbols of the State of Georgia.

The quartet on duty this particular morning included a young talkative fellow, an older gentleman in a wheel chair with an amputated arm, a skinny old guy, and a middle age man who appeared to be the manager of the operation. Collectively, between the four of them, there may have been three sets of teeth. Regardless, they appeared to be gregarious, fun-loving guys.

The sales staff at the roadside stand was very inquisitive about the bike trip and soon the skinny guy offered a bit of local lore. "See that place across the street?" he said. "That's the Sac-O-Suds. That's the place where the killin' took place in that movie *My Cousin Vinnie*." He went on to say, "When y'all get to Monticello, y'all see a lot of other stuff from the movie too."

When asked about the sweet grape-like smell that had been noticed over the last couple of days, the fellow in the wheel chair informed us, "Those are muscadines. Here try some." While munching on the muscadines, the skinny guy said, "You two ever try boiled peanuts?" When we said no, he immediately presented samples for testing. "They taste just like pinto beans," he said.

Since it would have been an affront to our new friends, we restrained ourselves from telling them that the pleasure of pinto beans had been absent from our lives. After careful consideration, the best way to describe the boiled peanuts was that they had the texture of "regular" peanuts without any readily detectable taste. In the continued interest of showing graciousness to our amiable hosts, we sung the praises of boiled peanuts and promised to enjoy them every time the opportunity arose.

To a couple of no-nothing Northerners, the four beer drinking, talkative fellows operating the roadside stand seemed to have the facility a bit overstaffed. That opinion was confirmed when the apparent managing partner stated, "Y'all are the first customers we've had so far today." The fact that the conversation was occurring at almost 11:30 in the morning was further testament to the lack of business. But business volume didn't matter to the four guys manning the stand, as long as the beer held out, the conversation among them would likely continue for however long they decided to stay open.

While walking back to the bikes, we agreed that running into the four fellows at the produce stand was a fortunate stroke of good luck. Not only did they offer a bit of local information, but they also provided further examples of the affable, outgoing, straight forward people who inhabited the rural South. The world could have ended yesterday and the four of them would have simply shrugged their shoulders and said, "Oh well, whose turn is it to buy the beer?" It would have been enjoyable to have spent much more time with them, but the warm morning dictated that it was time to buy some refreshments at the Sac-O-Suds and get back on the road.

"ME AND MY HUSBAND CAN'T EVEN EAT AT MCDONALD'S FOR THAT."

As accurately described by the foursome at the roadside stand, the remainder of the day's ride to Monticello included a rather

lengthy uphill climb from the river followed by repeated ups and
downs. The noontime heat and humidity made checking into the
Monticello Inn a welcomed end to the cycling day. Since other
options were not available, it was fortunate that the inn was a
clean, comfortable establishment. The Monticello Inn, however,
lacked the expansive lobby and reception desk of its big city counterparts. A sign on the office door instructed guests to check in at
the Dairy Queen next door. Two friendly ladies handled the procedure flawlessly.

The bikes were unloaded in the room and then remounted
for the short ride downtown for a recommended lunch at the
Tillman House. The converted old house offered real home
cooked Southern fare served cafeteria style by a husky guy with
a shaved head. After loading our plates to overflowing with
chicken dumplings, mashed potatoes and gravy, and string
beans, we found a table in the front room and began searching
for Jerry. The search proved unsuccessful, and an inquiry of a
waitress indicated that on this day he had been in earlier than
usual. While paying our $8.03 bill at the door, we remarked to
the young cashier that the food was very good and priced fairly.
She agreed and said in a charming Southern accent that took
special effort to understand, "Me and my husband can't even eat
at McDonalds for that."

The Monticello town square was similar in many respects to
the one in Jackson: Well-preserved, functioning stores surrounded a central park area complete with benches and a statue of a
Confederate general. Three elderly gentlemen occupied one of
the benches under a large perfectly shaped shade tree. The three
provided a photographic record of time standing still. A large
ornate courthouse, the same one that had appeared in *My Cousin
Vinnie*, occupied a large part of the square. A nearby bank sign
showed a temperature of 100 degrees. Although the town was a
perfect example of small town America, the afternoon in
Monticello felt every bit of 100 degrees.

A stop in Monticello would not have been complete without talking to the under paid County Commissioner who convinced us to visit the town in the first place. Jerry had given us his card, so a phone call was placed to his home to try to arrange a get together. A polite lady named Darlene answered the phone with a charming Southern accent. After my explanation of the circumstances behind the call, she patiently explained, "I'm Jerry's wife and he's out at an election night party." It was apparently primary election day in the Jasper County area. She further explained, "That party probably won't end 'till ten or so, will y'all be available later tonight, say around 10:00?" Unfortunately, we had found that for the last couple of months, 10:00 at night usually meant that our lights were dimming a wee bit. We also did not want to inconvenience this very accommodating couple by agreeing to the late hour get together.

The conversation with Darlene continued, however, and her pleasant demeanor made listening to her a real treat. When asked about Jerry's donkeys, she verified, "We use 'em to protect the herds from coyotes. We got two donkeys for a hundred head." A ratio of fifty cows for every deputized donkey seemed to be a pretty efficient use of protective force.

On a more serious note, Darlene explained that the couple had been in Rome for the funeral of Jerry's sister. She had died during testing for the source of heart problems. Our lengthy discussion with Jerry in the hotel lobby had caused some concern on Darlene's part. While waiting in the car, she wondered what had taken her husband so long to check into the hotel. We assured her that had the circumstances of their visit to Rome been known, we would not have taken so much of her husband's time. In a smooth melodic accent, she assured us that it had not been a problem.

Day 75 - 3535 Miles Down, 252 To Go

A PHOTO SHOOT?

Leaving Monticello at 6:30 AM to once again avoid the predicted oppressive heat, showed an early morning temperature of 70 degrees on the same bank sign. The customary up and down riding through rural farmlands with occasional small herds of cattle brought forth an unusually brilliant orange sunrise. Much of the day's selected route was mercifully shaded by nearby trees, especially a scenic stretch through Oconee National Forest.

Stopping at a gas station about eighteen miles into the day provided a restroom break and an opportunity for a brief chat with an elderly local gentleman. Assuming we were just out for a morning bike ride, the fellow was a bit taken aback when our response to his question of where we had started was Astoria, Oregon. "I'm dumbfounded," he said simply. We were never quite clear as to whether his expressed opinion was in reference to the magnitude of the accomplishment in general, or the fact that his two new acquaintances had somehow managed to make it to Georgia without doing major bodily harm to themselves.

The remaining ride into Milledgeville included some moderately challenging short climbs through another hot and muggy morning. Although it was a short day of only thirty-three miles on the bikes, our cycling clothes were soaked with perspiration by the time the outskirts of the former Georgia capital came into view. After a couple of difficult miles on a busy four-lane highway, we thankfully found ourselves in the lobby of a Hampton Inn.

Unfortunately, the short day's ride also meant a mid-morning arrival. According to the motel manager, a friendly fellow by the name of Harry E. (Sonny) Hine, our rooms would not be available for two hours. Because of the long wait, Sonny supplied an area off the lobby for storage of the bikes while a room was readied. As the bikes were moved into storage, he began inquiring of the trip and became more and more fascinated with the undertaking. After listening for a while, he asked, "Would you guys mind if I called the newspaper and told them about your trip?"

Being a little taken aback by his request, it took a few seconds to respond that, if he thought it was newsworthy, it was fine with us. A few minutes later, Sonny announced that the room was ready. After only about ten minutes in the room, Payton, a reporter for the *Milledgeville Union-Recorder* called to set up a 2:00 PM interview. Shortly after, Justin, a photographer, called to set up a 4:00 AM "photo shoot." A photo shoot? What was going on here? The attention was a little surprising.

A super-sized lunch of Mexican food at a nearby restaurant put us in the proper frame of mind to set down with Payton and his recorder in the breakfast area of the Hampton Inn. Payton was a twenty-nine year old native of the area and had graduated from Georgia College and State University in downtown Milledgeville. He was good at his job and asked numerous excellent questions about the trip. He also offered information and advice for the next day's ride. Since we wouldn't be in town when the paper hit the streets, he promised to mail a copy home.

After the interview, we joined Sonny and a young employee by the name of Rafael near the front desk. Sonny produced two Hampton Inn tee shirts and asked us to take them with his compliments. Rafael, a very inquisitive and friendly young man, asked as many questions about the trip as Payton had. He soon produced a camera and asked Sonny to take a picture of the three of us together. The attention in Milledgeville was a bit disconcerting, but the genuine interest of the folks at the hotel was much appreciated.

Promptly at 4:00 PM, Justin arrived for our photo shoot and asked that the bikes be brought back down to the hotel entrance for a reenactment of the ride into town. It did cause reason to wonder how many other news photos had been "reenacted" over the years. Maybe the conspiracy theorists really did have a point about the moon landing being staged.

Justin was also a recent graduate of Georgia College and State University and patiently worked with his two amateur subjects to set up the shoot. Yesterday the term "photo shoot" had not been even close to being part of our normal vocabulary. Today, the words were thrown about as though they were as common as "restroom break." It was remarkable that, in just a few short hours, we had become comfortable with the whole idea, and were actually beginning to enjoy the experience. The professionalism of the newspaper people and the hotel staff made the afternoon in Milledgeville a very memorable one.

THE GENERAL

After the photo session, a taxi was summoned for the short trip to downtown Milledgeville. While waiting in the hotel lobby for the cab, Sonny patiently provided a verbal travel guide of things to see and a recommendation of a good restaurant for supper. After discovering that a cab had been called, he offered, "I'll take you guys downtown myself." Sonny had already been more than hospitable, so further intrusion in his day was politely declined.

In retrospect it would have been advisable to have accepted Sonny's offer. The cab ride to downtown Milledgeville was endured in the back seat of a non air-conditioned Mercury Grand Marquis that most reasonably perceptive observers would describe as a "beater." The perspiration flowed freely by the time we mercifully exited the taxi in front of the Milledgeville Library.

The library was to serve as a location to check on e-mails and research future lodging. Unfortunately, the lady at the desk quickly informed us that, "Unless y'all are residents with library cards, there'll be a twenty-five dollar charge for using the computer." Seeing the looks of surprise on our faces, she said, "Try using the library at the Georgia Military College. It's just a short walk away." Although thinking it was odd to be sent to a private institution after deciding not to pay for the same service at a public one, the lady was politely thanked for her advice and we headed for the college.

The Georgia Military College (GMC) was situated behind picturesque pillars and a long brick walkway. The college was founded in 1879 and is a co-educational, liberal arts, junior college. The buildings and grounds were immaculate and there was a real feeling of the Old South throughout the campus. Since the fall term had not yet started, the campus was empty of faculty and students.

The library was located near the entrance and before long we found ourselves in front of Jane, the librarian. Sensing that the word military in the school's title may have some significance, I explained that I was a retired Army General in need of access to the Internet. She looked at "The General" with a fair amount of disbelief, but, nonetheless, began preparations to allow access to a computer. Realizing that the number of pay grades between a former Specialist and a real life General number in the hundreds or so, and that impersonating even a retired General was probably cause for time in the stockade, I decided to spill the beans to Jane. "I'm not really a retired General," I confessed. "No kidding," she responded.

A very friendly assistant librarian named Richard soon joined Jane. A passing temptation to offer a witty reference to the Dick and Jane characters in the grammar school reading book familiar to most middle age literates was discarded as inappropriate. The General charade had already shown that attempts at library humor might not have been an especially strong forte of mine. Merj's looks of agony at many prior efforts at humor were also factored into a decision to let this one slide. The most important reason for keeping thoughts to myself, however, was a desire to do nothing that would offend in any way the two cordial and helpful people whose acquaintance we had made in the GMC library.

Jane and Richard were interested in the trip and asked many questions. Their helpful and pleasant demeanor made answering each question an enjoyable experience. They talked of the history of GMC and were obviously proud to be affiliated with the school. In particular, they were insistent that we tour the large centrally located building that dominated the campus. The building had served as the Georgia statehouse in the 1800's.

Richard was a bit of an old car nut, so as Merj and Jane chatted about a multitude of subjects, Richard and I talked cars. He was in the market for a 50's vintage Chevy pickup truck and I was happy to be able to give him some ideas of where to find one. Richard listened with polite attention as a fellow car collector launched into a well-practiced description of his own cars back home.

Richard and Jane were two of the most accommodating and enjoyable people we had met to date. The otherwise empty library allowed the four of us to carry on an increasingly lighthearted conversation for a large portion of the evening. As we reluctantly left their company, both of them posed outside for a picture under the library entrance.

It was a short walk from the library to the side door of the former capital building. The old statehouse was of the Gothic Greek Revival architectural style and served as the seat of Georgia government from 1803 to 1868. During the sixty-five year period that the building provided a home to the state's legislators, Milledgeville served as the fourth capital of Georgia. By design, the statehouse occupied the highest point in the city and overlooked the nearby Oconee River. The decision that Georgia secede from the Union and join the Confederacy was made in the legislative chamber of the building in 1861. The structure was twice partially destroyed by fire and last restored in 1943. The present building was a replica of the original.

The door was unlocked so a pair of Yankees proceeded inside to explore a bit of Confederate history. The legislative chamber dominated the interior and was immaculately restored to a mid-

nineteenth century condition complete with a podium and desks
for the legislators. A balcony gave a second floor panoramic view
of the entire floor area. While strolling around the reconstructed
chamber, there was a real feeling of being in the presence of an
important historical event. The chamber and the rest of the building were restored to a level that was on par with any other historical structure that we had ever visited. Leaving the old capital, we
were both glad to have followed the advice of Jane and Richard.

The day in Milledgeville was an example of the benefit of
planning the day's itinerary from day to day rather than following
a predetermined route. In Rome, with most of the trip behind us,
and not believing there was much more to see in Georgia, we had
developed a mind-set of finishing the trip by simply finding a reasonably traffic-free, direct route to Hilton Head Island. If not for
the hotel lobby encounter, the two memorable communities of
Monticello and Milledgeville, four good ol' boys at a roadside
stand, numerous amiable Southern folks including County
Commissioner Jerry, and much scenic countryside and Southern
history would have been missed. The experiences in Georgia, and
the people that inhabited the state, had already become some of
the most memorable of the trip.

Day 76 - 3568 Miles Down, 219 To Go

JUST LIKE OVER THE HILL ROCK STARS

A predawn exit from Milledgeville was prompted by the need to
beat early morning rush hour traffic and the heat of yet another
predictably warm day. A mile and a half ride through commercial
districts followed by two or three miles of nicely manicured residential areas finally put us out of downtown Milledgeville. Traffic
got lighter as the day's ride turned onto a rolling, rural highway

that included a fairly significant sweat-producing climb. The top of the hill offered and opportunity to look back at a wide green valley covered in an early morning mist. Promises made to Merj that the current climb was the last one were being met with a noticeable grunt and unintelligible Scandinavian words. The credibility of the presenter of such proclamations was increasingly being called into question.

The serenity of the scenic rolling countryside was soon disrupted by an increasing number of semi tractor-trailers carrying an unknown white mineral. The frequency of the truck traffic was becoming a legitimate safety concern, so a stop at a small general store afforded an opportunity to take a break and find out about the contents of the trucks. The fellow behind the counter quickly explained. "Those trucks are haulin' chalk from the open mines around here," he said. The chalk was used to make paper coatings and squeak producing, chill inducing, markers for school black boards. "There's probably 400 of 'em that pass right by here on any given day." At least that many had passed us in the last few miles.

Playing dodge 'em with the chalk trucks continued until about four miles from the evening's destination of Sandersville. Soon after, the trucks were replaced by a steady rain that pretty much soaked us to the core. The rain, however, actually felt comfortable on the warm, sticky morning. Rain had been remarkably infrequent during the cross-country trip; averaging about one shower every thousand miles or so. It was further testament to the fact that much of the country had been experiencing drought or near drought conditions.

Another short cycling day meant a pre-noon arrival at the Sandersville Holiday Inn Express. The friendly hotel manager promised a room in a half-hour or so and showed us two restrooms off the lobby for changing out of the wet clothing. Emerging from the restrooms, feeling considerably better, the same fellow greeted us with unexpected information. "I called the paper and set up an interview for the afternoon," he said calmly.

What was going on here? After traveling 3,600 miles in relative obscurity, unusual interest had been shown on two consecutive days. In the latest case, the deed had already been done and no disagreement was permitted. As surprising as the attention was, it would be less than truthful to say that it wasn't at least a little flattering. We were beginning to feel like a couple of over-the-hill touring rock stars. The interview experience in Milledgeville had created a feeling of confidence as the time approached for interview number two. Merj, not sure whether the Sandersville newspaper experience would include a "photo shoot," began preparing an hour or so before the scheduled time. Nearly all of her interview prep consisted of time in front of the hotel room mirror.

The reporter from the *Sandersville Progress* appeared in the hotel lobby precisely at the scheduled time. The professionally attired young man was named Will Davis, and it didn't take long to discover that he was the paper's editor and publisher. Much like Payton from the previous day's interview, Will was very good at his job and asked a series of interesting questions. Two of his best questions related to the survivability of a long marriage after seventy-six days on the road and the cost of such an adventure. The answer to the first was a need to stay flexible. The answer to the second was a realization that this was a once in a lifetime experience, so digressions from the original budget had been tolerated.

When Will asked that we get back into the cycling garb and meet him in front of the hotel, we knew the answer to Merj's question about the possibility of a photo shoot. Four or five passes up and down the sidewalk finally gave him a photograph that would be at least marginally acceptable. There may have been a growing confidence when it came to interviews, but our photo shoots needed a lot of work. One had to wonder about Merj's lengthy photo shoot prep time. To properly stage a ride into town, it was necessary to get fully clothed in the normal biking attire. Among other things, normal biking garb included a helmet and sunglasses. When correctly attired, only a small portion of the human head was visible to anyone caring to look. Even if they weren't visible in the photo, properly prepared hair and full makeup were probably instrumental in the overall confidence of the female photo subject.

Day 77 - 3602 Miles Down, 185 To Go

"IT'S WEEDS, HE'S JUST LETTING THE FIELD REST FOR A YEAR."

The terrain south of Sandersville was of a variety that even brought an occasional smile to Merj's skeptical visage. The surrounding farmland was scenic in its own right, but the real source of her increasingly optimistic outlook was a noticeable flattening of the topography. The hills were finally behind her. My regular, confident claim that the previous hill was the last of them was apparently proving to be correct. If one throws enough mud on a wall, some will occasionally stick.

Outside of the small railroad town of Tennille, the regular pattern of cropland and gentle hills continued. The low morning sun cast shadows of the passing bikes and bike riders on a nearby roadside bank. The agility of the male half of the biking twosome allowed an interesting on-the-move photograph that would hopefully resemble the one of ET cycling across a full moon. It was entirely possible, though, that ET, while certainly not a handsome fellow, would have looked good by comparison to the two cyclists whose shadows were clearly defined on the roadside bank.

Soon, a very large field of an unknown crop appeared and became a source of mystery to us. The crop was of such interest that it was artfully photographed as though it represented a breathtaking mountain view. We carefully obtained a sample and sniffed it with no luck in identifying the nature of the barely detectable odor. With curiosity at a high level, I placed the sample in the front pack among the nine state dirt samples for purposes of future identification. It was quite possible that the unknown plant life may have found the accumulation of dirt to its liking and taken root right there in the pack.

While carefully packaging the precious cargo and preparing to get back on the road, a young mother with daughter in tow began to pull out of a driveway directly across the road from our makeshift agronomic laboratory. After two and a half months on the road, any shyness in approaching locals for information had long since disappeared. I approached the lady boldly, and motioned for her to roll down the driver's side window. It wasn't obvious, but it was possible the young mother was thinking that I was a perfect example of the type of individual she had warned her young daughter to avoid.

Regardless, she cautiously lowered her window, making sure to keep her finger on the up button at all times in case a quick closing and escape were in order. Sensing her slight apprehension, I calmly asked her, "What type of crop is that?" With a look of bewilderment on her face she responded, "It's weeds, he's just letting the field rest for a year."

After politely thanking the young mother, we waited until she was out of sight before bursting into laughter. Here we were, a couple of big time cross-country cyclists nearing the end of a summer long journey. We had been interviewed and photographed the last two days as though we were celebrities. Our egos were at their peaks. In spite of all the surprising attention and our own confident feelings, we didn't know the difference between a field of useful crops and a field of weeds. Egos quickly came back to pre-trip levels, and that was probably a good thing.

THE CHAIRMAN OF THE BOARD

Rolling into a very warm Wrightsville, Georgia, the encounter with the field of weeds was still a topic of discussion between the two of us humbled "gentlemen farmers" on bicycles. The mid-morning heat made a stop at an air-conditioned gas station/mini-mart/restaurant a welcomed respite. While parking the bikes in front of the building, it was obvious that a collection of old timers at a table near the window were more than a little curious about our presence. Four pair of eyes slowly followed our every movement as we secured the bikes and entered the refreshingly cool interior.

Once inside, a member of the assemblage soon approached. "Where'd y'all come from?" he wanted to know. The response of Oregon brought the usual follow up questions. One of the quartet, an elderly gentleman by the name of John, showed the most interest and said, "I saw you guys on TV a couple o' days ago." Although we clearly remembered two newspaper interviews, the appearance of TV cameras could not readily be recalled. We had to gingerly inform John that he might have confused us with someone else doing something even more spectacular on a bicycle.

After clearing up the minor TV flap, John launched into a rather detailed dissertation about the area and his own personal history. It didn't take long to be informed that football star Hershel Walker grew up in the environs of Wrightsville and still called it home. He went on to say, "Hershel went up North to play and he froze his (butt) to that bench and that brought him right back down here to play."

John had served in World War II with General Patton and was not shy in taking a bit of the credit for saving we "young uns" from Hitler. "On the way home from Europe, I lost a day and never got it back." It was assumed that he was talking about the International Date Line. Realizing, however, that since the International Date Line was located in the Pacific Ocean, to have lost a day would have required his taking the long way home from Europe. Since an answer may have consumed much of the hot morning, the lost day remained another mystery.

The discussion with John continued and he discovered we were from Ohio; trying to carry the conversation, he said, "I was just up there visitin' some friends. That's the state that's round on the end and high in the middle ain't it?" Boy, we'd never heard that one before. After telling John of my civil engineering background and that Georgia had recently been added to the list of states that I was registered to practice in, he opined, "Don't come down here, the roads are screwed up as it is." It appeared that John had little confidence in my engineering ability.

John continued to regale all within earshot of his philosophies of life, and while interesting, the increasingly warm morning was as usual making it imperative to get back on the road. Outside, one of his fellow diners stopped to explain that John was a morning regular at the restaurant and that he was know locally as "The Chairman of the Board." The title was appropriate and it was obvious we had not been the first visitors that he had decided to befriend. The morning stop had much the feel of Gomers's Filling Station in the old *Mayberry* television series. It also helped push the humbling weed field experience farther back in memory.

The remainder of the morning's ride toward Swainsboro was another very hot one through more rural countryside with shade afforded by an occasional grove of pecan trees. Unfortunately the earlier assumption that the road to the coast would be pool table flat was a little premature. The occasional ups and downs caused a reappearance of a now classic look of disgust on Merj's face. There would be no more optimistic predictions of a flat road from her bicycling companion. It wouldn't have made any difference anyhow. His topographic credibility had already been essentially reduced to zero.

Reaching the hotel in Swainsboro involved negotiating a road paving project and a couple miles of heavy commercial traffic.

Fortunately the day's ride was a relatively short 45 miles so the cycling portion of the day ended before noon. A bank sign next to the hotel showed a temperature of 96 degrees. A short time later, the same sign registered 102 degrees. It was fortunate that the local press in Swansboro had not learned of our arrival. Staging an entrance into town in 102 degree temperatures would not have been high on a list of desirable things to do.

Day 78 - 3650 Miles Down, 137 To Go

LOUIE

A predawn exit from Swainsboro consisted of easy riding through more scenic rural Georgia countryside. The comfortable, cloudy morning and low traffic volume made the route through fields of cotton and areas of green forests an enjoyable one. Occasional sightings of picturesque old farm houses and barns allowed opportunities to take breaks and continue pursuit of the obsessive old-barn photo complex. A couple of frisky country dogs broke the leisurely pace with a spirited sprint toward four bare legs. Fortunately, the level terrain allowed a slightly faster sprint on the bicycles, so harm to the two pair of well-tanned legs was avoided.

The pleasant morning continued through large stands of pine trees, planted in orderly rows for future harvesting, and beautiful groves of pecan trees. The pines lent a pleasant smell to the sticky early morning air. Soon after, the forested area was interrupted for a brief stretch by the appearance of white sand dunes. Although far smaller in area than the dunes in Oregon, they were unexpected amid the dense pines. Merj dutifully shoveled a half a truck load or so of the white sand into a zip lock bag to supplement the ballast already present on her cycling companion's bike. A short time later, a large Primitive Baptist Church set among the trees provided yet another interesting photo opportunity.

It had been a while since cattle of any significance had been part of the landscape, but that changed when a herd of beef cattle appeared around a long bend in the road. The cows casually raised their heads while slowly munching their morning meals under a stand of pecan trees. Merj became fascinated by their peaceful look and insisted that progress by halted to enjoy the moment. While instructing the second best photographer of our twosome to grab a camera, she walked to the fence line and began encouraging some of the nearby cows to join her.

Although it was never clear what was used to offer encouragement to her "adorable" bovine friends, surprisingly two of them did venture along side of her at the fence. There was a slight audible sound from Merj as the cows made their way; perhaps a mysterious Finnish chant was part of her technique. While enjoying the fruits of her cattle call, she instructed the picture guy to record the moment. It became apparent while lining up the "photo shoot" that an interesting old barn also occupied the grazing area some fifty yards to the rear. Unbeknownst to Merj, her cow interests and the old barn obsession had been satisfied in one photograph.

Even though clouds had helped keep temperatures down, a stop for refreshment became a priority. The need for drinks was soon satisfied by temporarily halting progress at a small cross roads market/barbecue. Orders were placed inside the small building through a secure looking sliding glass window, resembling that of an old fashion bank-teller. It was a scene reminiscent of the ones in movies that depict an individual talking to a jailed criminal through a bullet proof glass partition.

To add realism to the setting, the large woman behind the protective enclosure could have pretty much assumed the role of a crusty old warden, or the character of Louie from the old TV series *Taxi* as he handed out the day's assignments from his enclosed cubicle. It was a mystery as to what had made the store's offerings so valuable that extra security was needed to keep them from the general populace. Perhaps it was the pigs feet listed on the menu.

"I'M GONNA PRAY Y'ALL MAKE IT TO HILTON HEAD OKAY."

Just as Jerry the Jasper County Commissioner had said, towns in Georgia were, in general, evenly spaced every twenty miles or so. The day's ride was becoming fairly typical of those of late. It would only be about forty miles and would end in the fair sized city of Statesboro. The shorter rides were also necessitated by a need to lightly apply the brakes to our progress. The arrival at Hilton Head Island had been planned to correspond with the arrival of our two daughters. Had it continued, the recent rate of progress would have put us there a few days early; slowing down became a necessity. Having our daughters there was important to all involved, so a couple of extra days on the road were viewed as an opportunity to enjoy Southern hospitality for a little while longer.

The outskirts of Statesboro proved to be somewhat confusing, so we stopped for directions. The reluctance most powered vehicle drivers show when forced to ask directions vanishes when you are on bicycles. When a cross-country cyclist is lost on a hot, sultry Georgia morning he or she wants to travel not one more inch than required.

A young man mowing the grass in front of a large stately suburban home soon satisfied the need for directions to the hotel district of Statesboro. After getting the attention of the large, some might even say huge, fellow over the din of the mower, he shut down the equipment and walked to our side. While explaining our plight, he listened intently as rivulets of sweat ran down his face.

After due consideration, the accommodating young man responded in a concise fashion that left reasonable confidence that the hotel could be located. Although declining a drink of water from the bike mounted bottles, he said, "I'm gonna pray that y'all make it to Hilton Head okay." Our own sweat stained faces and clothing likely made the need for prayer obvious. Regardless, the thoughtfulness of helpful new acquaintances was again becoming more and more the accepted norm.

While preparing to leave, Merj jokingly asked if he had any problems with his boss. He grinned and responded, "He's okay, but there's only one guy that counts and that's Jesus. If you're blessed, and I'm blessed a lot more than others, the only guy I answer to is Jesus." Had the same question been asked of me, and meaning no disrespect to the deeply held religious beliefs of our helpful friend, my glib response would have been something like, "The first person I answer to is sitting on that other bright yellow Cannondale." The accommodating young man provided a genuine breath of fresh air on a very warm Georgia morning.

The evening in Statesboro was spent in a comfortably modern motel across from the campus of Georgia Southern University. The ride to the motel had passed the very scenic pine tree covered campus, and the school's football practice field where the team labored under the late morning sun. Georgia Southern's football team had reason to believe that their hot practice session would pay dividends by season's end, as the school had had a number of successes at the Division 1-AA level.

The evening in Statesboro was spent at a local mall and movie theater. Unfortunately transportation to the complex was provided in a taxicab found by perusal of the yellow pages. The cab, much like the one in Milledgeville, was an 80's vintage Mercury Grand Marquis with no working air conditioning and a barely working engine. The "cabby" was a contemporary sort of guy, intent on listening to the steady beat of loud rap music while arguing with his apparent date for later in the evening over a cell phone.

For a while there was some concern as to whether we had really entered a cab, or if the young rap fan had picked us up thinking we were a couple of hitch-hikers. The question was soon answered when, upon arriving at the mall, he leaned over the front seat and nonchalantly stated, "That'll be three fifty."

Day 79 - 3688 MILES, 99 To Go

_____

SLOW DOWN MERJ

Just as most Sunday morning rides had been throughout the trip, the Sunday ride out of Statesboro was a relaxing one even though the first few miles were through heavy commercial areas. The road soon left the business district and headed back into a rural countryside with large fields of cotton. At about eight miles into the day, the smooth flat paved surface turned into dirt and a couple of dogs took up chase. The increased cycling strength and skills acquired by almost 3,700 miles on the bikes allowed an easy escape from the canine pursuers.

A short time later, the small town of Brooklet came and went as thunder and lightning made an unwanted appearance on the northern horizon. A turn east on a lightly traveled, well paved, flat road made outrunning the thunderstorm to some point of safety a realistic consideration. Fortunately the thunderstorm appeared to turn to the west, so worries diminished as the riding continued free and easy through the cotton fields of southeastern Georgia.

Merj had developed considerably more strength and endurance since leaving Astoria nearly eighty days prior. Such was evident as she kept up a brisk pace while leading the way toward the evening's destination of Pooler. There were times when the thought crossed my mind of asking her to slow down a bit. Even though my bike was loaded with a few more pounds, much of it in the form of dirt and other "souvenirs," the fitness and confidence that she had gained was obvious. It was a rewarding feeling for both of us.

A customary mid-morning stop for refreshments at a mini-mart, provided an opportunity for a short conversation with a friendly lady behind the counter. Seeming interested in the trip, she asked, "Are y'all enjoying the Southern hospitality?" Proper conveyance of the hospitality that Southerners are known for was a legitimate concern on her part, so we quickly assured her that we had been the frequent targets of such hospitality. Back outside on the bikes, the threat of thunderstorms passed, and the decreasing cloud cover brought the usual heat and humidity. The light winds and flat terrain, however, made the riding relatively easy, although a presweat condition was the order of the morning. The easy cycling also allowed a side by side opportunity to reminisce about the previous eleven weeks.

Nearing Pooler, the road passed through the small town of Bloomingdale. Arriving in Bloomingdale was a significant event as it represented evidence of nearing the trip's final destination. An earlier training ride had involved transporting the bikes to the rural Georgia countryside for a fifty-mile loop, and Bloomingdale had been part of the circular route. Other signs of nearing Hilton Head also began making appearances. Chief among them was the Spanish moss hanging from live oak trees, the availability of the Savannah newspaper from sidewalk paper boxes, and our first sighting of a Piggly Wiggly grocery store. Feelings of accomplishment had begun to form, and the cadence of our pedals increased slightly as the finish line quickly approached.

Pooler was of sufficient size to allow a choice of hotel accommodations, so our resident hotel examiner carefully performed her assigned duties and proclaimed a Best Western as acceptable. The new hotel was located in front of a large structure that was home to the Mighty Eighth Museum. The museum looked very impressive from the outside, so it was decided to walk the short distance to examine its contents. Many displays, artifacts, photographs, airplanes and other paraphernalia depicting the history of the Eighth Army Air Corps during World War II were housed inside. It was an impressive display presented by an organization that was justifiably proud of its role in the defense of the country.

As had so often happened, the hotel desk clerk supplied useful information for the next day's ride into South Carolina. South Carolina would be our final state line crossing and was much anticipated. Between Pooler and the state line, however, lay a portion of suburban Savannah. Heavy traffic was expected near the Savannah International Airport and the nearby Port of Savannah. The courteous woman behind the reception desk, a native of Hanoi, Viet Nam who had come to the United States in 1975, patiently described a route that would hopefully provide a trouble free ride through the environs of Savannah. A very early departure was suggested to beat the anticipated rush hour truck traffic.

The State of Georgia had provided an opportunity to visit well preserved small towns that oozed charm, travel through scenic rural landscape, and most of all, experience the true Southern hospitality of her citizens. Since Georgia had been a state that we had frequented on a number of prior occasions, it's charming countryside and people came as a bit of a surprise. But then again, past visits had not included towns like Rome, Jackson, Monticello, and Milledgeville. By necessity the bikes had required avoiding large cities, but the casual suggestion of a Jasper County Commissioner that we visit his rural county had made for a very enjoyable overall experience. Georgia and her people had become one of our favorite states.

Day 80 - 3736 Miles Down, 51 MILES To Go

south carolina

"You got to get used to the pace of Southerners. Things move real slow in the South."

THAT'S SALT AIR I SMELL

The day's ride was one that represented entrance into South Carolina, and even though it would only be about 35 miles, it was the last serious day of cycling on the trip. The anticipation of seeing our children and dipping the front wheels in the Atlantic was building. The ride out of Pooler, however, was a concern as there was a nagging fear that something could happen in the very late stages of the ride to mar what had been a very safe and memorable summer-long experience.

The morning preparation ritual in Pooler was performed as it had been for the previous 79 days since any slight variation could be the cause of some sort of bad luck. Although neither of us considered ourselves superstitious, there was a feeling of, "Why take a chance?"

Leaving the motel in the predawn dark, Merj claimed that she could smell the salt air of the nearing Atlantic Ocean. Although not able to smell it myself, but realizing that my olfactory sensitivities were not nearly as developed as hers, the detection of salty air was accepted as fact. It was a good sign, but some troublesome cycling still lay ahead.

A carefully planned exit from Pooler included a ride through a residential section of town toward the expected busy Savannah airport and port areas. Cycling through the flat residential area was enjoyable as the darkness and sounds of the early morning added an unusual feel to the normal beginning of a day on the road. Unfortunately, the comfort of the residential area ended after just a few miles and the morning ride turned onto the busy highway leading toward the airport. The comfortable feeling in the darkness of the residential area was replaced by trepidation resulting from a fear of not being seen by the increasing number of vehicles on the road. Fortunately, the bright red flashing lights on the rear of the bikes supplied the necessary visibility to avoid unplanned confrontations with motor vehicles, and the airport area was traversed with no particular problem.

As expected, the number of large trucks increased noticeably as the ride passed the airport and closed in on the seaport. Dawn provided increasing light, and even though the road was being shared with some very large vehicles, the increased visibility offered a degree of comfort. A few miles past the seaport the traffic lessened and the cycling into Port Wentworth, the last stop in Georgia, was much less nerve wracking.

A stop at a gas station in Port Wentworth allowed an opportunity to collect thoughts and plan an entrance into South Carolina. In reality, planning a route was pretty easy; there was only one road that led out of Port Wentworth to South Carolina. It was a shame that, in five days, the route planning would no longer be necessary; we were finally getting pretty good at it.

Regardless, a flood of varying emotions began to make their presence known. The dominant one was a feeling of real satisfaction for being close to accomplishing a nearly lifelong dream. Oddly, I also began to anticipate the strange feeling of getting up in the morning without the expectation of a day's unknown adventures on the bicycles. We visualized the ride onto the island and the feelings that were sure to come with dipping the front wheels in the Atlantic. We were already experiencing a preview of the emotions that would arrive in a few short days.

The road to South Carolina traversed a very large salt-water marsh. The grass covered marsh extended for miles in both directions and offered beauty in its plainness. A view to the southwest over the slowly swaying marsh grasses showed the awakening skyline of Savannah. Part way across the causeway, a large sign welcomed visitors to the Palmetto State. A sign across the highway in the opposite direction, announced entrance back into the Peach State by declaring, WELCOME - WE'RE GLAD GEORGIA'S ON YOUR MIND.

Since the Georgia state line marker had been mysteriously absent outside Chattanooga, we recreated the Georgia crossing, even though we were at the opposite end of the state. Such an activity had a certain lack of authenticity, but it wasn't our fault that the people in the northern part of the state had decided to keep their Georgianess a secret. The guilt of the Georgia reenactment was soon followed by a real time celebration crossing the South Carolina line. In both cases, the "hold the camera at arm's length pointed back at the photographic subject" technique was incorporated.

South Carolina offered a smooth flat entrance with only a moderate amount of traffic. Road signs began announcing decreasing distances to Hilton Head. After a short time in the state, stopping for directions at a nursery cleared up confusion about the route. Ironically, the morning's ride traversed an area that had been previously frequented in the family car. Maybe it was the different perspective from the bicycle seat that caused our disorientation. It was a little embarrassing, but who cared! Even male olfactory nerve endings were beginning to sense salt in the air.

SQUAT AND GOBBLE

The last ten miles of the ride toward Blufton turned out to be one of the most harrowing stretches of roadway of the entire trip. A combination of narrow to non-existent shoulders and heavy traffic provided all the ingredients for a catastrophe. With nearly 3,800 miles behind us and the Atlantic Ocean within a stone's throw, the idea of something happening to prevent finishing what had started a summer before was unthinkable. As unthinkable as it was, the riding conditions were difficult enough to make it a real possibility.

A few miles from Blufton, and after a couple of unscheduled trips onto the safety of the grass along the roadway, a group of young males in a passing, beat-up van offered us the first outwardly negative commentary. One of the Phi Beta Kappas in the van yelled in an unflattering tone, "Get off the _____ing road." After an initial flash of anger and a response that somewhat mirrored their original request, a realization set in. Their observation was probably on target. We had no business being on that particular road at that particular time of the day. Unfortunately other options were not available.

Fortunately downtown Blufton appeared a short time later and a search began for a place to allow frayed nerves to heal. The search was short; the most popular eating establishment in town, The Squat and Gobble Restaurant, quickly became the location of much needed rest and recuperation.

The Squat and Gobble was a small, locally popular restaurant typical of many others that had been frequented throughout the country. A booth near the front window provided a good spot to plop down with a Coke, a *USA TODAY*, and begin the healing process. In a short time a very friendly waitress inquired as to our unusual mode of transportation and careful reiteration of cross-country experiences flowed freely. Before long, Paul, the owner of the restaurant, and a half dozen other people dining nearby joined in for good conversation.

Paul was an outgoing, gregarious fellow with a tinge of a Greek accent. He was in his mid-fifties and had immigrated to the U. S. some time ago. Paul was a former Navy SEAL and still had the build of a person who could secretly board an enemy vessel in the darkness of night and do considerable damage. A noticeable scar, probably the basis of an interesting story, showed itself on one of his legs. He was a charming fellow with an infectious personality. Unbeknown to us, before joining the small group assembled around the table, he had called the local newspaper to tell them about the two bicyclists holding court in his restaurant.

In quick order, Rob Dewig from *The Carolina Morning News* settled down in a chair next to our table and began asking questions. He was particularly interested in the tense ride into Blufton as it apparently reinforced his thinking of the need for a bicycle lane along the highway. The bicycle lane issue had evidently been under recent discussion by city fathers and had been getting a mixed response from the citizenry of the area. With the end of the trip less than twenty miles away and with the end of the day's ride only a mile or so away, time was of no concern, so the conversation was lengthy and relaxed.

As the interview was winding down, a photographer from the newspaper appeared with a request that the ride into Blufton be reenacted outside. An historic marker near the restaurant became the backdrop for another hundred-yard adventure along the busy roadway. After two attempts, the photographer pronounced success and the photo shoot was "a wrap." There was a feeling of relief that the reenactment had been accomplished rather quickly. The road into Blufton was difficult enough in real time. Redoing it only provided renewed opportunities for something bad to happen.

Since the day's ride was essentially complete and there was no need to hurry back to the bikes, it was decided to return to the Squat and Gobble to relax and share more stories with the staff and patrons. Soon Paul brought over a telephone and asked that we talk to a young lady reporter who had called from the Hilton Head Island newspaper *The Island Packet*. She arranged for an interview at the hotel that evening before riding onto the island and a photo shoot at the ceremonial dipping of the front wheels into the Atlantic Ocean. The notoriety was still a bit bewildering, but I think we were beginning to get used to it. After all, it had now become pretty much a foregone conclusion that almost three month's worth of bicycle seat time was going to reach a successful conclusion.

As the fun time at the restaurant drew to a close, Paul presented us with official Squat and Gobble tee shirts and said, "The meal's on me." Outside we posed for pictures with Paul and his son Dino in front of the restaurant. Paul, his son, the staff, and the patrons at the Squat and Gobble had caused the attitudes of the early part of the morning to completely change from anxiety and trepidation to relaxed contentment. Besides, the old touring rock star treatment was starting to feel pretty good.

The short remainder of the day's ride ended at a brand new Holiday Inn Express located just off Route 278. Reaching Route 278 was a significant achievement as it was the highway that led directly onto Hilton Head Island. Unfortunately, Route 278 was a very busy four-lane roadway that would prove a challenge to negotiate. It would be some time before there would be a need to venture out onto the road, so the worries could wait for a while. The conclusion of the trip was now very close. It was time to relax and enjoy the amenities of the hotel and surrounding area. If needed, we could crawl onto the island from the hotel.

The unwarranted star treatment continued in an unexpected way. Leaving the hotel for a walk to lunch, we were greeted with a heavy downpour. One of the bellmen, noticing the look of reluctance on our part to venture into the heavy rain said, "Y'all wait right there." To our surprise, he ran to his car, pulled it to our side and politely asked us to climb inside. He then proceeded to drive about two hundred feet to the back door of a nearby pub where he deposited his two passengers with a suggestion that it would be an excellent place for lunch. As the rain pelted off the roof of his car, considering other locations was not an option.

TIME TO KICK BACK

Since relaxation was the order of the day, an afternoon of leisurely e-mailing, note taking, and napping in comparative luxury provided a welcome change from many of the earlier stops. Surprisingly, although little energy had been expended, a renewed hunger had made its presence known by early evening, so a search began for a place to have supper. After getting a recommendation from the same helpful bellman who had supplied earlier transportation to lunch, a recently opened restaurant located about a half-mile walk from the hotel was judged to be acceptable.

The young waitress at the selected restaurant had enough of an accent to attract the attention of at least one of her nosy customers, so questions followed. As the inquisition began, she laughed, said her name was Maggie, and explained that her birthplace was Ireland. She had come to the United States with her parents at the age of twenty-one, and judging by her young looks, it appeared as though she may have arrived in America a couple of hours before our arrival at the restaurant.

After discovering our bicycling inclinations, Maggie told us, "I'm from New Jersey and I used to race mountain bikes professionally for Cannondale." We quickly informed her that Cannondale was also our bicycle manufacturer of choice. Neither of us was familiar enough with the topography of New Jersey to question the presence of mountains in the state, but apparently there were enough to present sufficient challenges to those who climb them on bikes for money. When told of our intent to ride along Route 278 onto Hilton Head Island, Maggie cried, without hesitation, "Are you crazy?" The questioning of our bicycling mental-health was getting a bit troublesome, especially from someone who claimed to be a former professional mountain biker. By the same token, with almost 3,800 miles behind us, who cared now?

The conversation with Maggie ended by her describing a recent trip to Cleveland for the wedding of a friend. The trip had reinforced her thinking that things moved faster in the North. She told us, "You got to get used to the pace of Southerners. Things move real slow in the South." This was not news, but in fact further verification of a rather admirable trait of the people who inhabited the southern portion of the country.

Day 81 - 3769 Miles Down, 18 To Go

EXTRA, EXTRA, READ ALL ABOUT IT!

The arrival of the rest of the family for the ride onto the island was scheduled in two days, so an extra day in Blufton was required to make the proper connections. The rest day allowed an opportunity to read the article that had been written about our trip in *The Carolina Morning News*. On the two previous occasions where articles had been written, early morning departures had precluded a chance to buy the newspaper. Though the papers would later be sent home, we as of yet had no idea of what had been written.

After a leisurely breakfast in the hotel lobby, a walk past a pair of newspaper boxes showed a rather surprising display. In the window of one of the boxes was the front page of *The Carolina Morning News*. On the same front page was a large color picture of the two of us entering Blufton along with a lengthy, well-written article. It must have been a slow news day in coastal South Carolina; somehow we had temporarily moved some of the other issues of local and national importance off the front page.

Buying a paper that had our picture prominently displayed on the front page brought forth the possibility of two reactions. The first was to simply put the fifty cents in the slot like any other day and find a bathroom to enjoy the paper's contents. The second was to buy the paper, look around for the first person available, and modestly exclaim, "See that right there? That's me!" Maintaining the modesty that had been dominant over the previous eighty days, the first option was chosen. Had there been anyone even remotely close to the paper boxes, though, it was quite possible that vanity would have displaced modesty and option number two would have quickly been selected.

The newspaper was a pleasant diversion, but the problem of dealing with Route 278 traffic had not magically disappeared. The general plan was to follow the road for about four miles to a hotel just off island. At the hotel we would meet up with family members for the climactic ride to the Atlantic. Although most of the final ride of about twelve miles or so on the island would also be along Route 278, much of it would be traveled on a bicycle path that paralleled the highway.

Since conversations with locals had proven successful in the past, the same technique was used in Blufton. Not surprisingly, a consensus quickly built that avoiding Route 278 was a necessity. To accomplish that end, it would be necessary to put together a patchwork route that included short stretches on the highway, jaunts through commercial parking lots, and side trips through adjacent residential subdivisions. Such an indirect route would increase the length of the day's ride, but it was only a few miles to begin with. Adding a mile or two would be a very small price to pay for increasing the likelihood of safe passage.

Days 82 - 3769 Miles Down, 18 To Go

WHO BELIEVES IN JINXES ANYWAY?

The next to last day on the bicycles began with a leisurely wakeup and breakfast. The shortest cycling day of the summer would require very little time on the bikes, so hills, headwinds, heat, food, water, restrooms, insects, aches, and team morale would not be a problem. Everything was not perfect, however, since the Route 278 traffic and dark skies awaited the mid-morning departure.

The day began with a leisurely ride through a Target parking lot, a mad dash along the road shoulder during the breaks in traffic created by a traffic light, and another leisurely ride through a GMC dealer's lot. Soon the route turned off on a side road and then ran parallel to the highway on a poorly maintained dirt road. After the turn onto the dirt road the skies opened and what there was of the road surface quickly turned into a quagmire. The thick mud made the cycling nearly impossible, but at the same time, gave a couple of middle agers a reason to laugh about their predicament and spend quality time in the mud.

After a short ride through the muck, the dirt road ended and the hard surface of a subdivision street began. A short break on the well-paved street provided an opportunity to use the water bottles to rinse the mud off gears and chains. A quick ride through the flat streets of the allotment, followed by a detour through the parking lot of a large outlet mall put us back on Route 278. The now time-tested practice of mad dashes during traffic breaks resulted in safely reaching the evening's hotel.

Shortly after checking into the hotel and getting out of the soaked biking gear, a young lady named Erin from *The Island Packet* called to set up an afternoon interview. The interview was conducted in the hotel lobby and included many of the normal questions. Erin, however, was especially interested in observations about the next day's completion of the trip. She planned on meeting us at the beach with a photographer to record the ceremonial dipping of the front wheels into the Atlantic Ocean.

Erin's questions prompted thoughts about the pending ride onto the island. Events over the last few weeks had moved quickly, and even with the extra day in Blufton, the end of the trip seemed to be arriving too quickly. Back in Kansas, when early thoughts began to form about the trip conclusion, there was a fear of jinxing the remaining fifteen hundred miles by giving them too much attention. The realization that we were actually going to complete the trip successfully was repressed until well into Georgia. Over the previous week, there was a feeling that, jinx or not, it was now okay to visualize pushing the bikes through the sand to the ocean. With the next day being the big event, there didn't seem to be enough time to properly prepare. But then again, maybe we were making too big a deal about the whole thing.

Our youngest daughter Sarah and her fiancé Doug arrived in the early evening and we spent an enjoyable dinner sharing the events of our respective summers. After dinner we spent hours looking through the pictures they had brought with them. Since the film from the road had been sent to a developer with instructions to mail them to our home, it was the first opportunity to see the hundreds of photographs that had recorded important events of the trip. Our oldest daughter, Jennifer, and her husband, Greg, would be arriving the next day. Everything was in place for the ride onto the island.

Day 83 - 3774 Miles Down, 13 To Go

THAT'S ALL SHE WROTE

Eighty-two days and nearly 3,800 miles earlier an adventure had begun that would culminate with a ride onto Hilton Head Island,

South Carolina on this morning. Random thoughts and reflec-
tions of the trip began making unscheduled visits to our minds. At
breakfast with the family, many of them became part of the discussion. The predictable memories of beautiful scenery and challenging climbs were discussed in more detail than most listeners
probably cared to hear. The remarkable aspects of the cross-country trip, however, were the collection of interesting and helpful
people that had been encountered and the fact that the trip had
been accomplished relatively problem-free. With a combined 160
person-days on the bikes, there had been no serious injuries, there
had been no dangerous encounters with two or four legged adversaries, and there had been no major weather problems. We felt
blessed and more than a little fortunate to have had circumstances
that were outside our control work out as well as they had.

The musings over breakfast were enjoyable and appropriate
for the last morning of the trip, but there were still a few miles
yet to conquer before the summer's worth of effort could be
declared a success. The busy mid-morning traffic in front of the
hotel on Route 278 reminded us that it was not yet time to
savor victory, as did nasty dark clouds hovering overhead.
Unfortunately, anything short of front wheels in the Atlantic
Ocean would render the trip incomplete.

The first half-mile toward the island was a continuation of the
previous day's mad dashes between breaks in traffic. Soon the first
of two arching bridges over the Intracoastal Waterway provided a
wide shoulder to allow relatively carefree riding to the small nature
preserve of Pinkney Island. A short crossing of Pinkney Island put
us again on a long, arching bridge, this one ending on Hilton Head
Island. Arriving on the Hilton Head side of the bridge was cause for
a preliminary mini-celebration and "photo shoot" with the family
next to a sign welcoming visitors to the island.

While feeling good about the current state of affairs, about
twelve more miles of riding was still required to reach the section
of beach that would be the official termination of the trip.

Although most of the remaining ride would be on bike paths, they wouldn't start for another two miles, so it was necessary to incorporate more of the traffic dodging techniques of the recent past. The absence of nearby paved parking lots unfortunately meant that a portion of the ride had to be done through mud and high grass well off the paved roadway.

The bikeways on Hilton Head Island form a convenient way for cyclists to traverse most of the island in safety and comfort. The city fathers have done an exceptional job of building a network of paved paths that allowed access to even the most remote sections of the island. Reaching the one paralleling Route 278 was cause for relief, and a feeling that it was now time to relax and slowly savor the accomplishment that was about to be realized. The leisurely ride along the bike path to the ocean had long been viewed as an opportunity to reflect and enjoy.

Unfortunately such tranquil expectations were soon forgotten as loud thunder claps and flashes of lightning created a need to significantly quicken the pace. Before long a light rain added incentive to reach the shelter of the underground condominium parking lot that would serve as the staging area for the excursion to the beach. The weather had unfortunately made the last few miles through the beautifully landscaped entrance to Palmetto Dunes a mad dash rather than one of calm reflection. The Spanish moss covered live oak trees provided a bit of an umbrella. Strangely, with about a half mile to go, the odometer on my bike shut down. After all the miles, it had chosen to give up so close to the end.

Entering the covered garage, the family awaited with a large banner that signified a finish line. We rode through the sign much as a sprinter broke the tape at the end of a race. There was a celebratory feeling among the two of us, our family, and a few curious bystanders in the dry comfort of the garage as the rain had now increased to a fairly heavy thunderstorm. The short trip to the beach would await the pending arrival of better weather and the folks from *The Island Packet*.

The rain eventually lessened and our entourage prepared for an event that had been anticipated since the journey began. As our family, the reporter, the photographer, and a few onlookers watched, Merj and I pushed the bikes onto the sandy beach. The wind swept waves of the Atlantic rolled onto the shore a few short yards away. After the assembled group readied their cameras, the front wheels of our bicycles slowly met the foamy surf. The trip was complete and a sense of tremendous pride and accomplishment washed over us. An undertaking that had its genesis forty years earlier had officially ended. The itch had been scratched.

With the trip now officially complete, Merj and I looked at one another and, simultaneously, a worry suddenly came over the both of us. What, we wondered, were we going to do tomorrow?

Day 84 - 3787 Miles Down, 0 To Go

————————

EPILOGUE

The return to Ohio brought a welcomed re-acclimation with friends, family, and co-workers, and a quick return to life's normal daily activities. Through the efforts of those back home, we found things in good order and generally in the same or better condition than we had left them.

Being away for the better part of three months had left a lot of catching up to do. We soon found that when getting together with friends and family the trip became a topic of discussion. Most had a genuine curiosity about it, and we enjoyed sharing a summer's worth of experiences with them in sometimes painstaking detail. A frequently asked question was what part of the country we had enjoyed the most. Because of an almost daily exposure to memorable sights, it was difficult to try to choose specific locations, but some had made lasting impressions.

In Oregon it was the coastal range and the high-desert. Idaho, one of our favorite states, offered the Sawtooth Mountains and Craters of the Moon. Wyoming's Teton Mountains and Colorado's picturesque ski resorts and Rocky Mountain passes were memorable for their beauty. In Kansas the sunrises had left an impression, as had the grain elevators dominating the skylines. Missouri's rolling countryside would remain with us, as would the scenic rural farms of Kentucky. Tennessee would be remembered for Nashville and Chattanooga, and Georgia, another of our favorite states, for its small towns with their characteristic Southern charm. Hilton Head Island, our final destination, was memorable for its wide sandy beaches.

More memorable than the scenery were the people we had been fortunate enough to meet across America. In an era of war, terrorist warnings, and worldwide tensions, we had wondered about the resilience and general mood of the country. Our concerns were answered on a daily basis by regular contact with average Americans going about their normal lives.

From the youthful optimism of a waitress in Oregon to the "leave things better than you found them" philosophy of a buckaroo in the same state. From the modesty of an elderly motel owning couple in Idaho to the independence of a tough 85-year-old mountain lion hunter in the high plains of Wyoming. From the grit of Colorado cattle herders to the honesty of a Kansas antique tractor dealer. From the serenity of a quilt shop owner in Missouri who "just wants to get to heaven," to the route planning helpfulness of a fellow Missourian card shop owner. From the diligence of an old car mechanic in Kentucky to the thoughtfulness of a slow talking Tennessee highway worker. From the Southern hospitality of a County Commissioner and the graciousness of a hotel owner in Georgia to the perseverance of a Greek immigrant restaurant owner in South Carolina. From Astoria, Oregon to Hilton Head Island, South Carolina, the chance encounters with those folks and with countless others had provided more than sufficient answers to our pre-trip concerns about the state of America.

After 84 days of viewing the country and its people at twelve miles and hour from the seat of a bicycle, there was a sense of accomplishment and pride. The feeling was more than that of the personal achievement of a near lifetime goal, but rather one of comfort in the spirit and optimism of the people across the country. Chances are there will be future reasons to doubt the strength and resiliency of Americans. But a summer of seeing regular Americans up close going about their lives gave two slow moving, middle age tourists reasons for optimism.

The summer adventure also helped ease my obsessive insistence on accuracy. The trip had required spending 319 hours, 18 minutes, and 58 seconds on the bike, which resulted in an average speed of 11.87 miles per hour. My acceptance of an average of twelve miles per hour was a step in the right direction. Besides, a book with the title of *AMERICA AT 11.87 MILES AN HOUR* just didn't have the same ring to it.

Oh, I almost forgot; Merj's state by state dirt samples. After just a few weeks home, Max, our Labrador Retriever, discovered them in the garage. Returning home from Saturday morning errands, we found the contents of eleven zip lock bags spread throughout the front yard. At least carrying what was probably a half-ton of dirt across the country had been a character building experience.

And the hundred-dollar bet with Bob; well, that got a little complicated. Bob gave every indication that the bet was off because of Merj's having traversed portions of Oregon in a motorized vehicle. Trying to convince him that the bet was really with me, and I had in fact covered "every friggin' inch" (minus the forced two mile truck ride in Wyoming), didn't seemed to make any difference. I had pretty much forgotten about the bet until we were having dinner with our wives and friends one Friday evening at a favorite local restaurant.

After finishing our meals, Bob stood up in the middle of the busy restaurant and tapped his water glass to get the attention of the large room full of diners. Not having any idea what he was doing, a thought crossed our minds that he may have temporarily lost touch with reality. Not to be deterred, Bob told the assembled restaurant patrons of our trip and then reached into a heretofore hidden paper bag and pulled out a glass and wood box that contained a crisp one hundred dollar bill hanging inside from two thin fishing lines. A professionally prepared plaque on the front of the box read:

PHILBERT

MOTIVATION FROM COAST TO COAST

THIS JUST KILLS ME

BOBBO

He was a man of his word after all.

Oh yeah, the snakes and flat tires. After 3,800 miles of riding along the highway shoulders of America, the tally of countable road kill stood at one porcupine, three deer, a jack rabbit, count-less birds and other small critters, more armadillos than anyone could ever imagine, and fifty-five dead snakes. As a matter of record, at no time during the entire trip did a snake come to life and bite Merj with each rotation of the front wheel of her bicycle. Merj, however, had the last laugh when it came to flat tires. The final count stood at male rider six, and female rider one.

And finally the *Boys Life* article from the 50's that had been the genesis of the trip. Although I was about ninety percent sure that the article had been as I remembered, small doubts began to creep into my mind as to the accuracy of my memory. Had the article really appeared, or had I dreamt it? If it had existed, did it really document a cross-country trip, or rather a week's bike ride across, say, Iowa? If the article didn't exist, the accuracy of the documented events of the trip would remain, but the reasons for doing it would no longer be valid. One side of me said to let it go. The other side said that I needed to find out for myself.

After a few weeks of internal debate and at the urging of a friend who was active in the Boy Scouts, a decision was made to pursue the old article. A call to the Boy Scout archives produced a lady who was very busy and would be unable to search for the article for some time. With curiosity now at a high level, a call to the Cleveland Public Library resulted in discovering that they had microfilm of the magazine back to its beginning in the early 1900's.

With a mixture of curiosity and apprehension, Merj and I headed to the library prepared to spend an afternoon in front of a screen scanning old issues of *Boys Life*. Based on memory, I asked for the years 1957 to 1960, I took the first two years, and Merj the second two. After only about twenty minutes, she casually said, "Come here and take a look at this."

On the screen in front of her was an article from the June, 1959 issue of *Boys Life*. The article was titled "Diary of a Bike Trip." It documented in a day by day fashion the journey of a fourteen year old Boy Scout named John Wilkinson from Los Angeles, California to Connecticut. While re-reading the article, it was as if almost forty-five years of time had vanished. The article was as I had remembered it. It also provided a certain level of satisfaction in finding that, even at middle age, long-term memory had remained intact. The afternoon in the Cleveland Public Library had supplied fitting closure to a childhood dream. Now, that itch had really been scratched.

ACKNOWLEDGEMENTS

Taking a book from hundreds of disparate thoughts to reality takes the help of many people. Since this one also included completion of a three-month, cross-country bicycle trip, a lot of others also contributed to the adventure that made the book possible.

During the trip, the very capable month long support of John and Aili Leivo proved invaluable in the heat and hills of the Rockies. Bob and Barbara Gardner's assistance through Kentucky and a portion of Tennessee was greatly appreciated in spite of Bob's questionable hotel picking skills. At home, daughter Jennifer Crissman regularly updated the web site, and her husband Greg efficiently handled paying the bills. Younger daughter Sarah took excellent care of the house and yard, and Pam Richards devoted many hours to transcribing audiotapes. Diane Kinsey's and Sharon Eckerle's encouragement after reviewing early drafts of the first portion of the book were important in keeping the writing fire burning.

Back on the road, countless people provided help in the form of directions, nourishment, comfort, and encouragement. At the risk of missing many equally important people who contributed to the success of the trip, some stood out. Included in the memorable group were Mickey at the Astoria Inn, Denny and his family at the Skyhook Motel, Clark Haglar "The Oldest Man in Idaho," Betty at Dr. Witnah's office, Leo Hennessy from the Idaho Department of Parks and Recreation, and Paul and Audrey Parton at The Pine Lodge Motel and RV Park. Also not to be forgotten were Bret Henson at the Henson Silver Guest Ranch, Bill and Dorothy Coats at the JC Motel, Honest Tom Kelsay of the Cimarron Tractor Company, Linda at the Kingman Library, Fred and Joan at the Maple Tree Inn, Bob from the Missouri Department of Transportation and Marlana at the Hideaway Quilt Shop. And, last but not least, Herman of the Tennessee Department of Transportation, Jerry the Jasper County

Commissioner, Harry (Sonny) Hine at the Milledgeville Hampton Inn, Richard and Jane at the Georgia Military College Library, and Paul at the Squat and Gobble Restaurant are all due our thanks. Many, many, others, most of whose names were never learned, deserve our thanks and gratitude for unfailingly offering assistance and friendship whenever it was needed.

A special appreciation is due the thousands of vehicle drivers who avoided making unscheduled contact with us during our countless hours occupying the right edge of the pavement. With few exceptions we were given plenty of room, although, admittedly the times that we weren't are indelibly etched into our psyche.

And thanks to the hundreds of people who sent e-mails of encouragement and news of the home front during the time we were gone. Word of mouth about the trip also offered an opportunity to make many new friends and renew old acquaintances. The e-mails were a real morale boost, and we tried to respond to every one of the folks who were gracious enough to contact us.

And finally, thanks to Merj, my companion for eighty-four days of adventure. As we crossed the country, she maintained an attitude that was remarkably positive considering the physical and psychological obstacles that paid us frequent visitations. Her experiences and observations became a big part of the story. Without her the trip would have been much more difficult. For sure the book would have been much shorter.